Murder, My Love

MURDER, My Love

The Great Crimes of Passion

Edited by

ERIC CORDER

ℙ✲ℙ

A Playboy Press Book

ACKNOWLEDGMENTS

Haas) by permission of Emile Burn, Executor of the literary estate of Edmund Pearson.

"First Night Murder," by Bruce Sanders. Copyright © 1962 by Bruce Sanders. Reprinted from *Murder in Big Cities* by permission of the author.

"The Picnic," by Stuart Palmer. Copyright © 1960 by Stuart Palmer. Reprinted from *A Study of Murder* by permission of the Thomas Y. Crowell Co.

"Memphis Serenade," by E. D. Radin. Copyright © 1953 by E. D. Radin. Reprinted from *Crimes of Passion* by permission of G. P. Putnam's Sons.

"Murder on Big Moose Lake," by George E. Minot. Copyright © 1928 by Marshall Jones Co.

"The Wicked Countess," by George Dilnot. Copyright © 1934 by George Dilnot. Reprinted from *Rogues March* by permission of A. M. Heath & Co., agents for the late George Dilnot.

"Rattenbury and Stoner," by F. Tennyson Jesse. Reprinted from *Famous Trials, Fifth Series,* edited by James H. Hodge and published by Penguin Books, Ltd., by permission of A. M. Heath & Co., agents for the late F. Tennyson Jesse.

"A Slight Case of Frigidity," by Dorothy Kilgallen. Copyright © 1967 by Richard T. Kollmar, Executor of the Estate of Dorothy Kilgallen Kollmar. Reprinted from *Murder One* by Dorothy Kilgallen by permission of Random House.

These stories have been condensed by the editor from their original lengths—"An Element of Farce" by Leonard Gribble, "Jim, Linda, Harry . . . and 'The Set' " by George Scullin, "Death and Times of a Prophet" by Stewart H. Holbrook, "Greek Tragedy" by Renée Huggett and Paul Berry, "First Night Murder" by Bruce Sanders, "The Picnic" by Stuart Palmer, "Memphis Serenade" by E. D. Radin, "Rattenbury and Stoner" by F. Tennyson Jesse, and "A Slight Case of Frigidity" by Dorothy Kilgallen.

NOTE: In the interest of privacy, the following names are not the actual names of the persons involved—Leta Vosburgh, Jim Anderson, Linda Anderson, Mr. and Mrs. Gilbert Sheehan, Mr. and Mrs. Harvey Collins, and Billy Hoover.

For
MALCOLM *and* BEVERLY BRALY,
who share the mountains, and neither of whom,
happily, is represented herein.

Contents

Introduction

PASSION is a crucible. It scorches, withers and finally burns the Apollonian veneer from our surface to expose the elemental, Dionysian core: The sublime falls to the orgiastic. We are revealed to ourselves, truly, only in our extremes. And passion whips us to the furthest extremity.

We are a young animal as evolutionary time is measured, still the infant progeny of aggressive hunting apes. Killer apes, it is argued. We do not yet wear our Apollonian cloak comfortably. We are not tamed. We want to run naked.

Passion is our gift and our curse. It molds saints; it molds monsters. It drives us to hurl ourselves toward the stars, and to sacrifice our brothers bloodily upon the altars of our fears. It creates heroism and betrayal, selflessness and slaughter.

Perhaps *the* prime font of passion is human sexuality; the "triangle" in particular, for most persons, is the most intense and difficult sexual relationship to control or to resolve satisfactorily. Thus, its destructive potential is high. This is a book of *crimes passionels* — murders deriving from triangles and forged in the conflagration of passion, reversions to primordial Dionysian solutions to the insoluble, murder done to satisfy frustrated desire, to relieve insupportable pain.

A sexual triangle is customarily conceived of as a man, a woman and the lover or mistress of one of them. But this is not necessarily so; the apex, the third point, may be several lovers, one of whom is handy at the moment, or an angry or jealous relative, or the representative of a chastising society, even a paramour from many years ago who vanished before the two principals met and bonded together. These variations are all represented here, along with several of the more traditional situations involving husband, wife and lover.

So the first criteria I used in selecting the stories herein were (1) that they deal with crimes of passion and (2) that they derive from a triangle. There were three more—entertainment, interest and special merit.

If you chuckle or find yourself charmed, you are being entertained. But if you are moved to tears, astonished, angered, shocked, or in other ways led to involvement, then you are also being entertained. The index of entertainment is the degree to which the subject can engage you. I attempted to diversify the modes of engagement so that repetition would not begin to blunt or bore. To prevent a sense of detachment or distance, the cases extend no further back in time than the beginning of the 20th Century. But cases whose details are so widely known and highly publicized that they are already familiar to everyone were ignored—except when the omission of a classic, such as the case of Stanford White and Harry K. Thaw, or of Dr. Bernard Finch and Carole Tregoff, would have torn a glaring hole in the fabric of the book.

The interest factor was questioned on two levels: First, the overview—did a particular piece contribute to a new understanding of such crimes? While not attempting to create a definitive work or to stamp the final page with a Q.E.D., I did feel that the book should give the reader a fairly solid grounding in the subject. This meant that the poles, and the major configurations of what lies in between, had to be fairly represented. Doctors, for example, typically display a nearly irresistible impulse to dismember the corpses of their wives or mistresses. Women, separated by continents and decades, turn to poison like moths to light, and are singularly fond of burning the bodies of husbands and lovers, or stuffing them into trunks.

The second level was the intrinsic interest of the specific

piece. Did it pose a puzzle? Contain something unexpected or startling? Or provide a unique variation?

Special merit is more difficult to define. In some renderings it was the author's sheer literary skill; in others it was the crushing power of events and perpetrators; or a high degree of ludicrousness; a probing analysis of character; a good evocation of former mores or a past milieu—something that gave a story added value and thus set it apart from its competitors.

Enough said. Like a road sign, an introduction should only indicate what lies ahead. I've had my say, and it's reflected in my selections.

I hope you'll find them satisfying.

I

The Woman Who Sentenced Herself

Derick Goodman

Few women have known a passion as great as that of sweet Yvonne Chevallier for her husband. She was wholly in love with the young doctor when she married him, and her ardor increased with each passing year. But as Pierre abandoned medicine, and his political ambitions mounted, he lost his feelings for Yvonne, until at last he felt nothing for her but haughty contempt. But her love for him never died, not even when he took a mistress, not even when she contemplated suicide—not even when she murdered him.

In 1948 the French penal settlements in French Guiana were officially closed and the last "bagnard"—convict—left the colony to return to his native land. The "bagne" of sinister memory which had inspired so many novels and melodramas was no longer in existence. The penal buildings and camps at Saint-Laurent-du-Maroni, Cayenne and the infamous Devil's Island were left for the jungle and the vegetation to reclaim. Five years later, they were in ruins, all that remains to mark the passage of a century and 70,000 convicts who had passed through the colony, nearly every one of them dying there. Only one ex-bagnard remained, Mouchaboeuf, the volunteer convict for the post of public executioner who guillotined dozens of his former colleagues. He alone dared not return to France.

But there are still French settlers there, and a large native population. Today, scientists have set up many advanced posts in the hitherto impenetrable jungle, seeking gold, uranium, and precious minerals. There is a modern hospital at Saint-Laurent-du-Maroni, and it possesses a large maternity wing. More and more native women are casting their old superstitions away and going there for their confinements. It was not always like this, however. The maternity wards were unpopular with the natives until that day in early 1953 when the big four-engined plane from Paris deposited a slight middle-aged woman with her two children on the tarmac. She was the new director of the maternity service for the colony. She had a lot of local prejudice to overcome but that was not all. She also had a terrible past to overcome: her name was Yvonne Chevallier and she had murdered her husband on the very day he was

3

appointed minister in a new French government, a bare two years previously.

Throughout her life, Yvonne Chevallier had always shown a surprising facility for hurting herself, bordering on mental masochism. But after complete acquittal for the murder of her husband, her voluntary self-banishment to French Guiana, the site of the infamous penal colony, one of the dead ends of the world, was an extraordinary example of self-abnegation. There are only two seasons there, six months' tropical rain, followed by six months' tropical sun. When you draw your mosquito netting over your bed at night, it is not to keep the mosquitoes out, but the blood-sucking vampires. There is little civilization, still less society. You are haunted by the gaunt ghosts of the 70,000 convicts who were punished there in the most revolting and inhuman ways. There can only be three reasons for going to Guiana: because you are sent there by the administration; because you have commercial interests there; or because you feel a Heaven-inspired motive to go there to assuage the suffering, as many nuns and priests have done.

In going to this hell on earth, Yvonne Chevallier provided a fourth reason. She went there to punish herself deliberately for the rest of her life. Human justice did not see fit to punish her, but Yvonne had killed the person she loved, hence her self-immolation. It is unlikely that she had ever read Oscar Wilde when she made her decision, for one of the reasons for the murder of her husband was her lack of literary knowledge. Perhaps the word "reason" is a little strong, but at least it was one of the beginnings of the affair. In what are known as "crimes crapuleux"—common criminality—in France, and indeed, everywhere in the world, motives are brutal and easy to understand. The gangster shoots a policeman, the burglar shoots the awakened householder. But in crimes of love—these cases of "crime passionel"—the earlier motives, the all-important beginnings, are as diaphanous and as complicated as a spider's web. Odd phrases, slight incidents, a wounding word which is taken too seriously, these form the beginnings of a crime passionel.

These slight beginnings lead to the *incidents,* the quarrels in public, and the deliberately wounding words, the gap which gradually widens between husband and wife, or lover and beloved. The incidents multiply until they become veritable motives. Suspicions harden, then one day you find a marked railway timetable, and a love letter signed by another woman. The quarrels intensify, the language becomes coarser and finally turns into gutter filth, the words used by "fishmongers' wives," to quote a French expression. A man is superior to his wife on the intellectual plane but inferior on the moral plane. A man becomes a celebrity, and his wife feels herself unable to maintain her dignity in her new surroundings of luxury. A man has a prodigious intelligence, is welcomed everywhere in literary salons for the wit and sparkle of his conversation. A woman is filled with prodigious love, but stammers and flushes when she tries to speak in public. Then the woman, because she is a masochist at heart, humiliates herself before the man, repeatedly throws herself on her knees before him. She writes him pleading letters which he ignores. But she knows the other woman, the inevitable third figure of a crime passionel, the other woman who is younger, prettier, vastly more intelligent, who is also in demand at the literary salons and cocktail parties in their large city. The man in question is no less than the mayor of this city. He is a member of the National Assembly and one day he will undoubtedly become a minister. The wound becomes ulcerated, and once the woman has paid that fatal visit to the gun shop—"Which is the one that kills without any doubt?" were her actual words—you know it is going to burst. And thus do these slight beginnings, these incidents, become motives for murder.

On the face of it, Yvonne Chevallier committed cold-blooded

murder. She poured four bullets into her husband, went down-stairs to tell the maid to keep the children quiet, then returned to the first floor and fired a fifth bullet into his back.

There are only two ugly buildings in Orléans, one of the most graceful of all French provincial cities, the hospital and the prison. Yvonne's life, her only real life, was to begin in one and to end in the other. In the space of time which elapsed between her entering the maternity ward of the hospital for the first day of work and her leaving the gates of the prison a free woman again, this little country midwife was to create the biggest furor in French public opinion for many years and was to cleave the country in two over a question of morality: should adultery be punished with death as in former days? In the case of Yvonne Chevallier, there was to be no doubt of the opinion of the public. In the darkness of early evening on November 7, 1952, a crowd of over 3,000 gathered in the heavy rain outside the Reims Palais de Justice, cheered and acclaimed Yvonne Chevallier as she left the court after her total acquittal. A little earlier, the same crowd had hissed "the other woman," Jeanne Perreau, and just as in the dreadful days of the revolution, had screamed at her: "A mort, à mort!"

Pierre Chevallier was a young doctor filled with promise when he met Yvonne Chevallier, a country midwife of his own age, in the Orléans hospital in 1935. There was a tremendous difference in their backgrounds. He came from one of the oldest and most esteemed families in Orléans. She came of honest but poor peasant stock. But, to bridge this difference, they possessed a common denominator, a devouring and almost animal instinct for physical love. The act of love which was so soon to unite them physically swept all obstacles from their path. Differences of intelligence, of background, never mattered in those halcyon days before the war. Yvonne gave up her practice in her country village and came to live with Pierre in his flat as his mistress. She was never accepted by his family, and this was one of the beginnings of the drama. In September 1939 he was mobilized into the army, and on his first leave he married Yvonne. It was wartime and he had to give her the security she deserved. But his family was not present at their almost secret marriage. Another of the beginnings. Judge Jadin was later to say to Yvonne as she sat in the dock:

"The Chevallier family never accepted you?"

"Yes, but only as one of the mistakes of Pierre's youth," she was to reply bitterly.

She was to bear him two sons, Thugal born in 1940, and Mathieu in 1945. Both are now with her in French Guiana.

Pierre Chevallier won the Légion d'Honneur, military division, for tending the wounded under fire before the capitulation of France, and then he returned to Orléans to throw himself wholeheartedly into the Resistance movement. He organized reception committees for the saboteurs parachuted from England and then, when his life was directly threatened by the Nazis, he joined the local maquis and rapidly became their chief. When the Germans began to retreat in July 1944, Pierre attacked them suddenly and threw them out of Orléans even before the Allied armies arrived there. He was the real liberator of the city, and in return the citizens elected him as their first postwar mayor.

From that moment onward, Pierre Chevallier never looked back in his career as a public man. His sycophantic friends pressed him to enter politics, and shortly afterwards he was elected Deputy for one of the radical parties. Yvonne fitted in badly with his new life, for he was a doctor no longer. Politics and municipal affairs took all his time. His reconstruction of Orléans was one of the masterpieces of public-works enterprise for the whole of France. He was here, there and everywhere, receptions, parties, banquets. It was a life which frankly displeased Yvonne. As a doctor's wife, she had been able to hold her own in conversation which, to be perfectly honest, was above her. She felt awkward at receptions and could not remember the names of her husband's friends. When forced to give dinner parties herself, she remained silent at her end of the table, stammering a few clumsy words when guests tried to converse with her. Her husband had neither the time nor the patience either to educate her or to put her at ease. All that remained between them at that time was their animal passion, and even this was fading on Pierre's part. Yvonne, on the contrary, was still madly in love with him. She was madly in love with him until the bitter end. But she had the supreme misfortune to be naturally clumsy in everything she did.

She had money but was unable to dress like other women in her position. She tried desperately to learn something of the subjects discussed at the parties and in the salons, but in her desperation fell back on learning by heart some of the literary and art criticisms in the weekly papers. It was fatal and it made everything worse. There is no need for a woman to simulate intelligence, but Yvonne was pathetic in her attempts to retain the love of her husband. In a word, she was dowdy. She was dull. Pierre had everything in life to be proud of except his wife. He felt he could not take her anywhere without bringing shame upon himself.

This is where Yvonne's self-pity and innate masochism began to play a large part. Thousands of other women have been able to adapt themselves to improved circumstances, women less intelligent than Yvonne, who was, when all is said and done, a certified midwife with a splendid reputation. Little by little, the situation became worse. The remarks began: "My God, when are you going to learn to dress yourself properly?" or "For Lord's sake, say something, don't just sit there. . . ."

Sometimes Pierre told her to be ready at a certain time in the evening so that he could return to pick her up in his car to take her to a party. He frequently forgot to go back for her.

Then came the first scene. He had been in Paris for a considerable time. Back in their house, Yvonne became more and more bottled up. When he finally returned, she threw herself at him weeping. "I can't stand it. I can't go on any longer," she sobbed. His mind on a thousand and one more important things, the doctor in Pierre diagnosed ordinary hysteria. He tried to bring her to her senses with brutal words. He was setting the pace and all she had to do was to keep up with him—if she could. If she couldn't, so much the worse for her! He hadn't the time to be always behind her, telling her constantly what to say, what to wear, almost which knife and fork to use. For the first time, she went on her knees before him, still sobbing. "The only thing you know how to do properly is cry," he said, walking out of the house.

Then came the blow she had been dreading, the physical break. Until then, and despite everything, one bond had remained between them, the act of love. Then Mathieu fell ill, and Yvonne had to put his bed in their own bedroom to watch over him at night. Pierre congratulated her on the decision and said he would put a little bed in his study for the time being. At that moment she did not realize it, but Pierre was never to return to their own big double bed.

Deprived of physical love for the first time in her adult existence, Yvonne fell back on drugs, veronal at night to chase away the sleepless hours, and maxiton—a stimulant given to French parachute troops—in the mornings to drive away the aftereffects of the veronal, a highly dangerous combination for the nerves. During the day, she chained-smoked and drank enormous quantities of strong black coffee. No human body can stand this sort of treatment for long. . . .

At the same time, she understood all too well the functioning of Pierre's physical self and his sexual needs. The suspicion grew that he must be finding satisfaction elsewhere. We have seen the beginnings, we have seen the incidents. Now we are coming to the third and more dangerous phase; we are to see the direct motives.

Yvonne finally overcame her scruples and went through the pockets of all of her husband's suits. She found what she had dreaded finding, a love letter from another woman. There was nothing special about it, it was just another love letter, but it was signed Jeannette. From the nature of Pierre's work which bound him even more closely to Orléans than to Paris, this Jeannette could not be far away. Then an old suspicion crystallized: Jeanne Perreau, wife of the owner of the biggest department store in the city, beautiful, intelligent, witty—and fifteen years younger than Yvonne. Could it be her?

From then on, everything Yvonne did shrieked of clumsiness. The ham-handed peasant in her came to the fore. She sent her maid with a note to Jeanne Perreau, asking her to give her the address of a mutual friend, and told the maid to wait for the reply. Naïvely, Yvonne thought she would have an example of the other woman's handwriting to compare with the love letter. In a modern age, the wife of the mayor of a city does not send notes by hand. She uses the telephone.

Sophisticated woman of the world, Jeanne Perreau did not fall into the obvious trap. She sent the maid back empty-handed and telephoned her reply, in cold and disdainful tones. The nights of veronal and the days of maxiton and black coffee were telling. Yvonne fell into a physical rage, lashing out at furniture and smashing ornaments. Then she rushed out of the house to Jeanne Perreau's home.

"You've been writing to my husband!" she accused Jeanne on the very doorstep.

"Never," said the young woman of the world.

"You're his mistress!"

"Where on earth did you get an idea like that from?"

"I know it, I know everything," Yvonne said desperately, but she knew she was losing ground in front of her implacable adversary. Moreover, she knew that once again she was making a fool of herself in public. Jeanne, on the contrary, was fully equal to the situation. With a friendly hand on Yvonne's shoulder, she led the mayor's wife into the house.

"Of course, we're good friends. There's no secret about that. But to imagine that because we're good friends we sleep together, really Yvonne! But you and I are good friends, I'm as fond of you as I am of your husband. We are all good friends and that is all Pierre has ever been for me. . . ."

And strange as it may seem, Yvonne left Jeanne's house, believing, at least for the moment, that there was nothing between the red-haired woman and her husband.

But that still did not explain away the existence of the letter. Somewhere in the vicinity was a Jeannette or Jeanne. That very night Pierre returned from Paris. Yvonne was waiting for him, the love letter in her hand. He took it calmly:

"Well . . ." was all he said.

"I think I have the right to demand an explanation!"

"Why?" Pierre replied calmly.

His calm drove Yvonne to fury:

"You're a bastard! You're a bastard!" she screamed at him. It was the first time she had ever spoken to him in that tone, and she regretted it the moment she had said it. But his reply did not help matters.

"And you're a real imbecile. You're so stupid you frighten me."

"But who wrote that letter?"

"Nobody."

"What do you mean, 'nobody'?"

"It's not your business and shut up. You make me vomit," he replied, using a stronger but untranslatable word for "vomit." He had replied to her purposely in the same sort of language she herself had used. The gulf between them had become an abyss.

Then came the general elections of June 1951. Pierre carried off a brilliant personal victory, topping all the electors' lists. He was only 42 and he was obviously destined for a brilliant political career. That night there was a magnificent reception in the mayor's parlor, with Pierre Chevallier as the undisputed star of the evening. He neglected his wife completely and refused to drink or dance with her. Then Jeanne Perreau arrived, and he made straight for her. They drank to each other's health and stood holding hands. Yvonne moved across to Léon Perreau, Jeanne's husband.

"Look, your wife and my husband are flirting together," she said.

"Nonsense," he replied equably, and moved ostentatiously away from Yvonne. As in all her impulsive moments, Yvonne once again made a fool of herself in public. She ran across to Pierre and tried to kiss him. He pushed her away almost brutally:

"Let's keep our more intimate moments for the home, shall we?" he said sarcastically. Everyone standing there could hear him. It could not have been worse had he struck her. Yvonne managed to get out before she broke down.

At home, Pierre continued to show her the same brutal indifference.

"Pierre, why do you behave like this to me?" she asked him shortly after the incident on election night.

"Because I've had enough of you," he replied, dismissing the subject.

Another time he said to her disdainfully:

"Could you really see yourself at big banquets in Paris?"

But Yvonne loved him. She was as desperately in love with him as she had been when they first met fifteen years before, perhaps more so. But she went on blindly smashing her head against the brick wall of his total indifference. She begged him to make love to her.

"I don't want you anymore," he said. "I don't even think I would be capable of making love to you anymore."

"But I'll do anything. I promise you I'll change. I'll be worthy of you. . . ."

"I don't want you," he said. "We'll divorce."

"Never," she cried.

"All right," he said wearily, "if you won't have a divorce, I'll put the children in a boarding school, and you'll only see me every six months. Oh, for God's sake," he continued, "stop blubbering. Your tears won't help matters."

But she stubbornly refused a divorce:

"I could never love any other man but you," she sobbed.

Physically, Yvonne was reaching the breaking point. Drugs and stimulants were taking their toll.

"Do what you like," he told her ironically. "As far as I'm concerned, you're a free woman. Don't you realize the advantage of the situation? You can have all the lovers you like, but be discreet about it; the public mustn't know that the mayor of Orléans is being deceived by his wife!"

Yvonne could stand it no longer. She took the children for a long holiday at the seaside. But even far away from her husband, she could not overcome her clumsiness. Perhaps it is unfair continually to accuse her of clumsiness, for she was always sincere. But her very reactions and initiatives aggravated the situation. She had only been at the seaside a few days when she wrote a long letter to Pierre, admitting all her faults and her inferiority complex. She promised him she would change and become a wife fit for him. Pierre never replied to the letter. At that stage it is difficult to see what he could have replied. The situation was becoming grotesque from every point of view.

Yvonne returned from her holiday and tried to commit suicide. She miscalculated the dose and only made herself terribly ill. But she had been close enough to death for the idea of death to have communicated itself to her in another and more insidious way: the death not of herself but of Pierre. She went to Paris and tried to see him at the Chamber of Deputies, but he sent an usher to say he was too busy. She took his secretary out to tea and astounded the young girl by asking her point-blank if she knew any details about her husband's mistress. No move could have been more ill advised or clumsier. And Yvonne's last words to the bewildered secretary were hardly the acme of discretion:

"There are some women who kill their husbands," she said bitterly, and added, "How I can understand them."

Yvonne left the secretary and went to the tiny bachelor flat where Pierre stayed when he was in Paris in the rue Cambronne. She had spent so pitifully few nights there with him, as he had always kept her away from his Paris life. She searched the flat from top to bottom.

As is often the case in affairs of crime passionel, the object which sealed Pierre's fate was of pathetically little importance. A railway timetable with a pencil tick against the times for the Paris-Chatelguyon trains. Nothing more, yet it was to lead to murder, to five 7.65-mm.-caliber bullets being fired into a man of 42.

For Jeanne Perreau was at that moment spending *her* holidays at Chatelguyon. There was no need to search further. Jeanne Perreau could lie as much as she liked but the proof was there, in the form of a tiny stroke with a pencil.

In cold fury, Yvonne returned to Orléans. She went straight to see Jeanne's husband, Léon Perreau. She told him Jeanne was her husband's mistress. Perreau managed finally to calm her down, saying gently—but without conviction—that it was all nonsense. She went home finally, but returned to see him the next day.

"I'm going to cause a scandal," she announced curtly.

"You can't cry that all round the rooftops," Perreau said, horrified. "Look, your nerves are shot to pieces. Why don't you go and see a doctor, a psychiatrist?"

She left Perreau, seized with a hysterical desire to laugh. A psychiatrist for a deceived woman. . . . Hardly had she arrived home when Pierre, warned by his secretary and Perreau, telephoned her from Paris. His language to her had never been so coarse:

"Are you going to stop mucking me about?" he demanded harshly.

"What do you mean?"

"You're a cow," Pierre told her.

"You, too."

The tone of the conversation was set. The language became cruder and untranslatable. Yvonne, seeking to wound him, told Pierre she was deceiving him with another man. He replied, using a particularly vulgar term, that he "couldn't f—— well care less" and hung up.

Yvonne returned yet again to see Léon Perreau. This time Perreau placidly admitted he knew of the liaison between his wife and Pierre Chevallier. Later, at the trial, he was to admit that his wife had told him of it on the very first day! Yet strange as it may seem, he had chased away a former lover of his wife's but it appeared to tickle his vanity that her second extramarital lover was the mayor of Orléans and a Deputy to boot!

Yvonne left him like a woman in a dream. She went to the police station and applied mechanically for a gun license. Yes, her husband was an important political figure and she was afraid he might have dangerous enemies. Unsuspecting, the Commissaire granted her the certificate on the spot. The unfortunate officer was later demoted to an unimportant post, which ruined any hopes he had of making a successful career in the police. The next morning, she went to Monsieur Meunier's gun shop and repeated the story she had told the police, asking for an automatic "which kills without any doubt" and 25 cartridges to go with it. The gunsmith recommended a 7.65-mm. Mab automatic, and she left his shop with the gun in her handbag.

That night she heard on the last news bulletin on the radio

that René Pléven had succeeded in forming a new government. Her husband's name was on the list of new ministers as Secretary of State for Technical Education, Youth and Sports. It was a brilliant beginning. With a final access of tenderness, Yvonne sent a long telegram of congratulations and love to Pierre. But the end was at hand.

Then she thought of the automatic and telephoned a great personal friend, a nun, Sister Sainte-Françoise, asking her to come to the house at that late hour. The Sister came and Yvonne told her everything, concluding:

"I am going to commit suicide, Sister. It will be better that way."

"Yvonne, you do not have the right to do that. . . ."

But Sister Sainte-Françoise's well-intended words about duty and children and resignation and putting yourself in the hands of the Lord did nothing to help Yvonne. Her nerves had definitely broken now; one moment she was opting for suicide, the next for murder. Suicide, murder—murder, suicide. Her reverie was interrupted by the telephone. Pierre was calling from Paris:

"I'll be coming in early in the morning to change. There are two important ceremonies and I'll be in a hurry."

She had tried to say something but he had already hung up. Not a word about his ministerial appointment, no word of thanks for her long and affectionate telegram. The rest of the night, more and more black coffee, more and more tobacco, more and more maxiton. There was no thought of suicide now; it was murder, murder, murder beating in Yvonne's tortured mind as she paced the living room, waiting for dawn. Dawn and waiting for the morning paper delivery. The name of Dr. Pierre Chevallier in the headline of the local paper—Our mayor is minister. His name on the front page of the Paris paper. His picture in both. A hurriedly put-together article in the local paper, filled with praise and lavish adulation for the mayor. No word of Yvonne. There would never be any word of Yvonne. She was not worthy of him. She was an imbecile, clumsy and maladroit. She had no finesse, no intelligence, no culture. He had told her so, time after time. She was just a little peasant girl; he was an important politician. Cow, imbecile, deceived woman. He had everything. She had nothing. But she had something. Black coffee, maxiton. Yes, she had something. Yvonne Chevallier had a brand-new Mab automatic pistol hidden in her linen chest upstairs.

The sound of a powerful car outside. Yvonne looked out of the window. There it was, just as Pierre had always dreamed it would be, the official six-cylinder black Citröen and chauffeur allotted to all ministers, the red-white-and-blue cockade displayed proudly in the windscreen denoting his parliamentary rank. It was the fulfillment of Pierre's dreams. Once upon a time it would have been the fulfillment of Yvonne's dreams. . . .

Her younger son, Mathieu, was standing beside her. Quickly, Yvonne took him in her arms:

"When Papa comes through the door, run towards him and say: 'Bonjour, Monsieur le Ministre.' "

The front door opened and the mayor of Orléans, the Monsieur le Ministre of only a few hours' standing, came in. Mathieu ran gaily towards his father piping: "Bonjour, Monsieur le Ministre."

It was obvious that Pierre was wildly happy. He picked his son up and kissed him. Then he put him down tenderly and rushed upstairs to change. He had not even glanced at Yvonne, standing in the doorway of the living room, her fists clenched tight with emotion, her heart pounding under the action of the drugs and enormous quantities of black coffee she had taken. She followed him to her own bedroom where he still kept his own shirts and underwear in another highboy. Swiftly he stripped, until he was down to his underpants. Yvonne handed him a clean shirt, then blurted out:

"Pierre, can't I have some kind of an explanation?"

"I've got no time now, I'm in a hurry."

"But I must have an explanation. . . ."

There was a pause as Pierre unfolded his shirt. Then he said in brutal, cutting tones:

"I've no desire to explain anything to a whore."

Cold fury replaced Yvonne's nervous agitation:

"It's not me, the whore. It's your girl friend who's the trollop!"

"I forbid you to speak of her in those terms," Pierre replied, his own anger rising rapidly. He seized Yvonne cruelly by the hair and said:

"She's worth more than you. You, you're worthless!"

Yvonne struggled in his brutal grip:

"She's a prostitute."

Pierre let her go and turned his back on her, saying:

"I don't mind what she is, and I'm going to marry her."

He started to dress himself before the mirror, chanting like a schoolboy: "I'm a minister, I'm a minister," executing a sort of war dance of triumph at the same time. Then he turned his head and said over his shoulder:

"She will divorce, and you will divorce. I'll marry her, and you'll stay in your own dung!"

Yvonne was appalled. This was worse than anything she had imagined:

"And the children?"

"They can go to a boarding school; I don't care."

"But Pierre, listen to me. Pierre, you are the only man I have ever loved, the only man I have ever known. I've never deceived you with anyone!"

Desperation. Fever pitch. Yvonne prostrated herself on her knees before her husband. He became more and more vulgar:

"Muck off. I've got other things to do than listen to your claptrap. Muck off; you stink!"

Yvonne put out a despairing hand and touched his thigh.

At that moment, Pierre made a particularly revolting and obscene gesture which was not even described before the court, so foul was it, accompanied by an equally unprintable expression. She ran to her linen closet and seized her automatic:

"If you marry her, I'll kill myself," she screamed at him.

"Go ahead and kill yourself; it will be the first sensible thing you've done in your life," he told her mockingly.

"But I'm serious," Yvonne said, brandishing the loaded automatic. "I will kill myself!"

"Well for God's sake kill yourself, but wait until I've gone," he added in mock seriousness.

The end. The final insult. The final sarcasm. The final humiliation. Breaking point.

Yvonne walked slowly towards Pierre, firing steadily from the hip as she moved. Four shots in swift succession, each hitting the target; the thigh, the chin, the middle of the chest and the forehead. The mayor of Orléans and the new minister slumped to the floor without a cry.

Downstairs, little Mathieu heard the shots and cried out.

Yvonne rushed down to him, seized him in her arms and took him out to the cook. Then she returned to the scene of tragedy. What happened next? All we *know* is that there was a fifth shot and the bullet hit Pierre in the back.

Yvonne said that she knelt beside her husband's body and intended to commit suicide with the last cartridge. But at the penultimate moment, her eyes fell on a picture of their elder son on the wall before her. She got up and the automatic "went off accidentally."

A few minutes later, the telephone rang in the main Orléans police station. The mayor's wife wanted the Commissaire urgently. Commissaire Gazano picked up the receiver. He heard Yvonne Chevallier stammer over the line:

"Monsieur le Commissaire, come quickly. My husband wants you urgently. . . ."

Two hours later, Yvonne Chevallier, heavily veiled and

dressed in black, stepped into the police car which drove her to Orléans prison. It was just fifteen years since she had met Pierre Chevallier at Orléans hospital. The two ugliest buildings in the otherwise beautiful city. . . .

It is no trite remark to say that public opinion is a fickle thing. Nothing could be more true and never before in France was this more clear than in the Chevallier affair. In the beginning, the whole of the man-in-the-street's sympathy was for the murdered minister. The woman-in-the-street's sympathy as well, for Pierre Chevallier had been exceptionally handsome, distinguished and even "sportif," a quality much appreciated by French women. He had a fine war record, a fine resistance record. He was a genuine hero. Orléans was officially quoted as the best reconstructed city in France, thanks to Pierre Chevallier.

There was nothing handsome about Yvonne. She was the sort of woman with long, angular features which invariably come out badly in photographs. Her physical state did not improve them. At the preliminary hearings before she was remanded to the Assizes, the newspapers, with no particular law of libel to restrain them, called her a shrew and a termagant. It goes without saying that they had already dubbed her the "Assassin of Orléans." French newspapers will frequently call you an assassin without bothering to find out if you are anything more than a suspect, or even whether the victim has died or not! But at the same time, public opinion had not yet universally condemned her, for there was the all-important question of the *other* woman. Contrary to general English belief, the French are an extremely sporting race and even have extremely advanced conceptions of "le fair play." Sometimes the French push their sporting instincts to the extreme, and court battles take on the aspect of a sporting contest with accompanying cheers and boos. The background to the Chevallier

affair could never occur in England, where adultery is undoubtedly as rife if not more rife than in France but is also undoubtedly more discreet. The French push their ideas of sport
into the bedroom with a certain spirit of "let the best man win."

The English lower, middle and upper-middle classes do not
look on amatory activities as a sport at all. They regard the act
of love with the same traditional respect as they regard their
overcooked Sunday roast joint and frequently soggy Yorkshire
pudding. Perhaps it is no mere coincidence that there is a
certain temporal connection between the sacred Sunday roast
and the English predilection for making love on Sunday afternoon. In any event, such matters are never a subject for conversation in these classes as they are in France.

It was thus with the Chevallier case. Yvonne Chevallier was
a shrew and a bitch, said the newspapers. All right, said the
public, for the moment, we will take your word for it. But
before we condemn her definitely, let's hear all about the
other woman, because you never know. And to date, nobody
seems to have disputed that Yvonne was a good mother and a
good housewife. It even appears that she was a good lover, so
perhaps there is more to this case than meets the eye. Let
us have "le fair play."

And the miracle took place between the appearance of the
morning newspapers on November 7, 1952, and the afternoon
newspapers on the same day, after Yvonne Chevallier had
spent the morning in the dock. For in that short space of time,
Yvonne became the victim instead of the accused. Few trials
have ever opened in such an atmosphere of passion in France.
In the Dubuisson case which was to follow a year later, the
public turned out in force because they wanted to hear all the
dirty details. This was most definitely not the case in the
Chevallier affair where there was only one fundamental question at stake: the right to punish for repeated and aggravated
adultery. This was the classical example of crime passionel and

in a strange way it signified that France was getting back to
normal after a difficult postwar period when the papers had
been filled with nothing but such boring subjects as the Marshall Plan, the necessities of rationing and successive financial
crises.

The case opened at Reims before the Presiding Judge, M.
Raymond Jadin, with M. Raymond Lindon, the Advocate General, appearing for the prosecution, and Maître Aquaviva, a
distinguished if somewhat tear-jerking lawyer, for the defense.
Strangely enough, he was to have little need of his powers of
persuasion, for the judge and the Advocate General conducted
an extremely capable defense for Yvonne Chevallier themselves!

Pale, with enormous dark patches under her eyes, Yvonne
Chevallier appeared between the ritual two gendarmes in a dark-
gray tailored suit and a white blouse. Her hands moved continually, rolling and unrolling a handkerchief into a ball. With
the customary phrases the case opened and then came the first
surprise. Judge Jadin, of ferocious reputation, called Yvonne
"Madame." Stupefaction in court! The correct term is
"Accused." . . . She sat in the dock as the judge himself traced
the background to the crime, which you have seen in the preceding pages, with a gentleness hitherto unknown in a French
court of law. She bowed her head almost in shame as he said
softly:

"You loved him and were in love and were his lover in the
fullest sense of the words. . . ."

It was true. Nobody had ever denied it. The feeling in court
began to change rapidly. It is one thing for a man to turn to
another woman when his wife no longer loves him, no longer
wants to be loved by him, is sullen, bored or indifferent. But
this was not the case.

"Your life became an insupportable burden," the judge said,
after he had come to yet another example of Pierre Chevallier's
brutal indifference to the mother of his children. Yvonne sud-

denly burst into tears. The two doctors who were present as a precautionary measure looked worried. But she controlled herself with an effort and rubbed the ball of handerchief into her eyes.

"It was terrible," she managed to stammer. The doctors looked relieved. They had obviously expected hysteria.

Only at rare intervals in retracing the events which led to the drama did Judge Jadin allow himself gently to chide Yvonne. Referring to the long letter she wrote to Pierre when she was on holiday at the seaside, he said:

"These confessions, this humility, did you really think this was the way to conquer a man's heart?"

"He had told me so often that I was stupid, an idiot," Yvonne replied helplessly. "I was so used to hearing it all, it was only natural that I admitted it in writing. . . ."

Finally Judge Jadin came to the actual scene of the murder. When he reached the joint just before the shooting, when Pierre Chevallier, clad only in his trunks, had made the terribly obscene gesture together with the unspeakable remark, Yvonne could stand it no longer. The expected hysterical crisis came, and Jadin recessed the court to a loud murmur of sympathy from the spectators. A quarter of an hour later Yvonne returned, looking better, and the interrogation continued.

"You had the pistol in your hand. You repeated, 'I will kill myself!' "

"Yes."

"He turned round and yelled at you, 'Kill yourself then!' adding almost immediately afterwards, 'But wait until I've gone.' "

"That is correct."

"At that moment the drama occurred. You walked towards your husband and you fired at him!"

Yvonne's voice was barely audible: "Yes, Monsieur le Président."

Judge Jadin skated expertly over the thin ice which covered

the dangerous circumstances of the fifth shot, fired after Yvonne had returned to the scene of the murder, accepting her explanation without demur.

The painful account of the shooting terminated, Judge Jadin tried to formulate a brief résumé of the psychological side of the case:

"Would it be true to say of you that you had remained more of a mistress, a lover, than a wife or mother?"

"I loved my children, too," Yvonne said, with more vigor in her voice.

"You had an animal passion for your husband. You should have dominated it and, in any case, have realized that you did not have the right to take life. You let this passion overwhelm your whole life without ever trying to control it. I understand your Calvary but it still did not give you the right to kill. . . ."

Yvonne was crying again in the dock, but softly this time. This was no longer hysteria. It was a lonely woman crying because she had killed the thing she loved. . . .

It was the turn of the witnesses. The first was the psychiatrist who had examined Yvonne, Dr. Gourion. He stressed that Yvonne had been exceptionally frank with him and had tried to conceal nothing. He had never examined anyone so willing to try to help him. Then he came to the key of the whole affair:

"She never thought that her husband *could* deceive her. This is a point of her character which is of essential importance in the circumstances; adultery for her was a sin from another world. I don't mean to say that she did not know of its existence, but she considered it as a sort of monstrosity, a form of sickness which could never occur to normal people. It was beyond her conception. . . . It was an absolutely stupefying revelation for her when she discovered that her husband was deceiving her with another woman. She was seeing another world which was completely foreign to her, and her subsequent actions could be compared to a bird which batters at a light-house, blinded by its brilliance."

Dr. Gourion would not commit himself on the question of an inferiority complex, but contented himself with saying:

"I noticed a certain humility in Madame Chevallier, due to the intellectual superiority of her husband. She was the 'nurse' who had married the 'doctor.' The passage of the years accentuated this humility and she had difficulty in following the ascent of her husband. If I may résumé the situation; Madame Chevallier had retained the mentality of a teen-ager in love with a student. . . . To conclude, she had suffered considerably from what I will call depreciation. A physical depreciation because her husband refused her intimacy; and mental depreciation because she judged herself inferior to him. She despaired of ever reaching the level of the person she had never ceased to love. That was the state of mind of the accused when she killed."

We have had the physical facts, we have had the mental theory. Now for the *sauce piquante,* the third party, the *other* woman. But first for her husband, Léon Perreau, the cuckolded husband, immortalized as a figure of fun in French song and verse from time immemorial. "Le Chef de Gare, il est cocu . . ." runs the song. The tune was in everyone's head as he took the stand. Judge Jadin continued with the questioning himself:

"You knew your wife was Pierre Chevallier's mistress?"

"Exactly."

An odd word, exactly. Nothing more or less, but presumably implicit approval. Exactly.

"What did you know about their liaison?"

"Not very much, to be perfectly honest."

General laughter in court, Judge Jadin frowned disapprovingly, but at once the atmosphere became less tense.

"You knew the liaison existed, all right?"

"That wasn't difficult; my wife told me about it on the very first day," Perreau replied unexpectedly.

This time, Judge Jadin had to warn the spectators severely against laughter in court.

"Astonishing frankness!" Jadin remarked disagreeably. "Your wife just told you she had taken a lover, like that?"

"We had come to an agreement between us, my wife and myself. We were only good friends. It was only our three children who kept us together. But for . . . other things . . . we led our own ways."

"I will spare you my remarks on your apparent conception of marriage," Judge Jadin said dryly. If he had hoped to embarrass Perreau, he was disappointed. The little, slightly balding man in the witness box seemed to be almost enjoying his self-appointed role as the cuckolded husband. Jadin tried hard to shake him out of his complacency, but all that resulted was a dialogue which might have come straight from the pages of Molière, or Beaumont and Fletcher.

"What did you think when Madame Chevallier told you her husband had told her on the telephone that he was going to divorce her, and would make you divorce your wife to marry her?" the judge asked.

"It was rather a shock," Perreau admitted.

"In other words, you didn't mind being deceived but you didn't want to be abandoned?"

"But I had three children," Perreau replied indignantly.

"One day Madame Chevallier asked you what you would do if your wife had a child by Pierre Chevallier?"

"That's right."

"And you replied that you would be there to assume the responsibility of fatherhood?"

"Exactly," replied this remarkable husband using his favorite word.

"And another time she asked you what you would do if they went off together and you replied: 'In that case you could come and stay with me and I'll build up your morale'?

"Do you realize that because of your complacency, you carry a heavy responsibility in this affair?" Jadin demanded.

"I didn't really have any choice," Perreau said, obviously not realizing it at all.

"Nevertheless, Pierre Chevallier wasn't your wife's first lover. You chased the first one away, right enough. Why were you so firm with the first?"

"My wife didn't want to go on with the affair," Perreau said frankly. Few comedians could have got a better response from the audience.

"You are a real *protector*," Jadin said ironically, playing on the double meaning of the word in French which also exists in English. The double meaning was completely lost on Léon Perreau, who replied complacently:

"Oh, that first lover disgusted me, but not the other."

The trouble was, Perreau was so obviously sincere!

"In other words, you approved of Pierre Chevallier?"

"Well, yes. It may sound strange but I liked him."

Jadin asked him if it was true that his wife had written to Pierre Chevallier saying, "My husband will step aside on condition that we find him a lucrative job which will interest him and take up his time."

Perreau admitted this was true, and this time even Advocate General Lindon jumped to his feet:

"So you would have consented to separate from your wife after all for a good job?"

"Exactly."

"And I suppose it was by chance that your wife's brother was decorated with the Légion d'Honneur on the recommendation of Pierre Chevallier?" Lindon roared at him.

"Oh yes, that. I'm forced to agree it's true. . . ."

After this somewhat revolting performance for a man and a husband, Léon Perreau was allowed to leave the witness box. There was not the slightest point to Maître Aquaviva cross-examining him for the defense, as everything he had said was already of inestimable value to the defense.

"Call Madame Jeanne Perreau!"

The stir in court rose to a murmur, then Jeanne Perreau walked unconcernedly to the witness box. Here was the *other* woman at last. You did not have to look at her twice to understand Pierre Chevallier's temptation. Sensual, yet extremely attractive features, a beautiful complexion, sleek red hair under an attractive lincoln-green leather beret, combined with complete mastery of herself and an absolute disdain for her surroundings and the majesty of justice. The murmur changed to loud boos and catcalls, and Judge Jadin had to threaten to clear the court. Her green eyes flickered contemptuously at the public as she took off her gloves unhurriedly to take the oath. She wasted no time in coming to the point.

"Jeanne Perreau, thirty-four years old, no profession. I met Pierre Chevallier in 1947. He and his wife and my husband and myself went out together. I became his mistress in 1950."

Bull's-eye first time! Jeanne Perreau had wasted neither time nor words in coming to the point. In the dock, Yvonne Chevallier kept her eyes cast on the floor before her and did not once raise her eyes to look at the red-haired iceberg in the witness box. But Jeanne was galloping even too fast for the judge.

"Don't go so fast," Jadin told her. "When were you alone with him for the first time?"

"In the train going to Paris. We traveled together and he invited me to dinner."

"And you became his mistress?"

"Oh, no, a long time afterwards," Jeanne exclaimed. "Six months later. I made him wait for it," she added.

Jeanne had spent every Tuesday and Wednesday night with him in Paris once the affair had begun.

"You loved him?"

"Yes."

"He loved you?"

"I believe so."

"You had another lover before Pierre Chevallier?"

"That has nothing to do with this court," Jeanne said defiantly.

"That's for me to decide," Jadin told her unpleasantly, and asked what had happened when Yvonne had gone to see her.

"She asked me all of a sudden, 'Are you my husband's mistress?' I had to reassure her."

"You lied to her."

"Yes, but I felt very sorry for her," Jeanne said, then added, "But I admit that I didn't feel sufficiently sorry to break with Pierre."

"You have a great responsibility in this case. You found many material advantages in your liaison," Jadin told her. Jeanne objected. Pierre had found it difficult to live on his Deputy's salary after having closed down his medical practice, she said.

"But your brother nevertheless received the Légion d'Honneur?"

"That's correct," Jeanne admitted.

Maître Aquaviva had been fidgeting on his bench for some time, not yet having found any useful role to play in helping his client. He finally decided the moment had come for histrionics. He leaped to his feet and swung an accusing arm at the red-haired woman on the witness stand:

"And you never felt any shame?" he roared.

Jeanne looked at him almost in pity, as if she were trying to understand a rather rude person butting into a private conversation.

"No, never. I was in love with him," she said as if surprised by the imbecility of the question.

"And you have no regrets for what has happened?" Maître

Aquaviva hurled at her in his best theatrical voice. Jeanne looked at him with further surprise registered on her face:

"But naturally I have."

She turned to leave the box but Aquaviva waved his arm at her:

"Stay there Madame," he commanded.

She shrugged in a resigned manner and waited for the rest of his thunder. From her expression, it was a bad few minutes to pass, but an inevitable few minutes, like having to go to the dentist.

"Madame, I am telling you," Aquaviva roared, "there above," he waved his arms towards the ceiling, "there above exists the Supreme Court. One day you will be called upon to answer for your acts, but I personally am not awaiting that day to tell you that it is you who should be in the dock beside Madame Chevallier. You are the principal guilty person here; you should be ashamed to the depths of your soul!"

This was what the public had come to hear. Their sporting instincts aroused, they clapped their hands instinctively in their appreciation of Maître Aquaviva's fine performance. The judge did nothing to stop the demonstration.

The hearty applause finally died down and Maître Aquaviva cleared his throat in preparation for an encore. Unfortunately he did not have the time to pronounce it. Replying to him in cold and extremely contemptuous tones, Jeanne said loudly, as if wanting to silence the remaining spectators and Aquaviva himself:

"My liaison with Dr. Chevallier was a private affair between myself and my conscience. I have no need for any other judge. I loved him, and he loved me. And as far as my husband was concerned, I did not want to leave him; he is an excellent companion and always loyal."

The applause for Maître Aquaviva turned to loud boos at this speech. Judge Jadin gave the public final warning that he would clear the court if there were any further disorders. Jeanne

Perreau, her green eyes flaming with temper this time, turned abruptly to the judge:

"I've got something else to say."

"Proceed."

Yvonne Chevallier jerked her tear-stained face from the floor and stared at this beautiful creature who faced the court filled with anger:

"I loved Pierre, I still love him and I am sure that you are never punished because you love someone!"

And without waiting for permission, Jeanne Perreau walked off the witness stand and strode, head high and mouth set in disdain, through the pathway between the public benches. As she left the courtroom, those inside could hear the crowd outside calling for her death.

If there had been something primeval and magnificent about her performance, it could but strengthen Yvonne Chevallier's defense. No possible amount of cross-examination could have produced such damning words. Jeanne may have been booed and hissed, but it was impossible for an intelligent man not to have some admiration for her. She was a one hundred percent woman.

It was the unpleasant task of Maître Mirat, appearing for Pierre Chevallier's family, the *partie civile,* to brave the obvious tide of opinion in court and seek to reestablish the character of the former mayor of Orléans. His difficulties were made yet more onerous because Judge Jadin himself was manifestly seeking to defend Yvonne Chevallier, and after all, a Presiding Judge is still a Presiding Judge, even when he has given every indication of having formed a quite personal bias in an affair of crime passionel. I know that jurists in England will throw their hands to the heavens in despair at the account of this case, but nothing is exaggerated. And you must bear in mind that, as I explained previously, the judge *conducts* the case in France in a far more positive manner than in England where he listens, considers, and interrupts when an issue is not clear and he wants a further explanation, or to explain a point of law. The judge examines the witness in the first instance in a French court, then the prosecution and the defense can cross-examine and draw out the testimonies. And it was clear in the Chevallier case that Raymond Jadin had decided which side he was on from the very beginning, when he called Yvonne "Madame" and not "Accused." It was absolutely unheard-of in a case involving a capital charge in which the offense was freely admitted. Yet there it was, and Maître Mirat had to carry out his duty to the Chevallier family. He produced two witnesses who, had they been handled in a different manner, would have undoubtedly altered the issue somewhat. Monsieur Pierre Carré, editor of the influential provincial newspaper, the "Courrier du Centre," told the court of an incident which had occurred in 1947:

"We returned from Paris in the same car with the Chevalliers one evening. They were late in arriving and were quarreling violently when we started. In the car, Madame Chevallier didn't stop insulting her husband for one moment. When we finally reached Orléans the doctor remained alone with me for a moment. He said that he expected his wife would try to kill him one day.

"His wife had violent fits of temper which frightened him. That very evening he asked me whether I would take on the responsibility for bringing up his children if anything happened, because he assured me his wife was incapable of bringing them up herself.

"Dr. Chevallier asked me to perform this task several times. Only a few months before the drama, he had a heart attack and said to me, 'If I die, do not forget that you are going to be the guardian of my children because I have no confidence in my wife. . . .' In fact the very day before he was killed he told me his wife had caused another scene and wanted to confirm again that I would agree to become the guardian of his children if anything happened."

An odd testimony—although the witness was undoubtedly biased because his best friend had been murdered, there was a definite ring of truth in Pierre Chevallier's concern for the upbringing of his children. But it was to be confirmed by the next witness, Monsieur Bouilhaguet, the Deputy Prefect of Montbéliard, who was also with Pierre Chevallier the day he met his death. After saying that his children were his "major preoccupation," Pierre Chevallier sold him that he was considering sending the elder, Thugal, to a boarding school. His friend replied that he thought Thugal was rather young for that, and Chevallier replied, textually, the Deputy Prefect stressed:

"You yourself know that my children are half-crazy. I've already waited too long. It is absolutely necessary that I free them from the influence of their mother."

Then Monsieur Bouilhaguet stressed that Pierre Chevallier had always been extremely discreet about his private life—"an almost inhuman discretion" as he put it.

"People have said that Pierre Chevallier was guilty of gross conduct toward his wife. Allow me to express my surprise, for Chevallier's behaviour in his day-to-day life was the exact opposite," he concluded.

Maître Mirat did not press the question of the fifth shot, the only really unexplained factor in the crime. For Yvonne Chevallier had made three separate statements, each different, about this strange fifth shot, coming a matter of minutes after the first four, after she had left the room of the crime, gone downstairs, spoken to the cook, and returned upstairs. In her preliminary statement she said that all five shots had been fired in rapid succession. But Pierre Chevallier's chauffeur, waiting outside in the ministerial car, said that this was untrue; the fifth shot had come some time after the first four. On being confronted with this statement, Yvonne Chevallier said that she had fired the fifth shot "without aiming," to remove the temptation of suicide (as she had only loaded five cartridges

into the magazine). Then finally she came out with the story
about seeing Thugal's photo on the wall, in support of her second theory or claim. It could have been a damning piece of
evidence for the prosecution had they wanted to stress it, for
a fifth shot fired several minutes after the others shows a cold
and lasting determination to kill, and it also could be considered as a *coup de grâce*. But Maître Mirat contented himself
with saying that Yvonne could not be considered as an entirely
truthful witness, as she had told several different versions to
explain this vital point. It surprised nobody in court when the
lawyer dropped the question of the fifth shot entirely and almost
apologized for his appearance, saying that he was there merely
"to defend the memory of a dead son." A most uninspiring
performance, altogether.

Then came the turn of Advocate General Lindon to wind-up
for the prosecution in his final speech, which, to be perfectly
frank, could take its place in a law-student's manual as a fine
example of a speech for the *defense!*

"In beginning my requisition," he said, "I want to stress
that to prosecute does not necessarily mean to crush the oppo-
nent. I am not constrained by my duty systematically to bran-
dish the Sword of Justice. . . ."

An audible sigh of relief came from the public benches,
where there had always been an unhealthy suspicion that the
prosecution might try to pull a fast one at the last moment;
such things have not been entirely unknown in a French court
of law.

"I am not going to be as severe as the law would dictate,"
Lindon continued. "I want to examine the psychological reasons
which made Yvonne Chevallier act as she did, and we will see
afterwards where her faults lay and how we must judge them.
. . . Yvonne Chevallier loved her husband, she adored her
husband, she loved him physically to the point of idolatry and,

at the same time, she was his slave and his mistress, rejoicing in his successes, wanting to help him everywhere and for always. . . . But her passion, based on simple and elementary motives, was too exclusive, all-devouring even.

"For at a certain moment, Yvonne Chevallier began to have doubts about herself. Is she worthy of this great man? She is afraid of appearing inferior, to spoil things for him by her very presence. So she closes her shell, she remains invisible, not wanting to spoil the triumphant advance of Pierre Chevallier in any way. The drama began at that moment. . . .

"She then has a presentiment of this other love and discovers its existence. It is a terrible revelation for her. She might have been able to tolerate a passing adventure, but never the possibility of a divorce. The torture begins for her, the torture from which she will never be free. The degradation of her spirit accompanies the degradation of her body; she is a sick person lost in a storm.

"I want to try to see what sort of a man Pierre Chevallier was during this time. You have been told what a public figure he was, filled with a great sense of duty, impatient to accomplish his great tasks. Nobody can doubt his courage and his honesty as a political figure.

"But I am less certain of him insofar as the honesty of his private life is concerned. . . ."

Lindon then read extracts of love letters between Pierre Chevallier and his mistress. Pierre had written: "Chérie, when I think of the hours we passed together the other night . . ." Then further on in the same letter he had said: "I have absolutely no further feelings for her, not even the sentiments of pity I had mentioned to you previously."

"He refused her this pity which even her rival granted her," Lindon roared. There was something rather unhealthy, almost obscene even, in this speech for the prosecution which seemed bent on pulverizing the character of the late mayor of Orléans. The Advocate General realized he was perhaps going too far and abruptly changed the subject.

"Jealousy was driving her crazy. Her husband's successive refusals to make love, his clear intentions of divorcing her, were marking her like red-hot irons. Is she capable of following the ascension of her husband? Is she too stupid, too gauche, too maladroit? But no, not at all. She will willingly be the slave of a great man, providing she has a little place at his side.

"He becomes minister and for a moment she thinks that everything will be all right; after all, shouldn't ministers set an example? And she sends her son to say 'Bonjour, Monsieur le Ministre'. . . . All the thanks she received for this touching thought was for Pierre Chevallier to ask for clean linen, clean linen which would serve him during the intimacy he would enjoy on the following day with Jeanne Perreau. . . ."

As an appeal for the defense, it was heartrending. As a speech for the prosecution, it was utterly and completely beyond explanation.

Once again, Lindon realized he was going too far and cleverly came back to earth—and to his duty as prosecutor in a case of what at least in England would be termed premeditated murder.

"Do I need to say that we must feel sorry for Yvonne Chevallier? I do not think so. Should we absolve her? If she has the right to a considerable degree of extenuating circumstances, I must now stress just what constituted her responsibility. Was she completely responsible for her action? It must be stated that she lied about one important fact—the moment when she fired the fifth shot."

Everyone sat up attentively. How was the prosecution going to handle the tricky question of the fifth bullet in the back? Lindon continued:

"She had stated first of all that the five bullets were all fired at once. It was not until she heard the contradictory evidence of the chauffeur, who said he heard a burst of shots, followed several moments later by a fifth detonation, that she admitted she had lied.

"Was the fifth shot an accident? Personally, I consider it was a sacrilege. Yvonne Chevallier fired at her husband's corpse. . . ."

And thus the prosecution dismissed one of the most important facts of the case. Maître Aquaviva sat back with a sigh of relief, and Linden continued:

"Yvonne Chevallier acted as if her own happiness was the only important thing in the world. Public figures belong to the nation. Should sacrifice have been necessary, she should have sacrificed her own feelings and not this man filled with promise for the future. She committed a crime which I cannot absolve. Therefore I am going to propose a solution which appears to be both wise and fair. I am not going to ask for a sentence of a hard labor or penal servitude. But neither do I want to see her acquitted.

"Do not render a novelist's notion of justice. I must remind you that you are not judging a divorce but a murder; a woman has killed. The question at stake is to know whether adultery deserves the death sentence, for that was the verdict which Yvonne Chevallier pronounced on her husband. You cannot acquit her. Neither can you give her a suspended sentence, for this would mean in effect saying to her: Go off and remake your life afresh and don't kill anyone else!

"For Yvonne Chevallier, I claim a short prison sentence—two years for example. I am personally convinced that the accused understands the virtue of redemption. She has already spent fifteen months in prison awaiting trial. She knows she has committed an irreparable act and she has never once asked for provisional liberty [bail]. In this I see the extent of her remorse.

"If you free her this night, gentlemen," Lindon told the jurors, "it will mean that you have given her absolution in the eyes of the public. Think, gentlemen, what this would mean. It would mean that every woman could hide a pistol containing five cartridges in her bedside table and use it at will, with the peace of mind that she would be acquitted for her act. . . .

"In finishing my speech, may I be allowed, in my somewhat theatrical red robe, to make the same remark as Sister Sainte-Françoise made in her black robe?"

Lindon turned dramatically to the dock and said:

"Yvonne, you do not have the right to do that!"

There was not the slightest need for Maître Aquaviva to bother to make a speech for the defense after the Advocate General's magnificent peroration in Yvonne's favor, but he could not resist advancing a few final heartbreaking and tear-jerking considerations.

"Gentlemen, think of her two sons. Must they grow up alone in the world? Return this unfortunate woman to her children. Gentlemen, acquit her and you will leave this court with a clear conscience!"

As is almost invariably the case in crime passionel, it was the sound of her own lawyer which finally made Yvonne Chevallier break down. Pouring with tears as he spoke of her children, she repeated hysterically in the dock: "I didn't mean it. I didn't mean it. Forgive me. Forgive me. . . ."

Most of the public were weeping by this time, too, and even the gendarmes showed signs of being touched, lending Yvonne fresh handkerchiefs from their own pockets. Asked by the judge if she had anything final to say before the jury withdrew, she whispered, "No, no, forgive me."

The jury was out for exactly 40 minutes. They had three questions to consider: Did Yvonne Chevallier intend bodily harm to her husband? Was her act premeditated? And did she shoot with intent to murder? The court kibitzers were betting that the jury would dismiss the last two charges and find her guilty of the bodily-harm charge, so that Judge Jadin could sentence her to two years' imprisonment on a form of manslaughter charge.

But when the jury returned, the foreman of the ten men stated they had found Yvonne Chevallier "Not Guilty" on each charge. Amidst thunderous roars of applause from the spectators, Judge Raymond Jadin formally acquitted Yvonne for the murder of Dr. Pierre Chevallier.

She was a free woman once again.

But there was a minor mystery concealed behind the decision of the jury which, at one moment, had decided in favor of the two-year sentence. Their decision to acquit her totally stemmed from the same motive which was later to condemn Pauline Dubuisson—"present-day bourgeois morality." For it appeared that one detail was responsible for her acquittal. A juror asked for an exact explanation of the obscene gesture Pierre Chevallier had made when standing naked except for his trunks, and the exact vulgar expression he had used to accompany it just before he was shot.

Judge Jadin was called and he read the part of Yvonne Chevallier's testimony which had not been read in court for reasons of natural modesty. The ten jurors were so shocked when they heard the evidence that they decided at once to acquit her.

Several months later, Yvonne Chevallier received the Church's absolution for her crime from Msgr. Picard de la Vacquerie, Bishop of Orléans. Then she left for the penal colony of French Guiana.

Perhaps the last words in the affair were spoken by one of the leading personalities of the colony to a journalist who went there to write an article about Yvonne Chevallier's new life with her children.

"How is she considered here?"

"As a woman who likes her job and who does it well."

And when the journalist asked about the past, the other explained gently that in the former penal colony, the past does not exist for anyone. It was like the Foreign Legion, he said, you were there and that was all. In this tropical land of heartbreak, discretion was the first article in the code of behavior.

But if the past does not exist for her neighbors, it is unlikely to have been forgotten by Yvonne Chevallier. How often must she relive those unpunished moments when she walked towards her husband, steadily firing mortal bullets into him? And how often must she relive the macabre moment when she fired that strange and totally unexplained fifth bullet into a dead man's back? For if no person had the courage to say it in court, I will say it here:

The fifth bullet, fired after she had gone downstairs and returned, was no question of sacrilege, as the Advocate General pretended. She was too simple for such thoughts. It was a deliberate bullet, fired symbolically in cold blood into the flesh which had *deceived* her. It epitomized the hairline between love and hatred. And in firing it, Yvonne Chevallier at last proved to herself she was not only equal but superior to the body on the floor.

II

The Dumbbell Murder Case

Thomas M. Disch

"If at first you don't succeed, try, try again"
is the maxim that best summarizes Ruth Snyder
and Judd Gray. Ruth was a bored young wife
with a loveless marriage, a handsome lover and
a zestful enthusiasm for widowhood. Judd was
a corset salesman with a passion to unloosen her
stays. Together they committed the single most
inept murder of the century.

THIS," said Damon Runyon, "is a dumbbell murder." He was referring not to the weapon but to the murderers, Ruth Snyder and Judd Gray, who were, yes indeed, dumb as they come. It was the secret of their success, and in terms of the size of the headlines and the number of column inches devoted to their crime, few murderers have ever been more successful. The public loved them. Ruth, especially. While she was waiting for her execution she received 164 offers of marriage. In crime, as in network television, the lowest common denominator always wins.

Imagine the worst Late, Late Movie you've ever stayed awake through, starring no one you have ever heard of. It opens with an establishing shot of a World War I recruiting poster. Legs pass by, and the camera follows the most interesting pair of them into an office building, through a door that says Tiffany Studios. Our heroine turns to face the camera and removes a floppy, flowery hat. Pretty, but a *bad* actress. Her mouth opens with each chew of gum. Her lips are on wrong. The idea she tries to convey is that she is sexy. What comes across is that she's cheap. And a bad actress. Ruth May Brown.

Now she is sitting behind a 1914-vintage telephone switchboard, doing her nails. The boss buzzes. He wants her to dial a number. She repeats it in a bored singsong, and then we watch her left hand—the right is still wet—dialing . . . the wrong number.

Cut to the office of *Motor Boating,* a Hearst magazine. The phone rings. Our hero answers. Albert Snyder. His boss, the editor of *Motor Boating,* described him this way: "Our world is made up of good, solid, silent men like this. He was a man's man, a real man, like scores of your own good friends and mine; a quiet, honest, upright man, ready to play his part in the drama of life without seeking the spotlight or trying to fill the leading role. Perhaps he was slow to make friends, though in his bowling club he was the life of the party."

All of this is visible in a glance. It is also clear that he is going to be murdered, for the soundtrack develops an ominous theme at this point. First, he bawls out Ruth for calling the wrong number, and she apologizes in a throaty not-quite-Lauren-Bacall voice. Then, fool that he is, he calls back to apologize.

A dissolve to Ruth, more smartly dressed now but chewing that same stick of gum, sitting behind the telephone switchboard of *Motor Boating* magazine. Good, solid, silent Albert places a present on her desk. When he is gone she unwraps it. A box of chocolates. "The cheap jerk!" she mutters. But when she opens the box there is a solitaire diamond. She places the ring on her finger.

"That diamond," she said later, "had as much as any one thing to do with my consenting. I wouldn't have given that ring up for anything after once I had it on my hand. I didn't know then what counts in life."

Ruth was ill on the day of their marriage. She managed to get through the ceremony, but Albert spent the night alone in his bachelor apartment.

In the first years of her marriage to Albert Snyder, Ruth discovered that what counted in life was romance, and it had passed her by. What was the use of falling in love if you ended up in a frame house at 9327 222nd Street in Queens Village with a sickly, cranky brat of a daughter and a husband who wanted to spend his evenings reading a book? Or he would build boats inside of bottles. Or go bowling with the boys. *Madame Bovary* has a slightly different plot, but it's the same general idea. Emma Bovary and Ruth Snyder were both bored for years, actively and desperately. The main difference between Emma and Ruth was that Emma lived before murder mysteries were invented. You are what you read.

Enter romance, in the form of Judd Gray, a traveling salesman working for the Bien Jolie Corset Company. A married man with a remarkable physical resemblance to the business-suited Clark Kent aspect of Superman, complete with spectacles and dimpled chin. In the autobiography he wrote in Sing Sing, *Doomed Ship,* he gives this account of his own character:

"I was a morally sound, sober, God-fearing chap, working and saving to make Isabel my wife and establish a home. I met plenty of girls—at home and on the road, in trains and hotels. I could, I thought, place every type: the nice girl who flirts, the nice girl who doesn't, the brazen out-and-out streetwalker I was warned against. I was no sensualist, I studied no modern cults, thought nothing about inhibitions and repressions. Never read Rabelais in my life. Average, yes—just one of those Americans Mencken loves to laugh at. Even belonged to a club—the Club of Corset Salesmen of the Empire State—clean-cut competitors meeting and shaking hands— and liking it."

But then, in June of 1925, at a Manhattan smorgasbord restaurant, he met Ruth Snyder, shook her hand, and, alas for them both, he liked it. The actual seduction was accomplished soon after in the office of Bien Jolie Corsets. Ruth had accompanied him there after-hours so he could retrieve a case of samples. Ruth complained of a sunburn. Judd offered to rub her back with camphor ice. She burst into tears. One thing led to another, and soon Judd was fitting her with one of his company's corsets. They were in love.

In Judd Gray's case there is no doubt that this was the Real Thing. Ruth's beauty enslaved him. Her wit captivated. No longer the tight little virgin of ten years before, she knew at last what a man wanted, and she provided it. He was fond of embracing her ankles and performing menial tasks for her. They drank. Ruth, who had been strictly beer and pretzels in Queens Village, advanced to rye and ginger ale. Judd, who had been almost a teetotaler, guzzled. Sex! Whiskey! 1926! And at the peak of his passion, at the crest of delight, he would cry out, "Momsie!" Or maybe just "Momie," which was his other pet name for her. She called him Bud.

And Ruth? Had passion transformed her as vividly? Just a few weeks before the murder, Momsie wrote a letter to Bud that conveys, better than words, the state of her feelings:

My Own Lover Boy—

Gee, but I'm happy. Oh, ain't I happy. Tomorrow's my lucky day.

I'm so happy, dear, I can't sit still enough to write what I'm thinking of.

You excuse it this time too, won't you, hon?

Went down to the movies in Q's and saw *Johnny get your hair cut*. Jackie Coogan is certainly a sweet kid and a marvelous actor, I think. Wouldn't be a bad idea if I had a haircut—it's beginning to luku-lika da wop. Wassa gude writin—huh? All I keeping thinking of is U.A. & you, you darn lovable little cuss. I could eatcha all up. Could I get lit & put out this blaze what's so much bother to me? Ah yes—hon, let's get good and "plastered"; ain't that a nice word? Beginning to think I'm already that way on nothing.

Hurry home, darling, I'll be waiting for you.

> *All my love,*
> YOUR MOMIE.

Meanwhile, back at 9327 222nd Street, Albert was receiving one custard pie after another, smack-dab in his long-suffering face. First his Buick fell on top of him when the jack slipped. Ruth may or may not have helped. Certainly a light bulb had lighted up in the balloon over her head. A month later, while he was once again under the Buick, its motor running, she brought him a glass of whiskey. He drank it. As he was falling asleep he noticed that the garage door had swung shut. Groggily he crawled to the door, opened it and escaped asphyxiation.

Some leaves flutter from the calendar. Albert is having a snooze on the living-room couch. He wakes choking. The gas cock of the heater, directly above his head, has been turned on. During another nap on this semifatal couch, Ruth comes into the room to turn down the radio. As she does so, she treads on the gas tubing of the heater. It comes off. When she returns home much later from a sudden shopping expedition, Albert is out on the street gasping for air.

She tried bichloride of mercury in his whiskey. After repeated insufficient doses he developed mithridatism, a tolerance for the poison.

Albert began to suspect something amiss. Ever an obliging victim, he recommended the writings of Mary Baker Eddy to his murderess. Christian Science, he suggested, would purge her of these homicidal tendencies. Ruth didn't study Christian Science, so there is no way of knowing if Albert's suggestion would have worked. In the same guileless spirit, Albert also gave his signature to three insurance policies. The top policy was for $1000. The second and bottom policies (Ruth assured him these were just duplicates) were for $5,000 and $45,000, and the latter was a double-indemnity contract. Should Albert now come to a violent end, he was worth $96,000. Ruth was in the enviable position of betting on a race she had fixed herself.

Murder, like schizophrenia, is a last-ditch attempt at communication, a way of expressing otherwise inexpressible feelings. Viewed in this light, Ruth's first few failed attempts represent the prattle of an infant, charmed to discover labials, dentals and fricatives but still unaware of language as such. The murder she achieved with Judd Gray was much richer expressively—baby's first complete sentence, as it were. A very simple sentence, admittedly, but simplicity has its merits. One good graffito is worth a thousand bad novels.

What Ruth had principally lacked in her previous attempts was an accomplice. She was, after all, murdering Albert for love. Any other motive would have wounded her self-esteem. The woman starring in the title role of her life could be forgiven any transgression, so long as it was done for love, and what better proof that this was the case than that her lover should assist in the crime?

Judd Gray was not easily persuaded. Ruth pointed out the beastly indignities that her husband inflicted on her nightly. Judd deplored them, but when Ruth then proposed that he learn how to use a revolver, Judd resisted her logic. She spoke in pathetic terms of her earlier solitary attempts and their failure. At last, by appealing to his sense of chivalry, Ruth persuaded him. He helped her murder Albert in much the same spirit he would have helped her cross the street. It was the sort of thing that is expected of lovers.

For two months they laid their plans and gathered the necessary equipment. A time was set—9:00 P.M., March 7, 1927—and a signal devised—there would be a light in the bedroom window. But when Judd came by at the appointed hour, the window was dark. Puzzled, he went around to the back door. Ruth was waiting in the kitchen. They embraced, and she explained that Albert could not be persuaded to go to bed. He was in the basement, chopping wood. Judd listened for a time to the rhythmic thunk of Albert's ax and decided that he was not in a mood to murder him that night.

He returned on the 20th. This time the house was deserted, the Snyders having taken Baby Lorraine with them to a party at their friends, the Fidgeons. Judd awaited their return in Ruth's mother's bedroom. Mrs. Brown was a practical nurse whose work often kept her away from home. Judd hung his hat and coat in the closet, then felt under Mrs. Brown's bedclothes for—no, not the sash weight; that comes later; not the pliers—a bottle of whiskey, which he downed (this, remember, is 1927) in one grand chugalug. A few minutes later he was down in the living room, hunting for another bottle, when the Snyders' car pulled into the driveway. He got back to Mrs. Brown's bedroom only a moment before Ruth came up the stairs with Baby Lorraine.

Baby Lorraine having been tucked into her bed, Ruth checked in with her accomplice. They embraced. Baby Lorraine was restless, and Ruth returned to tuck her in again. She changed into a nightgown and came back to Judd for more kisses and encouragement. All this while Albert was parking the Buick in the garage. Not that it makes that much difference, because even while he was in the next room, trying to get to sleep, Ruth would keep popping out of bed and into her lover's arms in the next room to discuss some last-minute detail.

Three in the morning. Albert is asleep. Judd removes his glasses and puts on a pair of rubber gloves. He opens his corset-sample case and removes (1) a bottle of chloroform, (2) a coil of picture wire, (3) a bandana handkerchief, (4) cotton batting and (5) an Italian newspaper he'd bought on the train ride into New York. He grips the sash weight in one hand (sash weights are the long lead counterweights that help windows move up and down; you never see them but they're always there) and Ruth's hand with the other. She leads him tippy-toe to Albert's bedroom.

For the first and last time in the two years they had been rivals, Judd Gray and Albert Snyder occupied the same space at the same time. Judd regarded Albert for a moment through an alcoholic fog. Then he lifted the sash weight high above his head and brought it down with his whole strength to smash— no, not Snyder's head; not yet—the headboard of the bed. Albert received only enough of a blow to awaken him. In the ensuing struggle Judd lost hold of the sash weight. Albert grabbed Judd by his necktie and began garroting him. Judd wheezed for help, and Ruth was obliged to perform the coup de grace.

Albert ceased to struggle, but Ruth, after her previous disappointments, was not going to leave it at that. She drenched the cotton batting with chloroform and plugged hefty wads into her husband's nose and mouth. Then, with Judd's assistance, she tied his hands and feet. An hour later, just to be sure, she coaxed Judd to return to the corpse and fasten a wire noose around his neck.

These chores accomplished, the murderers began to sprinkle "clues" about the house and destroy evidence that might incriminate them. First, there was Ruth's bloody nightgown and Judd's bloody shirt to dispose of. These were burned in the furnace, and Judd was provided with a fresh shirt from Albert's drawer. The sash weight was hidden in Albert's toolbox in the basement. The bandana and the Italian newspaper were carefully crumpled and tossed in a corner. Then, in an orgy of untidiness, Ruth tore about through all the rooms of the house, emptying drawers onto the floor, taking cushions off chairs, throwing pillows about and generally avenging her 12 years of housekeeping.

Now for the moment of farewell. Ruth bade her lover tie her arms and legs together and gag her, gently, with cheesecloth. She also asked to be knocked unconscious, but this proved to be beyond Judd's waning powers. A murderer he might be, but he was still a gentleman. Judd returned to the railway station, and Ruth, after enduring her bondage for a decent interval, slithered to Baby Lorraine's room and thumped on her door.

Baby Lorraine was dispatched to the next-door neighbors. The neighbors discovered Albert. The police were summoned, and this is the sad story Ruth told them:

While lying in bed she had heard footsteps. Leaving the bedroom to investigate, she had been attacked by two short men with black moustaches. Their faces were covered with bandanas. She suggested to the police that the men were Italians (this was just after the trial of Sacco and Vanzetti, Italians with moustaches), calling attention to the Italian newspaper they had left behind. They had thrown her onto her mother's bed, and then she must have fainted, for this was the last thing she could remember.

The police, naturally, didn't believe a word of it, and within a few minutes they had assembled enough evidence to convict her ten times over: the bloodstained sash weight, a bloodied pillowcase that Ruth had thrown into the laundry hamper, the smoldering remains of her nightgown. The jewels she'd claimed had been stolen were found under the mattress of her bed. At the foot of the bed was Judd's tie pin with the initials J.G. Nothing was lacking but a film of the murder, and Judd, by the time he reached the witness stand, almost remedied that lack by his testimony.

And at that, the jury took an hour and 37 minutes to reach a verdict.

The penalty for both of them was death by electrocution.

Ruth was undaunted. Indeed, in the months that were left to her she had a foretaste of that brighter world hereafter, for she had become a star. The newspapers were full of nothing else. Nobility and novelists had attended her trial to write about *her!* And, crowning glory, she herself was asked to write the story of her life. *My Own True Story—So Help Me God!* was published first in the Hearst newspapers and then as a pamphlet selling for 25 cents.

By this time Ruth had abandoned her earlier two-Italians alibi. Now she placed the blame squarely on Judd Gray's shoulders. "He turned on me," she wrote, "like a traitor and a liar. He made me a murderer condemned to die. He came into my home to steal another man's wife and take another man's life.

He drank himself into a delirium of murderous mania and killed Albert Snyder with his own hands. I shielded him. But the cowardly fear came up in him; when he saw he couldn't save his own precious skin, he turned on me. He is a low, cringing jackal, the murderer of my husband who is now trying to hide behind my skirts."

She also published work in a pathetic vein, turning to verse to express this more tender side of her nature.

> So many unkind words have been spoken,
> Each with a hurt in its aim,
> All over the globe they keep traveling,
> Causing us sorrow and pain.
>
> These words have crushed my dear mother,
> Changed happiness to despair,
> Lined her dear face with more wrinkles
> And added more silver to her hair.
>
> My baby, God's treasure, He gave me,
> Has suffered in her innocent bliss
> From a wrong befallen her mother
> Who longs to have her to kiss.
>
> You've blackened and besmeared a mother,
> Once a man's plaything—A Toy—
> What have you gained by all you've said,
> And has it—brought you Joy?
>
> And the hours when "Babe" needed my love,
> You've seen fit to send me away—
> I'm going to God's home in heaven,
> Ne'er more my feet to stray.

Despite endless stanzas that foresaw the same lost lamb restored to the fold, Ruth was by no means resigned to dying. With her lawyer's help she instituted a civil case against the Prudential Life Insurance Company, who had obstinately refused to fork out the $96,000 due her upon her husband's death.

Ruth's last grand blunder was worthy of her. Within minutes, literally, of entering prison after her sentencing, she converted to Catholicism. This remarkable conversion may have been due to the fact that the governor of New York State at that time was Alfred E. Smith. Ruth may have thought that a Catholic governor would be more likely to grant a reprieve to a murderess of his own faith than to a Protestant murderess. She could not have made a more disastrous miscalculation. Previous to her conversion, Smith had intended to commute Ruth's sentence for humane reasons. But to do so after she had publicly covered herself with rosaries would have been political suicide for Smith, who was then about to run for the presidency.

On the night of January 12, 1928, Ruth Snyder was electrocuted before 24 witnesses. Judd Gray followed her into the chair a few minutes later. She had made secret arangements with her attorney for her body to be taken to a private sanatorium where a doctor would be waiting to inject adrenalin into her heart. Recently the county clerk of Montclair, New Jersey, had been brought back to life by this means after seven hours of apparent death. The prison, however, refused to surrender her body until an autopsy had been performed. Ruth wasn't resurrected, and crime does not pay.

III

The Two-sided Triangle

Charles Naylor

Of all the widely publicized crimes of passion, none surpasses in irony and enigma the case of the minister and the choir singer. From the day that the dapper Reverend Hall and the demure Mrs. Eleanor Mills were found lying beneath their love letters in a three-way embrace with death, some of the finest legal and analytic minds have floundered trying to locate one of the essentials of every murder—the killer.

FIFTEEN-YEAR-OLD Leta Vosburgh was celebrating Saturday, the 16th of September, with a boy friend named Raymond Schneider. It was a summery day and early. They walked out from the center of New Brunswick, New Jersey, on Easton Avenue and made a left down De Russey's Lane, an unpaved road. After a few minutes' walk, they came to an isolated drive, overgrown and partially obstructed at the entrance to prevent cars from entering, since it gave access to the recently abandoned Phillips farm. They knew the trysting place well; everybody in New Brunswick did.

They had gone about 500 feet down this drive when Leta realized they were not alone; a couple lay fully clothed and quite still in the shade of a single crab-apple tree. She pointed, perhaps already knowing intuitively that something was wrong; it was, after all, only ten o'clock in the morning. Leta and Ray drew closer—and then in terror they ran.

Minutes later, having galloped across three fields to the home of Edward Stryker near Easton Avenue, they breathlessly told what they had seen to Stryker's niece, who called the police.

A while after, two patrolmen arrived. They'd had to cadge a lift from town, for it was 1922 and the average policeman had to improvise considerably. Leta and Ray led them to the spot and waited while the men made their inspection.

The corpses lay on their backs, the woman's head resting on the man's right arm, her left hand on his knee. The man had a Panama hat pulled over his face. What must have alarmed Leta initially—the supine couple had been liberally snowed

with sheets of paper (which would prove to be love letters).
A brown scarf covered the woman's lower throat, and when
one of the patrolmen lifted it he saw that her throat had been
slashed from ear to ear. The wound swarmed with maggots. A
man's wallet lay open on the ground near the two bodies.
Patrolman Garrigan, careful not to touch it, knelt to read the
name and address on the driver's license which was visible. It
had been issued to one Edward Wheeler Hall, 23 Nichol
Avenue, New Brunswick, New Jersey.

It was in the murky sociological matrix of a church choir
rehearsal that the Episcopal minister Hall, pastor of Saint John
the Evangelist, realized he was growing fond of his star choir
member, Eleanor Reinhardt Mills. She was, of course, married,
the mother of two. After her second child had been born in
1910, her life just stopped. Or at least it seemed to, and for
years she had lived only for romantic novels, the church (particularly its Ladies' Auxiliary), the choir (her soprano voice was
once described as "thin but adequate") and, ultimately, the
minister.

Reverend Hall—or Dr. Hall as his flock erroneously called
him (he hadn't received his doctorate in divinity)—was also
married. But that mattered little to the ladies of the church.
Minnie Clark, a Sunday-school teacher, had her eye on him,
too, as did many other women in the choir, and on one occasion Eleanor Mills was badly scratched by a contralto during
rehearsal. That notwithstanding, at the time of the murders
Reverend Hall and Mrs. Frances Hall had been happily together for 11 years. The marriage was childless. Mrs. Hall had
entered the minister's life through the church herself, as a
former Sunday-school teacher. Frances Hall, seven years the
minister's senior, had pots of money.

The murders were not particularly significant; few truly are.
But the papers gave them nearly as much column space as

would have been devoted, say, to a minor war, because the reading public is endlessly ravenous for scandal and sensationalism—which is a sad commentary on the quality of the lives of the reading public.

The crime was perfectly executed; no one knows to this day who did it—although the "what" and "to whom" were gruesomely obvious. The solving, on the other hand, was and always will be considered a miracle of incompetence. From the moment the two bodies were discovered under the crab-apple tree to the last day of the celebrated trial, it was one long bungle, studded here and there with gore, incest and the kind of potential for perversity that has made Peyton Place a synonym for Smalltown, U.S.A.

In addition to the wallet there was a calling card propped up against the dead man's left foot, and a recently arrived reporter from the New Brunswick *Daily Home News* asked Officer Garrigan whether he might pick it up and look at it. Garrigan said okay. The other law officer had, in the meantime, gone off to Easton Avenue with the hopes of locating a house with a telephone in order to call headquarters; that accomplished, he had headed back in the direction of the farm, but on the way he stopped a car and asked the driver, a local veterinarian, whether he would be able to identify a corpse believed to be that of the New Brunswick Episcopal minister. The man indicated that he could and followed the officer back. Yes, it was Reverend Hall.

The news had spread. People from the area appeared quickly in large numbers, delirious with excitement. By the time Detective Totten of the Somerset County prosecutor's office arrived (bear in mind that New Brunswick is at the very edge of Middlesex County), the calling card had been fingered and examined by all present, and much of the bark had been torn from the crab-apple tree for souvenirs. Also, all the high grass surrounding the two victims had been trampled, obliterating any possibility of determining whether or not there had been a struggle, or whether the victims might have met their deaths elsewhere and perhaps have been dragged or carried to the scene where they now lay, unnaturally, feet pointing in the direction of the tree, as neat as two pins. Evidence was disappearing quickly, and Garrigan and his partner were helpless to control the curious, souvenir-eager locals.

The Phillips farm, although convenient to amorous couples from New Brunswick, Middlesex County, lay unfortunately just over the border in Somerset County. Totten's team, unfamiliar with the area, had gotten thoroughly lost and taken 40 minutes driving the 12 miles from their offices in Somerville. Totten noted down as much detail as he could, though already the scene had changed significantly. His men salvaged the calling card (he noted that it bore something like "fly specks" and that, at least now, the card was propped up so that the printed side faced the feet of the dead woman); a card case containing driver's license, registration and membership cards; several love letters ("I know there are girls with more shapely bodies, but I do not care what they have. I have the greatest of all blessings, a noble man, deep, true, and eternal love. My heart is his, all I have is his, poor as my body is, scrawny as they say my skin may be, but I am his forever."); a two-foot section of iron piping; and a Peters .32-caliber cartridge case which had been lying in the grass.

Shortly before the Somerset men disappeared, and before an undertaker came and carried off the corpses, a green sedan drove into De Russey's Lane and stopped. Edwin R. Carpender, first cousin of the minister's wife, stepped out with his New Brunswick lawyer, former State Senator William E. Florence. They identified Hall's corpse and left quickly. They were visibly shaken.

The feelings that existed between the minister and the choir singer were no secret to the townspeople. They had been the subject of gossip for years. One of the Halls' maids, Barbara Tough, told the special prosecutor at the 1926 investigation, "I could easily see that Eleanor was one of his favorites." Hadn't she blundered into the church guild room once and seen the choir singer sitting on Hall's lap? Elsie Barnhardt, sister of Eleanor Mills, told of a Halloween party at which Mrs. Hall resigned herself to keeping out of the way when she realized her husband was seeking out Mrs. Mills for dance after dance. Another witness reported seeing the adulterous couple holding hands once in front of the Rivoli Theater in New York.

Mrs. Hall declined to view her husband's corpse. Some considered this a heartless indiscretion on her part, but the Somerset County Physician's comment to the undertaker may help to explain: "Better get them out of here in a hurry, Sam; they've been dead at least thirty-six hours." The prevailing opinion was that Frances Hall was the culprit, or at least that she had paid the killers. But her statement to the press, delivered by Miss Sally Peters, maid of honor at the Halls' wedding, spoke of robbery. The minister, according to the undertaker, had only 61 cents and two handkerchiefs in his pockets, but Mrs. Hall remembered the large, valuable and one-of-a-kind gold hunting watch he was carrying and $50 she knew to have been on his person. If this placid, gray-haired woman had been jealous, she certainly had kept it to herself. Eleanor Mills's teen-age daughter Charlotte, who had once been in Mrs. Hall's Sunday-school class, thought Mrs. Hall "austere." And she assured the press that Mrs. Hall had indeed known about her husband's affair—she would have to have been deaf and blind not to.

Mrs. Hall, however, was able to account for her own actions during the crucial hours:

The morning of the 14th was as normal and dull as one can imagine. The whole family—that is, Reverend and Mrs. Hall,

Frances Hall's peculiar and semiretarded brother Willie Stevens and little Frances Voorhees, a visiting niece—went off to buy groceries in the family Dodge. After lunch, the minister had to attend a P.T.A. meeting, and his wife took the opportunity to involve herself in making preserves. Minnie Clark stopped by for a few minutes. Hall returned from P.T.A. only to pick up ten-year-old Frances Voorhees and go off to a local hospital to distribute flowers. Seconds after the car pulled out of the drive the phone rang. It was Mrs. Mills. Would Mrs. Hall take a message for the rector: "You tell him that there is something about the doctor's bill for my operation that I do not understand."

The operation referred to relates to a puzzling facet of the case. Mrs. Mills had undergone surgery for a malfunctioning kidney the previous December. The rector and his wife were well-to-do and could afford extension phones and the maintenance of their rambling, inherited home, but Eleanor Mills, with two children and a ne'er-do-well husband, had difficulty paying the rent each month and when she needed to use a phone, it had to be the dressmaker's next door or a pay phone. The operation had cost $200, and if the Halls hadn't made arrangements to pay, the choir singer might have died ten months earlier. It was Mrs. Hall who drove Mrs. Mills to and from the hospital and visited her bedside many times and brought flowers. The ladies were, in a manner of speaking, friends.

Frances Hall told her husband of the call when he returned home that evening at six-thirty.

After dinner Mrs. Hall and little Frances went out on the veranda, as one does after the evening meal when nothing particularly distinguishes the day from any other. The phone rang again, but she didn't immediately get up to answer it, knowing that the two maids and Willie and her husband were about. The ringing continued. She went into the library and picked up the receiver at the foot of the staircase, but, hearing his voice, she realized that her husband had already taken the call on the upstairs extension. It was about seven.

She returned to the veranda, and a few minutes later she and Frances went into the library to play a card game. After another short lapse of time they were interrupted by the minister, who had come downstairs. He told his wife that he was going out to check on Mrs. Mills' medical bill.

According to Mrs. Hall's testimony, that was the last time she saw her husband dead or alive.

At nine she put Frances to bed and returned to the library, where she remained playing solitaire for two hours. She was only interrupted once, when Willie came down to say goodnight.

She worried. The reverend often went out during the evening on church business, but was usually home by ten. Still, there was nothing she could do, so she left the hall light burning and went to bed. "I got up in the night," she later admitted, "and came downstairs to see if by any chance he had come in and I had not heard him, and I looked around the house just to see if there was anywhere I had missed him coming in, and about half past two I was perfectly frantic about it—I did not know what could have happened."

She woke up Willie and they hurried to the church seven blocks away on the off-chance that the rector had fallen asleep there. But no; the lights were out and the front door locked. The only other place to look was the Mills's apartment—he had, after all, gone out specifically to discuss the hospital bill—but the lights were out there, too.

They returned home and both attempted to sleep, although for Mrs. Hall that was impossible. Early in the morning she called the police, without giving her name, and asked whether any casualties had been reported. "The one thought in my mind was that there might have been an auto accident, and my husband might have been injured and unable to communicate with me. . . ."

It wasn't until after breakfast that she returned to the church and there met Jim Mills.

It is almost reasonable that no one made the same concerted effort to pin the murders on Eleanor Mills's husband Jim as they did on Mrs. Hall; he was by all accounts weak and ineffectual. On the other hand, people like Frances Hall don't usually stoop so low as to shoot (or conspire to shoot) two people dead and then slash their rival's throat—ladies of her ilk don't do that sort of thing. The tabloids knew they stood a better chance of increasing circulation with the minister's wife (heiress to the Johnson & Johnson surgical-supplies fortune) on the front page than they did with Jim Mills, who had never made more than $38 a week, and they played her for all she was worth.

Until two years before the murders, Mills had worked in a New Brunswick rubber factory; but Reverend Hall—an ever-welcome guest at the Mills's apartment—used his influence to have the sallow-faced, long-nosed man hired as Saint John's sexton. Luckily, at about the same time, there was an opening at the Lord Stirling Public School for an assistant janitor, and Mills took that on as well. He told reporters shortly after the murders: "Dr. Hall was my best friend. . . . He was the kindest man I ever knew."

It was when she spoke with Mills at the church the morning of September 15 that Frances Hall learned the choir singer was also missing. Almost casually, later in the day when she again encountered Mills, he said from the porch where he was sitting, "Perhaps they have eloped."

Mills was not an angry or a vengeful man; in fact he seldom rose above a vague hurt, or indifference. It is significant that very soon after the bodies were discovered he sold a bagful of love letters to the *New York Daily Mirror* for $500.

A full month passed after the murders before the star (and virtually solitary) witness stepped forward. Her name was Jane Gibson. She was a widow and she lived with her son William in a ramshackle converted barn on her 60-acre pig farm—for which reason the newspapermen quickly dubbed her "the Pig-woman." The farm lay at the Hamilton Avenue end of De Russey's Lane.

She had been having trouble recently with "foreigners" steal-ing pigs and corn, so when she heard one of her dogs barking at about nine o'clock on the night of September 14, she went immediately to the front door to look out.

Creeping across her cornfield, barely visible, a figure was stealing away.

It would have been small victory to salvage whatever corn the man might have been carrying; much better to find out where the thief kept his stash. So she very quietly stole out, mounted an unshod mule and followed him. At Hamilton Avenue he boarded a horse-drawn wagon and turned up De Russey's Lane. She followed at a distance for about a mile— she had an idea of who he might be, and it occurred to her that if she were to cut across the fields on the diagonal she might head him off.

She had gone a short distance when she heard sounds that made her come to a dead stop.

Here the narrative splits.

According to Jane Gibson's first account, in that moonless spot she could just barely see four figures—what looked like two men and two women—standing near a crab-apple tree. There was a shot, and one of the figures fell. (This would be the single bullet that killed the minister.) Then Mrs. Gibson heard a woman scream, "Don't! Don't! Don't!"

Terrified and confused she tried to urge the mule away quietly. As she was leaving, the gun fired again several times, and another figure fell. Like Cinderella, in her haste to get free, the Pigwoman lost one shoe.

The following day she told the story again, with embellishments and corrections: The four figures had been arguing heatedly before the gun was fired. "Suddenly there were shots, four of them. I saw a man fall, and then I saw a woman fall." She added, "If I had only called out, I might have prevented the murders. But I was stunned and seemed to be powerless and I did not know what to do."

The next morning she remembered even more: Moments before the shooting a woman's voice asked, "How do you explain these notes?" Then the single shot, and the Pigwoman saw Eleanor Mills run off to conceal herself in some sumac bushes located near the abandoned farmhouse. Unfortunately the pursuers spotted her with a flashlight, dragged the screaming woman back to the tree and shot her. Three hours later, when Jane Gibson returned to the scene of the crime to retrieve her missing mocassin, she claims to have seen a sobbing Mrs. Hall prostrate over Reverend Hall's corpse.

During the first week of November Mrs. Hall received an interesting letter. It was from a neighbor of the Pigwoman, Mrs. Nellie Lo Russell:

"Dear Madam," it began. "In regard to September 14, Mrs. Jane Gibson was not at the Phillips farm at ten o'clock as I live back of her. She came over at ten o'clock or a little before to tell me that she had took my dog from a man on Hamilton Road. She set on the steps of my little shanty awhile and I gave her a dollar for bringing my dog. We talked awhile, and I came home about eleven o'clock. She has told me things that were not so. I don't think she can help it."

Mrs. Gibson's reaction was to invite newsmen to her house

and bring out a wall calendar. The entry for September 9 indicated that she had *that* day rescued Nellie Lo Russell's dog Prince from a "Polack."

The Pigwoman was above all else colorful, and the same forces that brought the unresolved case back before the Grand Jury again four years later—deeply entangling Mrs. Hall, her two brothers and first cousin, Henry Carpender, gratuitously—made the world listen attentively to her incredible whimsies. One day she would claim to have seen Mrs. Hall clearly by moonlight dressed in a gray coat; then, entering the courthouse for the hearing, she'd walk within inches of the minister's widow—for the first time since their supposed encounter—without a shiver of recognition.

Doubtless, the reason the Hall-Mills murder case crowded out election news, a Florida hurricane disaster and Gertrude Ederle's crossing the English Channel was that the now defunct *New York Daily Mirror* was then mounting an all-out effort to push sales over those of the *New York Daily News*. Through the *Mirror's* efforts New Brunswick grew cancerous with photographers, reporters and sightseers. The main street looked like a fireman's fair. The price for space in a rooming house skyrocketed. Crowds thronged to the scene of the crime each weekend, sometimes making the terrain a quagmire. They broke into the main house of the Phillips farm looking for souvenirs, and some clever gentleman went so far as to create a crime museum on the site. Just as things were about to reach the popcorn-and-postcard stage, there was talk of erecting a housing development over the whole mess.

The hearings, the trial and the newspaper interviews brought many interesting bits of information into the public consciousness. Much was said, but little accomplished.

We learned, for example, that Leta Vosburgh, the young lady who first discovered the bodies, had almost certainly been having sexual intercourse with her father the night of the murders, and that a few days before she had heaved a brick at her stepmother through a window.

We learned that John Gorsline, a Saint John's vestryman, married and father of a 13-year-old daughter, had been parking (or "sparking" as they said in those days) with Miss Catherine Rastall (another member of the Saint John's choir) on De Russey's Lane the night of the murders. They, too, heard shots.

We learned from Eleanor Mills's sisters, Elsie Barnhardt and Marie Lee, that the minister and the choir singer had intended to leave the country for Japan as soon as Charlotte, Mrs. Mills's daughter, was graduated from high school.

Four years after the tragedy, Special Prosecutor Alexander Simpson ordered exhumation of the bodies in order to perform new autopsies, and although deterioration of the tissues was advanced to a point where it was nearly impossible to tell, the doctor discovered that "the upper part of the windpipe and the larynx and the tongue were missing" from the corpse of Mrs. Eleanor Mills.

What became of the tongue? Who took the gold watch and $50 from the pocket of the minister?

During the third week of the trial, the Pigwoman, then recently taken ill, created perhaps her last real stir, arriving at the court in an ambulance and testifying from a hospital bed that faced the jury box. Equally a curiosity, her mother blurted out suddenly, "She is a liar. A liar, liar, liar! A liar, that's what she is! Ugh!"

When the trial finally came to a close and Jane Gibson, still bedridden, was told the news of Frances Hall's and her two brothers' acquittal, her reaction was classic: "Acquitted?" she asked. "Well, can you beat that."

It wouldn't be until 1964 that the famous lawyer, William M. Kunstler would make public the long-suppressed evidence he had uncovered while researching his book *The Minister and the Choir Singer*. He found two pages from the Pigwoman's calendar, of which the first, dated September 14, 1922, read: ". . . followed thief/lost him/open wagon/lost moc/Farmer fired 4/shots." The page dated September 17 disclosed simply, "Must have been/what I heard/and saw/on 14th."

We can be sure that if the minister's wife did commit the murders, the Pigwoman did not see it.

The case goes unsolved. Today, not only has the scene of the crime undergone a total face-lifting, but very nearly all the people involved, including Mrs. Hall, her brother Willie, the Pigwoman and Charlotte Mills are dead. Kunstler suggests that the murders might well have been committed by the Ku Klux Klan as a part of their drive to "clean up" communities throughout the country during the Twenties. It is easy to forget today that the Klan was once concerned with issues other than white supremacy, but—particularly in 1921 and 1922—they were making a determined effort to rid the country of all extramarital and "perverted" sexual activity. Generally their tactics for restoring morality went no further than to tar and feather an offender. But they were also fond of amputating the penises of the wicked and branding the breasts of the unfaithful with a triple *K*. Since the church was in those days the sociological common denominator, the Klan was very mindful of what church people said and how they lived. Often Klan members would interrupt a church service to publicly deny Klan involvement in some local atrocity, but on occasion the Klan did commit murder.

The Hall-Mills case confirms the famous dictum that one need only tell a lie long enough and loud enough for it eventually to be believed. Although there was absolutely no basis for believing Frances Hall to have been a murderess, it is her fate to be remembered as such by a whole generation of newspaper readers who will always believe her guilty of a crime she never committed. Paradoxically, a real villainess, the perjurous Pig-woman, is remembered as no more than a figure of harmless fun.

IV

An Element of Farce

Leonard Gribble

Dr. Hawley Crippen was no more a doctor than he was a man. A patent-medicine salesman, he was a milquetoast husband with an overbearing, theatrical wife who abused him without mercy. Then a gentle brunette entered his world, and everything—including Hawley—changed. Fortified with love, he devised a bizarre new formula for happiness: One of the more potent ingredients was murder; another and fairly unique one was the transformation of his beloved into his son.

THEY called him the Doctor, and he was something of a joke. He wasn't a doctor, but there was an element of farce in his life. It contributed towards a fabulous tragedy.

He sold patent medicines and he looked at the world through a pair of metal-rimmed glasses. His drooping moustache was an exact copy of the one worn by Sir Arthur Conan Doyle. But he didn't care for detective stories. Perhaps if he had, he would not have adventured in murder.

Hawley Harvey Crippen was a weedy-looking American, with none of the drive and thrust associated with transatlantic go-getters in the first decade of the 20th Century. Rather short, he appeared to be a quiet man of self-effacing ways who danced perpetual attendance on his wife, a blowsy, loud-voiced woman who used her married name as seldom as she conveniently could. Anyone who wished to bring a hard-rimmed smile to Mrs. Crippen's fleshy face called her Miss Elmore. She sighed whenever she spoke of the stage, and she used a phony American accent.

This overweight and overbearing female allowed her intimates to call her Belle and never for a moment suspected the name could be comic in the circumstances. But then she had no sense of humor. Unfortunately for him, neither had her husband.

Crippen was born in Michigan and claimed to be a graduate of the State University. He came to England, and his fortunes —or rather lack of them—forced him to undertake various ways of earning a living. When he married a music-hall artist with a Polish name he thought himself a man favored by the gods, and with Cora Mackamotzki for his wife he doubled his efforts to acquire money. He was more successful than was generally realizéd, largely due to the fact that he was prepared to do more than one job at a time.

But when the Crippens were settled in Hilldrop Crescent, Holloway, he was a man very much in love with someone who was in every way the antithesis of his fleshly spouse.

At that time he was making money as a dentist and working as an agent for a patent medicine. He had an office in Albion House, New Oxford Street, and on the door was the proprietary name Munyon's Remedies.

Working with him was a slim girl named Ethel Le Neve. At least she looked to be just a girl; she was really a woman of 27, but her slight figure and French looks made her seem a good many years younger. Ethel Le Neve, among her other duties for Munyon's Remedies, was Crippen's typist. She had gentle manners and the pale skin that often gives slender brunettes an almost ethereal appearance, especially when they have large, round eyes. Ethel Le Neve's eyes were very large and very round.

Crippen's home life was such as only a placid man, desiring peace and harmony above all else, could tolerate. His loud-mouthed wife openly sneered at his lack of masculine attributes and was extravagant and utterly without taste. She cultivated friends who pandered to her conceit, spent money recklessly on entertaining those friends and on clothes and jewelry to deck her gross body. The *ménage* in Hilldrop Crescent employed no servant, yet Belle Elmore was lazy and hated to rise before the sun was well up. More often than not her husband cooked his own breakfast and took hers to her bedside. He brushed his clothes and cleaned his boots before leaving for Oxford Street. During the hours he was at home he was at his wife's beck and call. He suffered her friends with their doubtful jokes and raucous voices, ate poor food and pulled his coat-sleeves over frayed cuffs. He endured, and was seemingly prepared to endure so long as his wife dominated him, not because he had a martyr complex but because he had no will of his own to urge him to do otherwise. He had no will because such love as he had known was dead. Belle Elmore had killed it wittingly and did not care. She had married a man she could keep under her thumb.

But the large, round eyes of the gentle young woman with the boyish waist fanned to flame an ember Belle Elmore had not entirely extinguished. It was farcical, as most things in his life were farcical, but Crippen developed a passion for his secretary.

Even more strange, it was returned.

The sad-eyed man with the walrus moustache, who was saddled with a stout wife of waspish temper, found himself devoted to a slip of a thing who spoke to him in a hushed whisper and returned his kisses with trembling lips.

Perhaps violence was the only solution. Violence or madness, and Crippen did not intend to go mad.

The parting came suddenly. When Crippen knew he must be rid of Belle, he did not pause; he acted. The mousy little man whose glasses often steamed over as he puffed through his whiskers became a man of action in the early hours of February 1, 1910, when he committed murder. And he was still in action when Inspector Dew of Scotland Yard arrested him and startled the world with a practical demonstration of how much it had shrunk since the 20th Century had dawned.

What probably set his adventurous steps irretrievably on the path to murder was a letter he received on January 31. He learned that his services with Munyon's Remedies had been terminated, which meant that the better part of his sure income had vanished. He would no longer be in a position to satisfy his wife's expensive tastes or pacify her anger by chinking new-minted sovereigns. He could no longer use her greed to make life tolerable for himself. The man who had drifted for ten years, ever since he came to England in 1900, suddenly found he had to swim for it. When he tried, his fund of energy surprised him.

Belle Elmore was seen no more after January 31, but on that night she was very much in evidence. The Crippens gave a dinner party, which must have been an appalling mockery for the host who had just been sacked. The guests were Paul Martinetti, a retired pantomime artist, and his wife. After dinner the Crippens and the Martinettis played whist, and the party broke up about half-past one in the morning. Mrs. Martinetti, for one, enjoyed herself.

"It was quite a nice evening," she said later, "and Belle was very jolly."

From which one can safely assume that Belle Elmore, unfortunately for herself, did everything she could to grate on her husband's jangled nerves.

When the guests left she probably had a headache due to the stuffy room and drinking too much. Her husband mixed her a potion, doubtless assuring her it was a sedative. It was—a very permanent sedative; hyoscine hydrobromide. It induced stomach pains, then delirium, afterwards coma and finally death. She was probably dead before daylight, when he proceeded to cut up the body. His wife had to disappear completely, so he burned the larger bones and buried the clammy flesh under a clay-and-brick floor in a rear cellar.

By February 3 it is conceivable that he was finished in the cellar, satisfied with the disappearance he had effected. He took some of his wife's jewelry to a pawnshop. It must have pained him to accept £80 for articles that had cost him much more, but he was in need of ready cash. A fortnight passed, and some more of his wife's jewels passed across the pawnshop counter.

With money in his pocket and Ethel Le Neve smiling above a few pieces of the dead woman's jewelry, he felt that perhaps he could climb back into the old orbit for a few hours and re-capture something of the old magic his association with music-hall artists had held. He took Ethel Le Neve to a dinner and dance given by the Music Hall Ladies' Benevolent Fund. Ethel was as happy as a kitten, and her delight removed the last of Crippen's doubts as to the wisdom of the visit—until he came face to face with Mrs. Martinetti. The woman who three weeks before had played whist with the Crippens stared at the brooch Ethel wore. It was a cluster of brilliants, which reminded her of one she had admired on Belle Elmore's dress.

"Where is dear Belle?" she asked, eyes raking Ethel Le Neve.

"In America, my dear."

"America!"

"She sailed on very short notice. On business, of course."

Crippen and Ethel melted into each other's arms as the orchestra began a waltz.

Afterwards Crippen awaited any repercussion. There was none. On March 12 Ethel Le Neve moved her belongings, which now included quite a few pieces from the dead woman's jewel box, to Hilldrop Crescent. It was a move full of obvious risk and sure to start tongues wagging.

By March 23 Crippen was ready for a change of air and scene. He took his ladylove to Dieppe for Easter. Popular be-lief has it that on the steamer trip from Newhaven he dropped overboard a small bag containing Belle Elmore's head. If he did, Ethel Le Neve knew nothing about it. Crippen had started by lying to her about his wife. He had continued by lying to his wife's friends. Inevitably, he had contradicted himself. He came back to England after that short Easter break to find rumors circulating as to why Belle Elmore maintained silence for long.

For two months Crippen waited for the rumors to die. But that is not always the fated end of rumors. Someone went to the police. Scotland Yard sent Chief Inspector Alfred Dew, a very painstaking officer, to make a few inquiries.

The Yard man's knock on the front door was answered by Ethel Le Neve. Dew saw that she was wearing one of the brooches described in the list in his pocket. He asked to see Mr. Crippen.

"I'll call the doctor," said the young woman.

Crippen appeared, told the story of his wife's trip to the United States, and when asked to show his official guest through the house, did so very readily. When they arrived in the rear cellar the short man with the weak eyes blinking behind his spectacles actually stood on his wife's grave while he continued to answer the Yard man's string of questions.

He came through the ordeal successfully, but at a terrible price. It wrecked his nerve. He knew he could not suffer such a mental ordeal a second time. Inspector Dew's quiet efficiency had thoroughly scared him.

He found himself again having to make a drastic decision, but this time it was not so difficult; he had grown used to action and he had come to believe in his luck. He would disappear, and with him Ethel Le Neve. It was the obvious and only solution. Furthermore, it would present the authorities with an insoluble problem of their own. All he required was a margin of time.

He made hurried plans, and Ethel Le Neve's wide eyes grew wider as she listened to them. But she loved him very dearly. She offered no protest, set no feminine obstacle to his wishes. Perhaps the New World might offer a new start.

The story of Crippen's flight with Ethel Le Neve is now part of the history of Scotland Yard. It was undertaken because Crippen no longer had faith in his power to maintain a deceit, and possibly because he realized that he must try to save the young woman he loved from threatened disaster. He must have realized perfectly well the danger to her of being arrested as an accessory, and knowing her timidity and gentle ways he foresaw that the only possible way of saving both of them lay in flight.

He purchased clothes for a youth and disguised Ethel Le Neve as an adolescent after cutting her hair. World War I was still four years away, and no one had thought of passports as an aid to international travel. Crippen and the disguised Le Neve left Hilldrop Crescent and fled to Brussels. There they put up at the Hotel des Ardennes, registering as Mr. J. F. Robinson and son. They stayed for eight days.

The *directrice* of the hotel was a woman with sharp eyes. She observed that Master Robinson wore shoes more like a girl's, for they had high heels. His figure resembled a girl's, and he seldom spoke. She sensed mystery, but was prepared to supply her own answer. She saw the couple as a teacher eloping with a girl student.

Curiosity, however, got the better of her judgment. She inquired about the lad and was told he was stone deaf. But when she saw the Robinsons conversing at their dinner table in agitated whispers she knew how much truth there was in the claim to deafness.

During that week Chief Inspector Dew returned to Holloway to ask more questions. He found the house empty and decided to make a thorough search. When he examined the rear cellar again, he detected marks that could have been the result of fresh cementing. He had the cellar floor dug up, and what had happened to Belle Elmore was no longer a secret.

Full descriptions of the missing pair were circulated, with portraits and samples of their handwriting. A reward of £250 was offered by Scotland Yard for information, and overnight Crippen's name became a household word throughout the British Isles.

On July 30 the Canadian Pacific liner *Montrose* left her dock at Antwerp. On board were Mr. Robinson and his silent son. Captain Kendall, master of the *Montrose,* saw the couple walking along the deck, noticed the son's mincing step and stared when the father's hand was squeezed affectionately. He had read the recent London papers carrying the story of the Yard's latest manhunt and he wondered if he had the runaways aboard his ship.

Like a sensible man, he sought to prove or allay his suspicions. He took occasion to have a chat with father and son and during the interview noticed particularly how badly the youth's clothes fitted and how indifferently cut was the unruly hair.

He sent a wireless message to Scotland Yard. In London a passage was booked on the White Star liner *Laurentic,* sailing from Liverpool. When she left for the Saint Lawrence, Inspector Dew was aboard. He reached Canada ahead of the Robinsons and made speedy arrangements for arrest with the Canadian authorities.

When the *Montrose* arrived off Father Point, in the Saint Lawrence, a pilot boat started for the liner. She carried, instead of the customary pilot, no less than four pilots. Three of them were Dew and two local detectives. As the detectives stepped aboard the liner, Dew glanced over the knot of interested passengers. With an anticipatory thrill he recognized the man he had crossed 3,000 miles of ocean to capture. He turned to the Canadian detectives and pointed.

"There's your man."

Crippen turned very white. For a moment he could not speak. When he found his voice his wrists were handcuffed. Then a scream rang out, followed by the sound of a falling body. Master Robinson had fainted.

Dew brought his prisoners back to England, and when he

arrived he turned over such evidence as he had found in Crippen's cabin and on his person. This included some more identifiable pieces of Belle Elmore's jewelry and a card on which Crippen had written:

I cannot stand the horror I go through every night any longer. As I cannot see anything bright ahead, and as our money has come to an end, I have made up my mind to jump overboard tonight. I know I have spoiled your life. I hope some day you will learn to forgive me. With last words of love,

Yours,
H.

Crippen never referred to that card. Was he toying with the idea of suicide, or was he in earnest? Was his mind made up, or was he daunted by looming shadows? Nor did he refer to the charge against him. The man of action had run down like an unwound clock. But some time later, when he realized the full implications of the evidence against him, he said to someone from the office of the Director of Public Prosecutions: "I am not sorry. The anxiety has been too much. It is only fair to say that Miss Le Neve knows nothing about it. I never told her anything."

For the first time in his life Crippen was able to rise beyond the element of farce that had mocked him repeatedly. The short man with the unkempt whiskers and staring eyes, who spoke with a slight mid-Western twang, achieved startling stature as he set himself to protect the woman he loved. He refused to make any statement that would involve her in any way. He left questions unanswered because to reply might implicate her. It has been said he sacrificed himself for her. Most probably that is an overstatement. He set himself to make sure she did not sacrifice herself. That he was genuinely in love with her there can be no doubt, and he was truly grateful for the love he had received in return. During the voyage back to Britain he asked Dew, "Would you object to my seeing Ethel again? Just once."

Dew asked, "You have a special reason?"

Crippen brought his gaze back from the ocean and stared straight at the Yard man.

"Things may go wrong with me," he said, "and I may never see her again. I won't speak to her. She has been my only comfort for the last three years."

Seen in perspective, Crippen is a pathetic little man who nerved himself to a brutal act. Just how pathetic he really was is indicated by those words to Inspector Dew, spoken at a time when Crippen must have known what he could expect from a trial in Britain.

That trial was debated for five days before a packed court. Perhaps the most telling fresh piece of evidence was the discovery of Crippen's purchase of the poison. He had bought five grains of hyoscine and signed the poison book. He claimed he had required the poison for some patients, but he could not remember their names. The prosecution produced a piece of flesh taken from the cellar of Crippen's home. In 1892 Mrs. Crippen had undergone an operation, and the piece of flesh preserved in Formalin contained the scar from that surgery.

The jury retired for less than half an hour, and their verdict was guilty. The Lord Chief Justice donned the black cap and pronounced sentence of death.

The day after Crippen's trial ended, Ethel Le Neve was formally tried as an accessory after the fact. The defense counsel's strong plea resulted in the judge summing up in the prisoner's favor. Ethel Le Neve was found not guilty by a jury who retired for only a few minutes.

Free, the unfortunate woman asked to be allowed to visit Crippen in the condemned cell. Permission was granted, and she took him her last gift, a portrait of herself. Shortly before he was executed Crippen said in a letter to her: "I kissed it, though, in spite of my greatest efforts it was impossible to keep down a great sob and my heart's agonized cry."

He was hanged at Pentonville on November 23, a modest little man who had instinctively shunned any glare of publicity throughout his life, but who had contracted the foolish habit of loving the wrong women at the wrong time.

V

Jim, Linda, Harry ...and "The Set"

George Scullin

The perfect wife does not always end up with the perfect husband. In Amesbury, for example, a lot of wives were simply ending up with somebody else's husband. It was "The Set's" way of waging war against the boredom of monogamy. Of course, nice couples like Jim and Linda Anderson didn't think this way, and Jim probably explained that to his friend Harry the night he brought him home for dinner. His Linda was the perfect New England wife. But then, so was Hester Prynne; even perfect wives have their little failings. . . .

U P in that odd northeastern angle of Massachusetts, intruding hard into the dark pine hills of New Hampshire, is the venerable, time-passed town of Amesbury. From its summits ancient mansions frown across at each other with inbred politeness. Lower down, on winding, criss-crossing streets, a modern business district has been imposed upon gabled structures that were old a century ago. Still lower, on the floor of the valley, is a litter of gaunt, red-brick factories that speak of better days. Amesbury once flourished as a manufacturing center, but now most of its former enterprises exist as—in the hopeful words of the Chamber of Commerce—"desirable industrial sites," and many of the townspeople find their employment across the river in Newburyport.

Newburyport, which against the wishes of its upper set also figures in this case, must be described as quite the opposite of Amesbury. From its boatyards, starting in 1630, sailed fleets of fishing boats, fleets of privateers during the American Revolution, and then, for a hundred years, fleets of the largest, fastest merchant ships ever to cut the seas in search of profit. That profit is still visible on High Street, three miles of the largest, most ornate wooden mansions in America.

It all began quietly enough. It began, in fact, with a whisper: "If the truth ever gets out about some of the parties around here . . ." By March 1953, Amesbury and Newburyport were both aware of a new group in their midst, known as "The Set." If no one knew any members of The Set, there were few in

87

Amesbury who could not talk knowingly of its monthly rituals, of the way in which young husbands put their wives in a jackpot, then gambled for new mates for the night. In Newburyport, from the mansions on High Street to the beer parlors on the waterfront, the talk was all of the same Set. The rituals were called "wife-swapping parties."

For a while it was just talk, but with the discovery of a body in June 1954, Amesbury and The Set became the focus of national attention.

Reporters sifting the limited evidence and the wide assortment of rumors could find only one point on which to agree: that the James Andersons were too nice a couple to be drawn into so sordid an affair. Newsmen referred to "the model family," "the beautiful wife," "the ideal husband" and "the perfect marriage," and for once the hackneyed phrases were accurate. Yet the Andersons *were* involved, and tragically.

In Amesbury today, Linda Anderson is remembered as the beautiful girl she was and the charming wife and mother she became, because that is a pleasant memory. She was born in 1927 to Mr. and Mrs. Gilbert Meacham and raised in their comfortable home. From her first appearance in Sunday school she was destined to attract boys; she had the kind of beauty that could be regal without being pretentious.

She met Jim in her freshman year at Amesbury High. James Anderson was small and slight during his high-school years— his Navy record shows he reached five feet, nine inches, 140 pounds—but he was the handsomest boy in his class. He was the All-American type, with brown hair, brown eyes, regular features and a wide, engaging smile. He was two years older than Linda, the only child of Mr. and Mrs. Thomas Anderson.

It was a case of love at first sight. Jim waiting on the school's front lawn to escort Linda home became as familiar a sight as Kraske's famous bronze Statue of Doughboy that is a photographic must for all tourists. Jim's plans, prompted by

his father and approved by Linda, called for his going on to
college to study electrical engineering, a field in which he
showed great aptitude. But World War II changed all that with
crushing abruptness, as it changed the plans of hundreds of
thousands of other young couples.

Impulsively, they married before Jim shoved off to join the
Navy. He was 19 and she was 17, and if that seems terribly
young for marriage, remember that there were uncounted
thousands of other young couples caught up by the same
urgent demands.

Suddenly the highly attractive Linda found herself finishing
high school wearing an almost visible "hands off" sign because
she was married. At a time when she would normally have
been enjoying male adulation at its peak, with dates for every
occasion, she was dutifully at home with her parents. Outwardly she evidenced no frustrations, but women who have
shared the same emptiness will say the frustrations were there.

With Jim's release from the Navy early in 1946, he and
Linda encountered another phenomenon, as baffling to them as
it was to their contemporaries. They met as married adults to
resume a high-school courtship. They made this difficult adjustment, but having passed the first step, they were confronted
with another. Amesbury, for the first time, faced the same
housing shortage that tormented the rest of the country. The
young Andersons had to choose between paying high rents or
moving in with one or the other of their families. They opted
for the high rents, in the meantime making plans to build a
house as soon as possible.

It was a mutual decision, which did much to consolidate
their marriage, and for the first time Linda could feel she was
really doing her share as a housewife. She began to blossom
after that, becoming absolutely radiant after the birth of Joanne
late in the year. She resumed her church work and entertained
frequently in her home. A year later Beverly was born, and

then, in 1949, Jim got the boy he wanted when Charles arrived.

With a growing family the financial pressure was on. Said one of his lifelong friends: "Jim was in a sweat all the time. Not having a college education bothered him. He was always trying to make up for it, studying on the side, but with three kids arriving in less than four years, he was always having to take on extra work, and then he'd be too tired to study."

Linda did not mind the self-denial. With her three fine children, her fine husband and her church work, she was a woman fulfilled, and if she had to scrimp, that was an honored part of the New England tradition.

Then Jim got his first break, a job with Columbia Broadcasting System's Hytron Laboratories across the river in Newburyport, working in the television-tube department. It combined his aptitude for electrical work with his ambition, and in a matter of weeks he was able to report to Linda another piece of luck. "There's a job open in my department as night foreman. That means from eleven at night until seven in the morning, but listen to this—it's a hundred and thirty-five a week. We can start building our house!"

They had already picked a site for what they always referred to as their dream home—about three miles north of town on the shores of Lake Attitash.

They started building in 1950, but even with Jim doing all the electrical work and devoting every spare minute to the project, they found themselves caught by sharply soaring prices. By the time their dream house was completed in 1951, they were desperately over their budget.

As Linda was to tell Amesbury Police Chief Edmund McLaughlin later, "It meant absolutely that I had to help out. It meant leaving the children with my parents, but there was this job in the diner in Merrimac, and what with tips, we could make ends meet."

It was a little more complicated than that. The job meant not only work but the emotional wrench of tearing herself away from three small children and a beautiful new home. While Merrimac is a pretty town only five miles west of Amesbury, and the diner, catering to local trade, is a far cry from a greasy spoon, events were to prove it was no place for Linda because any separation from her children at that point would have been hurtful.

Linda was only 25 when she first took the job, just reaching the full beauty promised by her adolescence, but along with her beauty, provocatively contradicting it, went a small-girl, almost baby voice. It was, in a way, a dangerous combination, her beauty and her voice appealing to the protective instincts of every male, but at the same time providing enticement because of its young innocence. Linda knew she was beautiful. She had been told so often enough and groomed herself accordingly, making every attractive detail of her features count, but never did she consciously combine beauty and girlish voice to become cutely coy.

She used the family's second-hand Hudson convertible to get to and from her job. She left for work around eleven in the morning, to avoid the noon rush hour, and arrived home between eight and nine, after the supper rush. The timing was such that Jim could have used the car for his night work in Newburyport, but neither liked the idea of Linda's being left out at the lake without transportation. Another car being out of the financial picture, Jim bought a motor scooter and drove the half-hour to work on that.

Several things started to go wrong during that year. The cottage on Lake Attitash was out in the wilderness, with the loons shrieking a ghastly laughter on the lake and all sorts of noises in the underbrush. Linda, alone with the children after Jim left for work each night, had to fight those minor fears herself—small fears, taken one at a time, but cumulative.

Then there was the problem of adjustment. At first they had thought they would have their mornings together after Jim returned from work, and their evenings together after Linda returned from work, and both would have ample time with the children. But Linda, returning exhausted at 8:00 P.M., was not up to greeting a husband freshly awakened from his day's sleep. Nor could she, freshly awakened in the morning, see him as a romantic figure when he wearily returned from his night's work.

At this critical point, Jim unwittingly removed himself further from the family by undertaking a new project. As he saw it, Lake Attitash offered several attractive possibilities as a boating and picnicking area, and to that end he began to plan a boat-rental service to open in the spring of 1953. Not having much capital, he bought old boats and devoted his spare time to repairing them.

In working all night on a highly technical job, and then working all his spare hours to build his own business, Jim was working virtually every hour. When Linda protested, he said, "Look, if we can make some money renting boats, next year we can open a resort store, sell supplies to picnickers and campers—the works. Then you won't have to work in a diner anymore. You can run everything from right here."

To Linda this rosy future seemed a long way off. She was impatient with her husband, and when Jim did take his first day off in months—to go rabbit hunting instead of taking her to Lawrence or Portsmouth or someplace where there was life— she felt deserted. At the same time, when one of her daughters asked, "Mommie, aren't you ever going to stay home to play with us?" she had the feeling of being the one who had deserted the whole family.

Ironically, it was Jim's sense of Linda's disturbed feelings that prompted him to make amends by throwing a party in January of 1953. Linda's own admission was that it was at this party that she first became an unfaithful wife, indicating that she yielded because for the first time in months she got the kind of attention her beauty had taught her to expect.

It is worth recalling that this is the land of Hawthorne's *Scarlet Letter,* and of Hester Prynne, the young woman who was forced to don the vivid *A*. It is also the land of the witch-hunts, in which a married man could and did denounce as a witch the strange woman found in his bed, having no other ready explanation. In Linda's mind, with her first adultery, she became a creature beyond the pale.

Now the story of Linda and of The Set becomes curiously mixed. The Set, it is said, consisted of some 20 couples, all very sophisticated members of the elite of Amesbury, Newburyport and Salisbury Beach. Occasionally guest couples from Boston and the art colony at Gloucester joined it. They viewed sex as a purely physical manifestation, of no more significance than dining, drinking or dancing with another man's wife, or another woman's husband.

Yet even in this "enlightened" atmosphere, jealousy sometimes intruded. While the wives were willing to concede that sex was impersonal and of no more significance than a sentimental waltz, they were not quite capable of watching, without jealousy, all male interest concentrated on two or three of the most attractive women. Here Linda's name is heavily underscored, as though by feline claws.

But The Set was resourceful. One night in June 1953, so the story goes, they were meeting in a sheltered cove on the bay side of Salisbury Beach, and the usual pairing-off of temporary mates took place. Still remaining around the dimming campfire were three or four ill-paired couples whose legal mates were somewhere in the bayberry brush. They were depressed; they felt inferior, as if they were the unwanted, the rejected. With alcoholic brilliance, one of them said, "What we should do is draw lots, or play spin the bottle, or something. Then it would all be fair, and there wouldn't be anybody left sitting around the fire feeling jealous."

The ultimate solution was the key game. From then on, the men tossed their remarkably similar brass house keys into a hat. A brisk shaking, and then the wives groped in the hat. To whichever master of the house the key belonged, so belonged for the night the woman who had drawn it. It was equitable, exciting and left no wife or husband room to complain.

Where was Jim during these wife-swapping parties? He worked nights, remember? But then a question: If Jim was not a participant—and he wasn't—whom did Linda have to swap?

At this point a curious figure enters. To go back a little: Working with Jim when he had been on the day shift at the electronics plant had been a young man named Harry Quinn, who on casual acquaintance was an engaging character. When Jim brought him home to meet Linda, Harry was very subdued; his wife was divorcing him, and the blow was numbing. Linda was two years his senior, which made her solicitude all the more flattering, and soon Quinn was a regular guest of the Andersons, frequently accompanying them on nights out.

By March 1953, Linda was finding in Harry Quinn all the attention and flattery Jim was too busy to give her. No longer was she the neglected wife, the harassed mother of three, an underpaid waitress in a diner. She had a lover younger than she, and she must have amazed him with the fierceness of her ardor. With the breaking of her marriage vows only three months earlier, she was in a restless, reckless mood. Attention and reassurance were not something to be yearned for wistfully; they were something she had to have, and in Quinn she found them.

For a time Quinn filled her needs, but then her implacable New England conscience caught up with her. Now she was not a woman who had impetuously sinned once, but a scheming adulteress, deliberately seeking ways to be with her lover. The enormity of her guilt overwhelmed her and drove her into a more frantic search for new excitements in which to forget it. She did not dare look at her past, and the distant future, filled with dire promises of puritanical retribution, was too awful to contemplate. Henceforth for Linda there could be nothing but the immediate now.

There is no evidence of when, where or how Linda entered The Set. It is only known that within it she found what she craved. Sophisticated couples. College graduates. Artists. Sons and daughters of prominent people. If they could make light of sex and call a little friendly adultery a liberating symbol of the new order, then a small-town girl who had never gone past high school had nothing to worry about.

Linda's search for excitement changed into a rapidly accelerating flight from reality. In the fall Quinn rented an apartment in Newburyport and gave Linda a key. She would visit him after work, cooking his suppers for him and otherwise taking care of his needs.

Probably the most remarkable feature of Linda's dual existence was her ability to be her naïve self in the presence of family and friends. She gossiped as eagerly about The Set as any of her friends, and her wide-eyed, baby-voiced astonishment at its scandalous conduct was too realistic to be doubted. Somewhere in the course of a year she had learned how to keep her two lives so separate that they didn't even meet in her own mind.

April 10, 1954. At 4:00 A.M. Jim sought out his superintendent and reported he was too sick to finish the night shift. It was well below freezing outside, but Jim chose to ride home on the scooter in spite of his boss's worried suggestion that he rest on a cot in the first-aid room. Thus for the first time in years he arrived home unexpectedly, some three hours ahead of time.

It is still a subject of speculation as to whom he found—or didn't find—when he arrived in the chill blackness of that pre-dawn hour. Was Quinn there, or was it that Linda wasn't there? Whichever, sometime that morning Jim and Linda had a quarrel.

At 11:00 A.M. Linda, her beautiful composed self, drove off to work, stopping first at her parents' home to drop off her children and visit a moment. She was composed all during her working hours. Jim was not. At three that afternoon his friend Kenneth Cook arrived to help him move some boats as planned, but Jim wasn't up to it. "I feel lousy," he told Cook. "I was sick last night and couldn't sleep today. Make it tomorrow, huh?"

If one side of Linda was calm and composed, the other side was tense, nearing hysteria. When she left work at 8:00 P.M. she could feel a pursuing wave, ready to come crashing down.

The quarrel resumed where it had left off. Jim, sick and exhausted to the point of collapse, was tormentingly reasonable. Maybe if he had been furious, acted the outraged husband, Linda might have accepted it or even welcomed it as her due punishment. But when he pleaded with her to think of her children, her parents, their marriage, he was appealing to the very things she desperately wanted to forget. Every mention of the children stabbed at her conscience. Every mention of her parents forced an agonizing surge of guilt. And Jim was pathetic, bewildered—if he had taken better care of her, he said, she wouldn't be in this trouble. He, not Quinn, had driven her to this.

An hour. Two hours. Three. "Think of the children." "Give up the partying." "Come back to us." Pleas more searing than epithets. Pound, pound, pound came the words. Children, parents, marriage. They were the only words Jim had. She had to shut them out. Silence them. There was the small pistol, the one she kept loaded for protection during her lonely nights. She sprang for it.

Jim was too slow. She shot him in the head before he could reach her. Terrifyingly, he did not fall. He grappled with her, bruising her chin, bruising her shoulder. She fired again. He fell, and crashing down with him came that pursuing wave. Now it was not Jim she was destroying, but the whole of her guilt. When she fell upon him, stabbing wildly with a steel knitting needle, it was her conscience she was trying to kill.

Her fury spent, Linda became icily calm. She felt no remorse. Any love she might once have had for Jim was as dead as he was. Now she was remembering an explanation she had heard somewhere for the absence of fish in the Merrimack River, something about the chemical plants upriver dumping enough wastes to turn the water into an acid bath. That would do it. Calmly she dragged the body out to the convertible and stuffed it into the trunk. She collected two 15-pound anchors from Jim's boats and a coil of wire from his workshop.

It was nearing 4:00 A.M., a good hour, and as it was Palm Sunday, there would be no late stragglers returning from parties. Staying to the back roads, she drove her burden to the Rocks Village bridge, and there in the center, enclosed in darkness, she wired the anchors to the body, one to a hand and one to a foot. The iron rail was four feet high and latticed with strap iron through which not even a child could fall, so she had to perform an incredible feat of strength to lift the weighted body—180 pounds in all—over the rail. But she willed herself to the effort, and her will was more powerful than her body. The corpse splashed heavily, and Linda drove to the cottage to sleep soundly.

Before going to work at the diner that Palm Sunday morning, she showed her bruised chin and shoulder to her parents and to Thomas Anderson, Jim's father, with all the plaintive, baby-voiced hurt of a woman who has been struck by her husband for no good reason.

"This time he has gone too far," she said. "If he doesn't apologize right away, I'm going to leave him."

When Kenneth Cook arrived at the Anderson cottage that morning, he found the place deserted and the doors locked. At 2:00 P.M. Jim failed to show up for the Sunday dinner his mother had prepared. Concern was shown when he also did not appear at work that night. But Monday morning Linda cleared all that up.

She told Jim's father, "He was waiting for me in the car when I came out of the diner last night. We drove over and sat in front of my folk's house, but when I wouldn't go out to the cottage with him he got mad all over again. He drove off, and now I haven't even got a car to go to work in. He's sulking, that's all."

But on Wednesday Mr. Anderson was worried enough to report to the police that his son was missing from home and job. Bizarrely, Jim had unwittingly connived at his own disappearance. Brooding over the way his marriage was falling apart, and thinking of happier days in the Navy, he had spoken in many places of a wistful desire "to go down South and see some of my old Navy pals." Investigating police heard this story from one of his friends at the plant, from the chef at the all-night diner where he ate and from a cousin. When they questioned Linda about this point, she became pitifully stricken.

"Now he's deserted us," she said with a small-girl's wail. "It's the end. I am going to get a divorce."

And on April 16, through a Newburyport attorney, she began divorce proceedings, charging cruel and inhuman treatment and desertion.

State police recovered the convertible a week after Jim's disappearance. It had been left only that morning in a parking lot in Everett, a northern suburb of Boston, and the key was in the lock. No attendant had parked the car, but one early-arriving worker said he thought he remembered seeing a man walking away from it. When the police examined it for signs of violence, they discovered that the trunk had been cleaned with benzene, but neatness was no crime, and there were no traces of blood.

Linda closed the dream house and moved in with her parents, bringing only her clothes, a davenport and a chair, that furniture being needed to fill out the rooms her parents had set aside for her. Dutifully she was home every night not later than nine-thirty, just as she had been while Jim was in the Navy. So perfectly did she fit the picture of the wife who had been wronged that by June even Jim's friends had come to think he had flown the coop.

June 2, 1954. The spring floods had surged down the Merrimack and were gone. The day was warm, the tide abnormally low in the marshes. On the south side of the river, midway between Rocks Village bridge and Wickford Point, a woman bird watcher carefully stalked through the marsh grass hoping to sight nesting waterfowl. When she could go no further without sinking, she pulled out her binoculars and began scanning the outer pools. Instead of waterfowl, she sighted a half-submerged corpse in that final stage of decomposition that shocks even hardened coroners.

Police could not force a boat through the marshes to the pool in which the body floated, and no approach could be made on foot. Only by extending fire ladders across the muck were they able to reach the body. It lacked a hand and a foot, and nothing but a few shreds of outdoor clothing remained on it. The features, even the teeth, had been battered beyond recognition. The fingers of the remaining hand were in shreds, only a few tatters of skin still adhering to the thumb. But a few grueling hours later Medical Examiner Daniel Leary announced that the victim had been slain by two small-caliber bullets through the head and numerous fine stab wounds, as from an ice pick. The body had been in the water for about two months, he said, and its battered condition was probably due to its having been dashed against submerged rocks during the violence of the spring floods. He set the age of the victim as near 30; weight, approximately 150 pounds; hair, brown. He accounted for the missing hand and foot by pointing to a broken strand of wire still attached to the remaining ankle. "I think you will find," he said, "that the body was torn away from weights attached at the points where arm and leg are severed."

Thus quickly had Medical Examiner Leary produced an accurate picture of the cause of death and the manner in which the corpse had been dumped. But in two months, swirled along by the floods, the corpse might have been carried down the Merrimack from as far as 50 miles away. The police, judging by the unnecessary thoroughness with which the murder had been carried out and the characteristic manner in which the body had been disposed of, concluded they had the victim of a gangland execution on their hands. They notified Boston, but the police there, after a hopeful check of their undesirable characters, found them all unpleasantly accounted for. The next step was to see what could be done with the tatters of a thumbprint.

The most painstaking effort produced only a loop here, a ridge there and a whorl near the ball of the thumb, not enough to work on. But there was the missing-persons report filed on James Anderson, age 29, weight 150, hair brown. The Navy Department produced his fingerprint record, and when the loop, the ridge and the whorl where superimposed on the whole print, they fitted into place like three pieces from a jigsaw puzzle. If that was not conclusive evidence, two fillings from an unbroken tooth were identified by a Newburyport dentist as Jim's.

That put the case squarely in the hands of Amesbury Chief of Police Edmund McLaughlin and Essex County District Attorney Hugh Cregg.

McLaughlin went to work digging up everything he could find on the murdered man's habits. Cregg interviewed Linda.

"Jim didn't have an enemy in the world," Linda assured him. "No one, absolutely no one, would want to kill him. He could get hotheaded, but he never hit me but that once."

No one could have been more convincing. It was Linda Anderson, the mother of three, speaking. She couldn't have shot Jim. Jim had deserted her, and if he was gone, how could she have killed him?

McLaughlin was doing a little better. He moved into the dream cottage with laboratory equipment and a team of experts. An X-ray machine peered through the plaster walls in search of buried bullets. Chemists went over the walls and furniture for traces of gunpowder. Ultraviolet lamps sought in eerie blueness the stains of blood that would show up black. And under that intense scrutiny, though the murder was two months old and the house had been cleaned with a powerful detergent, they could see the murder happening in front of them. The first gout of bloot, the pool where the body had come to rest, the trailing smear leading out the back door.

A Rocks Village resident read the first reports and remembered that around April 11, in an hour of insomnia, he had heard a heavy splash in the river and then seen a car near the center of the bridge turn on its headlights and drive away. McLaughlin sent a frogman down, and an anchor was located, of the type used by Jim.

McLaughlin discovered lighter areas on the walls, dust-free, as though articles of furniture had once stood there. Linda readily told him she had taken the davenport and chair and just as readily released them for laboratory inspection. She hadn't picked up the furniture until two weeks after Jim's disappearance, she said, and it was no surprise to her that the floors had been scrubbed, "because I always kept a clean house." When tests revealed dried droplets of blood concealed in the floral design of the upholstery, she gasped in horror, "I've been sleeping on it!"

McLaughlin and Cregg had to concede that Linda would hardly take bloodstained furniture into her parents' home if she was guilty. Had she had the faintest doubts, she could have destroyed the furniture.

Science had identified an all but unidentifiable corpse, located the death scene, blueprinted the murder in ultraviolet light and traced the body's course from cottage to bridge to swamp. But at no point could it identify the killer or provide a motive.

Wrote Linda to Quinn: "I can feel your arms around me. . . ."

There was only the circumstantial evidence pointing to Linda, and that was useless. The guilty Linda had ceased to exist, so thoroughly eliminated that the widow was as eager to see Jim's killer captured as anyone, despite the fact that Jim had beaten her.

Reporters continued to dig, but simply went from one rumor to the next.

To their rescue, driven by envy over the publicity Linda was getting, came Harry Quinn. He knew all there was to know about wife-swapping parties, he said, and he implied that he also knew all there was to know about Linda. McLaughlin picked him up, grilled him and then threw him out. Quinn was aggrieved. He complained to reporters that no one really appreciated what a great lover he was.

The fact was that McLaughlin had gotten all he needed from Quinn. On his mind was the age-old rule that the man with the most gossip is probably the man with the biggest interest in the crime. Once more Linda was brought in, and this time was asked, "Would you mind taking a lie-detector test?"

Linda could hardly refuse. She was taken to Boston for the test and answered 120 questions so convincingly that her human interrogators could only believe in her innocence. But the machine, utterly immune to her beauty, her baby voice, the pathetic wringing of her hands, had a different verdict.

In Lawrence, McLaughlin and Cregg questioned her more pointedly, supported by a staff of male and female officers. It was a closed session. Known are the persons present. Known is the fact that her confession covered three pages of single-spaced typewritten copy. Known is the fact that District Attorney Cregg refused to make the confession public.

That was on June 26. On June 27 every newspaper from Calais, Maine, to San Diego, California, was carrying the story of Linda's confession and the perfidies of one Harry Quinn. According to the degree of revulsion of the reporter, Quinn was described as Blabbermouth, Kiss-and-Tell, Boastful Beau and Lover Boy. But Quinn was grateful for his press notices. "Man, you don't know what this case has done for me," he said. "I can hardly fight the girls off."

Linda's trial took place on November 29, 1954. Suspense in the courtroom was so taut the long-dead air was vibrant.

Judge Fairhurst entered, and there followed the solemn ritual by which the court was declared in session. Then Attorney Leary was on his feet declaring, "Over my wishes, my client pleads guilty to second-degree murder."

It was all over. Judge Fairhurst sentenced beautiful 27-year-old Linda to life imprisonment, and the case was officially closed.

But there was to be an anticlimax. If Blabbermouth could not be linked directly to the murder, there still remained on the Massachusetts books that same law that had once condemned Hester Prynne, the adulteress who wore the scarlet *A*.

The next day Harry Quinn was brought before Judge Fairhurst for trial without a jury. He entered smugly, convinced of his immunity, and for the first half-hour couldn't believe what was happening to him. One by one the witnesses appeared against him. By the time they had finished, Blabbermouth had been reduced to Blubbermouth, tearfully protesting he was just an innocent boy caught up by the excitement of the case. "Maybe I kissed her once or twice," he pleaded, "but that was all."

"I don't believe you," said Judge Fairhurst. "In reference to the conduct of this man, he can take a large measure of the responsibility for wrecking that family. That girl is going to be doing penance for a long time. I feel he should do penance for a long time, and that is what is going to happen to him."

Thereupon he handed down the limit—three sentences on three counts of adultery, each one for a year in prison, with the added provision that they be served consecutively, one after the other.

VI

Murder Among the Lovebirds

Janet Flanner

In murder, as in life, it's often not what you do, but the why and the way of it. Herein are two totally different ladies of love: the gauche 19-year-old Violette Nozière, and the elegant middle-aged Germaine d'Anglemont. Both committed murder, but the spectators at court interrupted the trial of one with threats of lynching, and the trial of the other with huge bouquets of flowers. *Vive la différence!*

MAYBE our grandmothers were right and female standards are, on all sides, not so high as they used to be. Certainly an eclectic comparison between the mediocre murder recently committed by the 19-year-old Parisian Flapper Mlle. Violette Nozière, and the stylish assassination achieved by the consummate Mme. Germaine d'Anglemont, age 48, indicates a deplorable decline in the younger generation. Madame d'Anglemont shot her lover like a lady, because she was jealous; Violette Nozière killed her father like a cannibal, because she wanted to eat and drink up the savings that were his French life and blood.

Even in their private lives—or as private as could be, considering that both females publicly lived on love for sale— Germaine d'Anglemont cut the grander figure, since, though an uneducated foundling, in her long life she had learned to dine with royalty, own a smart house, accept diamonds and take such an intelligent interest in politics that senators and deputies had been her slaves. And even the gentleman she finally shot was a chief magistrate.

Though her doting parents had educated her over their heads and means in a Paris private school, in her brief career Violette Nozière had learned merely how to drink bad cocktails with penniless collegiates, was at home only on the Boule 'Mich,' gave her mother's engagement ring to a lover rather than received any gem from him and certainly never met any member of the government until, on trial for parricide, she made the acquaintance of her judge.

Germaine d'Anglemont was the last of the silk-ruffled, scented, hard-lipped, handsome prewar *courtesanes,* and she made a fortune. Violette was, one fears, not the last of the fake-silver-foxed, hard-toothed, modern young monsters, of mediocre looks and without any sense of the business of life. Being up to date, her crime cruelly lacked the grand manner.

Since she was faintly intellectual, Violette Nozière character-istically chose poison and patience as her weapons. Though she did not succeed till August 1934 in putting her father into his grave and her mother into the hospital, she practiced up on murdering them in March by giving them, "as a nice new tonic" with their evening coffee, six and three tablets of veronal, respectively, which they hungrily swallowed, since both were passionate patent-medicine gourmets.

At shortly past midnight after the March evening meal, contented with their coma, their daughter set fire to the flat's modest parlor curtains, walked across the hall, roused a neigh-bor with a scream of "Fire!" and a brainy afterscream of "I think the electricity must have short-circuited!" The local fire brigade was called, and the next day M. and Mme. Nozière made the second page of the Parisian newspapers for the first and last time—thereafter they were unfortunately to be front-page stuff—for being unconscious from suffocation in what was called "A Bizarre Conflagration." Murder in an odd form was on its way to the Rue de Madagascar, where the three Nozières dwelt till they started on their separate paths toward cemetery, clinic and prison.

In the five months which followed, the immodest Violette did nothing unusual—for her. She continued her afternoon and evening life on the large sidewalks, the small hotels of the Boulevard Saint-Michel (Latin Quarter) where, from the age of 15, she had been playing hooky from the costly female seminary for which her parents had scrimped so that she might star in mathematics. But though majoring in geometry, Vi knew less about Euclid than about a lot of other men. At her trial it was brought out that she was not only a nympho- but also a mythomaniac—or a natural tart plus a born liar.

On the Café d'Harcourt terrace she picked up men with a dual purpose, the second being to tell them fantastic fibs—that she was an heiress; that her grandmother owned a château; that an aunt had millions, an uncle billions; that she herself was noble; that she was a trigonometry professor; that her father was a director in the French railways. He was, in a way. He was the locomotive engineer on the Paris-Vichy fast train; her grandmother's "château" was a cottage where, after her granddaughter's arrest, the old peasant humbly died of shame among her cabbages. Indeed, only two things unusual were performed by Vi during those fatal five months. She continued to try to kill her mother occasionally; at any rate, whenever the girl prepared breakfast for her, *maman* was deathly sick after, so Vi must have been putting something into the coffee—besides chicory, that is. (Her father, having just fallen out of his engine cab onto his head, was momentarily in the hospital and so drank *his* bad coffee without ill results.)

Violette's second odd act was to fall in love. The emotion was great, since she eventually killed for it; the object was slight—an 18-year-old gigolo law student with sleek hair, slack morals and American horn-rimmed spectacles, worn like a foolish foreign trademark on his French phiz. His name was Jean Dabin; his father, in Vi's mythology, was also probably a railway director—i.e., in reality a whistle-blowing petty stationmaster on the Paris belt railroad.

Violette's love for Jean was the only true passion in her life, except that for murder. To him she gave all she had—herself plus 100 francs a day, which she got from other men by night. She also promised to give him a secondhand Bugatti and a first-rate September holiday, for, as she said, she was shortly expecting to inherit 180,000 francs, or the exact sum her father had saved up from a lifetime of driving the Paris-Vichy express.

On August 23 her patience and poison and passion finally

focused. Violette Nozière repeated what she had tried out in March, except that she increased her father's dose to 20 powdered veronal tablets and her mother's to six. This time she also gave herself a small dose of milk of magnesia, as she was feeling liverish. Then she curled up in a chair for a nap by her parents' couch while they died—she hoped. At 2:00 A.M., when she called the same neighbor, she this time screamed—since she had turned on the kitchen range without lighting it—"Gas!" and, as a new afterscream, "I think the pipe has burst!"

The neighbor was, of all men to call in twice, an electrician and gas fitter by trades. Whatever he had failed to smell in March, this time he smelled not only gas but a rat. So did Vi, at dawn in the city hospital, sitting tenderly by her mother's bedside. (The authorities had refused to let her sit tenderly by her father's slabside in the morgue.) Sensing danger, she calmly rose and walked out into the new Paris day and what for one week seemed limbo, since no one could find her. By dinner, her news photo as "Wanted for Parricide" was all over Paris. Police hunted her everywhere, except at the Bal Tabarin (where she spent the first night after her crime, gracefully waltzing) and on the Boulevard de la Madeleine, where a white-faced, neurotic, not very pretty young creature plied her trade while whispering crazily to her customers that her father was a railway director, her grandmother owned a château, and she herself was an heiress—to 180,000 francs. Oh yes, she was surely an heiress by now. . . .

On the sixth day she was trapped into a second rendezvous by a gallant young male who had recognized her face on the pillow from his newspaper he'd tossed onto the chair. Arrested, she told the truth, probably for the first time in her life. At any rate she said she was glad she'd killed her father, who she claimed was a satyr, though her relief at hearing that her mother was yawning back from the jaws of death may have been a lie.

Her trial for murder in the autumn of 1934 was melodramatic. It opened in the Paris Assizes with a five-minute silence for King Alexander of Yugoslavia, who had also just been murdered in Marseilles. In the three days which followed, Violette fainted frequently, was occasionally nearly lynched by angry crowds and was constantly hectored in court by her mother, who was sentimentally suing her for damages for having robbed her of the sweetest husband woman ever knew.

In addition to other details, the jury was swayed by the fact that Violette had also robbed what she thought was her mother's corpse of 1000 francs pinned to the maternal corset. With lust for money to spend on her lover in cafés (for bad martinis) accredited as her miserable motive, the jury judged her guilty of the uncivilized crime of parricide, whereupon the judge read what remains the most medieval death sentence preserved in modern French law: "She is to have her head cut off in death upon a public place in Paris. She shall be taken there barefooted, clad only in her chemise and with her head covered by a black veil. Before the execution shall be done, let the clerk in a clear voice read aloud this Judgment." Because women are no longer guillotined in France, and if they were, no matter whom they'd killed, they would be allowed to die dressed and with their boots on, the rare sentence was followed by unusual silence in court, suddenly broken by Violette's vulgarly shouting, "Curse my father, curse my mother!"

To the outraged gendarme who dragged her away, she shouted in one of her illuminating afterthoughts, "Fetch my handbag with my powder, rouge, money. I must have dropped it in the prisoner's box." What was most precious she had clearly left behind her in court. Thus passed from youth into lifelong imprisonment the best-educated, worst-mannered young murderess in French annals. Killing the author of one's life is, in any land, the most thankless of crimes. But it was the fact of the girl's having rudely slept in the intimate presence of the dead and dying that caused the French jury to cut her off from civilized society as long as she might live.

The jury in the same Paris court which had just tried Germaine d'Anglemont for having shot her late love, Causeret, had only cut her off from civilized society for 11 months. And even that period of sequestration was a cultivated *passetemps,* since she spent it as prison librarian; both before and after murdering, dear Germaine was ever the bookworm. Her crime, trial, sentence, were all as cynical and sociable as her origin. Born a love child, humbly named Huot, whose father only made her acquaintance when she was age 11, at 12 Germaine had won the catechism prize in her orphan asylum, at 14 had her first flirtation, at 15 her first carriage and pair and the stylish name of D'Anglemont, which she picked out of a dime novel. The week before Mlle. Huot became Mme. D'Anglemont, she had been noted—pretty but shabby—in the then famous Jardin de Paris Café, the noting being done by a tableful which included Catulle Mendès, the poet; Henri Bernstein, the playwright; Prince Fouad, later king of Egypt; and other gentlemen of the 1905 *belle époque,* one of whom asked her how she got there.

She said she had run away from home penniless and had got into the café by pawning her umbrella for three francs with the *vestiaire.* The gentlemen handed her 500 francs ($100 in those lovely days) to get some decent clothes, three francs to get her umbrella, and invited her to dine. Her second lover, according to the list the Paris judge indelicately read out at her murder trial 34 years later, was a Dutch millionaire named Van Horschoot; the third was an Argentine tutor the Dutchman had hired to complete the girl's education—though she seemed to know a great deal already; the fourth love was the Prince Franz Josef of the royal house of Bavaria, who died of a broken heart because she wouldn't marry him.

Among the innumerable others she did not marry were the Polish Count Wielsinski, who instead of a wedding ring could only give her diamonds and pearls; the Aga Khan, who merely gave her a diamond (though it was 18 karats); Camille Picard, today Deputy from the Vosges; a Monsieur France, who was 70 and in sugar; a Monsieur Astruc, at whom she once threw an expensive Gothic statue of the virgin; and a Dr. Morgilewski (whom she never saw again for 13 years, till the fatal day when she telephoned him to come round professionally as she seemed to have shot one of his successors). The mass of parliamentarians she also enmeshed finally dwindled down, in her forties, to the late lamented Chief Magistrate Causeret, young, promising politician, fickle, married, father of children and, what was worse, son of the pious Rector Causeret of Clermont University.

"If I've omitted any of your lovers, pray excuse me, Madame," the judge said ironically at her trial. "The list is already so long. You were a *courtesane de haut vol*—a high flyer; you are also, alas, a good shot." It was her custom to practice in the shooting gallery near the Rond-Point, where Ivar Kreuger brought his fatal suicide gun. She kept two pistols in her boudoir alongside a statue of Saint Thérèse—all three useful as weapons to a woman in a jealous rage. For it was for jealousy that she murdered Causeret. She had him followed through the streets of Paris by a hunchback female detective (a masseuse, when spy work was scarce), who reported that he had gone to a department store to buy suspicious silk pajamas, instead of going, as he had announced, to talk politics with an old gentleman.

At noon, five minutes after Causeret had returned to her smart Place Beauvais flat to lunch, there was still nothing to eat on the dining-room table, but there was a corpse with only a bullet in its stomach in the boudoir. As Germaine later admitted to the jury, she had been a little hasty—the handsomest apology a murderess ever made.

At her trial the jury also was hasty; in one minute they saw it would be useless to condemn her, since they also saw, all around the court, the visiting politicos who would demand and obtain her pardon. The jury therefore judged her guilty, but with a cynically strong recommendation for mercy, which to the judge's mind meant a sentence of 11 months. Thus the quality of mercy was for once strained, since six years is a normal clement "stretch" for French female killers. Along with her 11 months, Germaine d'Anglemont also got bouquets of flowers in court, and her friends shook hands, kissing hers.

In her trial, justice was not done. Yet injustice would also have been accomplished had not a D'Anglemont's punishment been infinitely less than a Nozière's. For in a way these two were test cases, illustrating the modern French attitude toward murder, which can be summed up thus: The manner of killing is as important as the manner of living.

VII

Death and Times of a Prophet

Stewart H. Holbrook

The life of a prophet is rarely easy, and often he is misunderstood and poorly used by his time. Franz Edmund Creffield—or Joshua the Second, as he was known to his followers—was no exception. Of course he did differ from his predecessors in some respects: his satyriasis, for example, and the absolutely total devotion of his remarkable God-given energies to the "salvation" of souls that were strictly female. . . .

O_N what precise date a shaft of divine light transformed Franz Edmund Creffield from an obscure rural evangelist into prophet Joshua the Second in all his glory is not known. Neither is the exact spot where the visitation took place. But the year is certain; it was 1903, and the neighborhood of the miracle was Corvallis, Oregon.

Troubles follow in the wake of a prophet as naturally as water runs downhill. If the prophet has a set of Old Testament whiskers and a chronic case of satyriasis, then the troubles are sure to be multiplied and likewise interesting.

This particular backwoods Joshua had both the whiskers and the affliction. And when he raised his voice in holy anger, as he did on one remembered occasion, the vast city of San Francisco shook horribly in the grip of an Act of God, then went down, writhing and smoking, in one of the greatest disasters within the memory of living men.

Driving up the lush green Willamette Valley from Portland to Corvallis, one scarcely wonders that this land once produced a veritable prophet. It is amazing there have not been more of them. Here was the Promised Land where the creaking covered wagons came to rest at the far end of the Oregon Trail; where the immigrants shouted "Glory to God!" and drove their stakes, naming their settlements Amity, Sweet Home, Salem, Aurora and Corvallis—which last is said to mean heart of the valley. Here along the many creeks is beaver-dam soil, richer than the delta of the Nile. Vegetables grow as large as the pictures on the seed packages. Enormous prunes and the finest walnuts on earth hang heavy on the trees. Vetch and clover grow thick and big enough to stop the wheels of powered farm machinery.

117

The climate is damp and mild. Seldom is there more than a trace of snow.

Here and there along the 90 miles the highway plunges into groves of Douglas fir, tall and mighty even before Lewis and Clark and the Hudson Bay Company came. To the east rises the backbone of Oregon, the majestic peaks of the Cascades, and on the west are the Coast Range mountains, faintly hung with mist and haze in season, brooding, black, faraway hills to make a prophet out of almost any man.

In the heart of this valley is Corvallis, seat of Oregon State College, a spick-and-span town that holds court for Benton County, sells things to farmers, makes considerable lumber, has a daily paper, a radio station and a library of 130,000 volumes, including "a 15th-Century antiphony composed of Gregorian chants in Flemish, handprinted and illuminated on parchment and bound in calf over the original board covers."

Corvallis is sedate enough today, as serene as any campus town in the land. It has, in fact, been sedate throughout most of its three-quarters of a century. Only during the days of Joshua the Second, when signs and portents were on every hand, did Corvallian blood run hot and fast.

Unheralded, Franz Edmund Creffield made his first appearance in the Corvallis of 1902 in the form and style of a Salvation Army worker. He was 35-years-old, smooth-shaven, short of stature and had large brown eyes. He retained a slight but noticeable accent from his native Germany.

A few months later, or early in 1903, he either left or was discharged from the religious group and seems to have disappeared for a time. It was likely during this obscure period that the great light beat upon him and he talked with God somewhere in the tall forests that edged close to the town. In any case, he was soon back in Corvallis.

In 1903 no man could be a true prophet who did not have a beard, and when Creffield emerged from the timber he was wearing an astonishing growth. It was of the veritable Moses type, flowing down over his chest and spreading to left and right, unruly, wild, burgeoning like everything in the Willamette Valley, while over his shoulders tumbled falls of unkempt hair. Both beard and hair were of a reddish golden brown.

He was Edmund Creffield no longer, but Joshua the Second, sole prophet and for a short period sole communicant of the Church of the Bride of Christ. Even the tone of his voice had changed; it no longer had the supplication, the humbleness, of street and field evangels. It now boomed like muffled thunder, and in it, many came to think, was the authority of Jehovah.

It must have been that the Corvallis of the time, in spite of its several churches, was lacking somewhat in spiritual life, at least so far as the women were concerned. In those days, of course, there were no movies, no serial radio dramas, no bridge clubs to entertain and thus protect the dim minds of vapid females; so it is conceivable that in Corvallis, as in any other American town, time often seemed interminable to those who live chiefly to kill time.

And it is conceivable, too, in view of the record, that this brand-new Joshua possessed a magnetic if not downright hypnotic personality. Within a month he had a sizable cult of converts. It was all done so quietly that even the town fathers, who fancied they knew almost everything that went on locally, were wholly unaware of the great harvest of souls that was going forward.

The first meetings were held openly in the homes of converts, of whom at least six were men. At this period the prophet seems to have had no particular message other than that the ways of the world were all wrong and should be changed. One by one the male converts dropped away, leaving Joshua and a stooge known as Brother Brooks to carry on with the increasing flock of girls and women.

If you think that the apostasy of the few men was discouraging to the prophet, then you don't know how an Oregon Joshua works when he gets going full gospel-style. The meetings in the homes of converts were continued; but they now were held in the afternoons, when menfolk were away.

There must have been a female Judas in the flock, for it was presently whispered around town that never before had there been seen such manifest workings of the spirit as Joshua Creffield brought about. Pulling down all the blinds of the meeting place—so this she-Judas reported—Joshua began a chant, swaying to its rhythm, waving his arms and calling upon what he addressed rather familiarly as the Full Spirit to descend upon the meeting.

The girls and women soon began to sway. They chanted; they moaned; they "spoke in tongues" and cried aloud while the prophet seemed to gain in stature and his normally calm eyes sank deep into his head, where they glowed like two pits of fire. The swaying and the chanting went on.

Suddenly, like a thunderbolt, the prophet's voice boomed out: "Vile clothes, begone!" The whiskered fellow then disrobed, and without urging on his part, many of the women present did likewise. There was nothing coy about it, no sense of shame. They threw off their peekaboo waists, their skirts and their multitude of petticoats; they tore wildly at their whalebone corsets, meanwhile moaning like all get-out.

"Roll, ye sinner, roll!" thundered Joshua: And roll they did, some in chemises, some without, all over the bare floor, with Joshua and Brother Brooks rolling happily among them.

Either at this or at a subsequent meeting Joshua began to expound the canons of his sect. He had already announced that he and his followers were members of the Church of the Bride of Christ. Now he let it be known that the Lord had commanded him to select from among his followers she who was to become the Mother of a Second Christ.

It soon became apparent to the faithful that Joshua was going about his quest for a second Mother in a thorough and searching manner, which manner was obviously of the empirical school. Several married women left the sect at this point, taking their daughters with them. But many remained, and new females appeared at every meeting. So many came, in fact, that Joshua and Brother Brooks felt the need for more room.

On Kiger Island, in the nearby river, the prophet and his stooge, with girls and women helping, built a large wigwam of poles covered with boughs. The boughs were interwoven cleverly and tightly, and the entrance was closed with a curtain. It is recalled that one of the most willing workers was a beautiful and young ash-blonde girl, Esther Mitchell.

Their hands torn and covered with the pitch of Douglas fir (*Pseudotsuga taxifolia*), but with their eyes shining with the light of Gospel, girls of 14 and women of 55 toiled on the pretty wooded island. Some brought small tents that were set up, and small wigwams also were built.[1] Throughout the summer of 1903 meetings were held on the island almost every afternoon, and the vast workings of the Spirit could be heard on either shore of the mainland.[2]

With cooler weather and heavy rains, the island retreat was not a happy place to roll about in the altogether. A new and

---

[1] Years afterward an ex-member recalled that one of the small tents or wigwams of the island retreat was the "whipping place," where Joshua switched this or that girl or woman to "drive out the devils." But this ex-member was unacquainted with the name of the late Marquis de Sade.—S.H.H.

[2] Even the Oregon State Agricultural College at Corvallis was affected by the workings of Joshua. Miss Ellen Chamberlain, who was a teacher there in 1903, wrote me: "—— was a young girl in my history class, very attractive. After a two days' absence from class I asked her brother, also a student, what had become of his sister. He was evasive, obviously

suitable spot was soon found in the residence of O.P. Hunt, in Corvallis. Mr. Hunt was a respected citizen, a member of a pioneer family, and Corvallians were shocked one day in early fall to see a large sign over the door of his house: "Positively No Admittance, Except on God's Business." A smaller one attached to the gate repeated the warning. Now things began to happen to quiet Corvallis. A reporter of the local *Times* viewed the premises and wrote:

> Certain caprices of religious fanaticism have been manifested at the house that are so unusual as to suggest a condition bordering insanity. Walks about the house have been torn away. Much of the furniture of the house has been reduced to ashes in a bonfire held last night in the yard, on the theory that God wills it. The shrubbery and fruit trees and all the flowers have been digged up and destroyed. Kitchen utensils have been beaten to pieces and buried. . . . It is reported that house cats and dogs have been cremated.

Joshua and Brother Brooks were taken to the courthouse for a sanity hearing. Joshua sneered at the proceedings and told Deputy Sheriff Henderson not to "talk that way to God's anointed." The men were found sane, but officers advised them to leave town. Brother Brooks said nothing. Joshua merely laughed quietly as he went out the courthouse door.

In the meantime Mr. Hunt—but apparently not his women-folk—had discovered that he wanted no more of Joshua and

---

embarrassed. But I found out that ——— was too taken up with the Holy Roller meetings to think of school. One day a bit later this girl went to the college president's office and asked if she might pray for him. He assented and called in Prof. Crawford and one of the lady teachers. They told me how beautifully, how fervently she prayed for them, to do more for the spiritual welfare of the students. The next day I found this girl in my room, sobbing. I tried to reason with her. She was adamant. I was glad to know her mother had come to be with her son and daughter, but alas, the mother soon became a victim of that satanic influence. . . . As I recall it, both mother and daughter were later committed to the asylum."—S.H.H.

his sect. In the meantime, too, prints of a photograph that had been taken many weeks before began to circulate in Corvallis. The name of the unbeliever who took this picture has been lost to history, but his little Brownie camera had a good lens. The picture was what today would be termed a candid camera shot, and it was taken during one of the spiritual orgies of the cult on Kiger Island. The film was small but as clear as crystal; it showed Joshua, quite naked, amid nothing less than a bevy of naked local matrons and girls, some of them standing, some rolling in the lush wild grass. Several were easily identified. The film, it is said, was soon worn out in making reprints.

No movie ever made created such a furor as this two inches of silent, static film. There was an immediate uproar, as enraged fathers and injured husbands had their kids and wives packed off to the state hospital and to the home for wayward girls. Some 15 of Joshua's sect were at once taken out of circulation, while others got warnings to which they paid little if any heed.

Then, on the coolish evening of January 4, 1904, a band of silent men called at the house where Joshua and Brother Brooks had quarters. None of the men were masked, nor was there any attempt at concealment of the affair, and nearly all of the mob were citizens of high standing. Without a word this band took the two long-haired men to the edge of town, where a pot of tar was heating over an open fire. They were made to strip, then given a coat of tar and feathers [3] and told to keep out of Corvallis.

Brother Brooks was never again seen in town after the party at the tarpot. It was different with Joshua. Mrs. Hunt and her

---

[3] I am told by one who was present that the mob was particularly careful to see that Joshua's coat of tar and feathers covered all of him.—S.H.H.

young daughter Maude searched for and found the feathered prophet hiding miserably in the woods. They brought him to their home. The sticky coat was removed, and a few days later Joshua dropped his biblical name long enough to marry Miss Maude Hunt. The marriage proved something of a local sensation, for it isn't often that the daughter of a respected pioneer family ties up with a man who has just had tar and feathers scraped off his hide. The marriage also doubtless eased the minds of many Corvallis males; they could well believe that now the prophet's search for a second Mother was done.

But the search *wasn't* done. Leaving his new wife at the home of her parents in Corvallis, Joshua went to Portland to commune with a married woman who had been a follower in the palmy days of the Kiger Island colony. She and the prophet were presently found *in flagrante delicto* by her husband, who swore out a warrant in which he called the prophet's holy search by the vulgar name of adultery.

Police had been waiting for something tangible like this to work on. But now they couldn't find the prophet, and to stimulate the search for him O. P. Hunt, the prophet's own father-in-law, offered a reward of $150 for his arrest. Maude Hunt Creffield secured a divorce. Things looked dark for Joshua the Second.

Nearly three months thus passed with the prophet supposedly at large. Then one day in June, young Roy, adopted son of O. P. Hunt, made a startling discovery. Crawling under the Hunt home in search of a tin can in which to carry worms on a fishing trip, the youngster was frightened near out of his wits when he suddenly found himself looking into the great blazing eyes of a bearded man.

Backing out of the hole as fast as he could, the lad ran screaming to his father. Mr. Hunt came and peered into the hole, then called the police.

The cops came and hauled the prophet from his den under

the house. He was, as one of the officers remarked 30 years after, a sight to behold—naked, dirty as a hog, hairy all over as a water spaniel and most wonderfully endowed by Mother Nature withal. His beard grew down to his stomach and was bushy as a clump of black alder. But he was as thin as a fence rail. He was weak, too, and could scarcely stand.

"You're Creffield, ain't you?" asked a cop, no doubt recalling folk tales of surviving specimens of *Pithecanthropus erectus.*

"I am Joshua." The voice that came from the long beard was weak, yet obviously the voice of a prophet.

It was a weird tale that the officers and Mr. Hunt pieced together. For more than two months the prophet had lived day and night in his lair under the home of his ex-father-in-law, unsuspected by menfolk of the house. He had existed on jars of fruit and scraps of food that Mrs. Hunt and other faithful (who were admitted to the secret) could smuggle to him. He had thrown away all his clothes before he entered the den. The only covering he had when taken out was a ragged and filthy quilt.

Creffield was put on trial before Judge Sears in Multnomah County Court in Portland. He readily admitted what the court charged were improper relations with the Corvallis matron, but he said that such things were not at all improper in a man of God such as he. "Christ," he said in the usual manner of mountebanks, "broke the Sabbath day, and the Jews put Him to death. I've broken your laws, and you will undoubtedly do the same to me. Like Christ, however, I will rise again and ye all shall suffer."

The jury was made up of forthright men. In 12 minutes, or about the time it took them to go to the jury room and back, they brought in a verdict. It was "Guilty." Judge Sears asked Creffield if he had anything to say before sentence was pronounced. He did; he had a lot to say. In a rambling yet fervid harangue, during which he misquoted considerable scripture and called the saints to witness, he told the court and the jury that he forgave them, for they knew not what they did.

"Two years in state's prison," said Judge Sears, a man of few words.

"God bless you," replied the prophet, and impious deputies laid hands on him and whisked him away to Salem. He was dressed in at the pen as Number 4941 on September 16, 1904.

Fifteen months later the prophet was released. The warden, of course, couldn't know what a baggage of trouble and tragedy he was turning loose. His beard gone, his hair cut close, Joshua left the scene of his triumphs and trials, going at once to Los Angeles, then as now a lodestone for prophets of all kinds. He didn't stay long, but was soon in San Francisco. How he lived during this period of exile is not known, but one should consider that no prophet has ever starved in California.

Very soon Corvallis learned that Joshua was writing letters to 17-year-old Esther Mitchell, she who had attended the prophet's meetings on Kiger Island. He wrote her that God had at last made it clear to him that Esther and no other was to become the second Mother. This had been revealed to him in a message direct from heaven. What young Esther replied is not known, but events that were soon to pile up would indicate she was favorable to the message. The prophet also sent a letter from San Francisco to Mr. Hunt, his former father-in-law, at Corvallis:

God has resurrected me. I have now got my foot on your neck. God has restored me to my own. I will return to Oregon and gather together all of my followers. Place no obstruction in my way, or God will smite you. Joshua II.

That was clear enough. And from San Francisco, too, the prophet wrote his ex-wife, Maude Hunt, then living in Seattle with a brother and a sister-in-law, Mr. and Mrs. Frank Hunt.

Maude replied that she would remarry Joshua if he would come
to the Puget Sound metropolis.

The prophet, now in full beard again and ready for anything,
came north, stopping neither at Corvallis nor in Oregon but
going directly to Seattle. He and Maude were married by an
orthodox minister, and now he made plans for a triumphant
return to the state that had used him so shabbily. He would,
he vowed, go to a primeval spot that he knew on the Oregon
coast and there establish a colony for the faithful, a true Garden
of Eden in which the flock could live in a manner best suited
to them and their beliefs, free from the profane gaze of scoffers.
It would take a little cash, obviously, to purchase this Eden,
which he had visited, and he suggested that Mr. and Mrs. Frank
Hunt dispose of their Seattle property and buy the land for the
Glory of God.

So hypnotic was this bearded man with the startling eyes that
the Hunts did just that. They sold their Seattle house and
bought the strip of land in question. It was south of Waldport,
Oregon, fronting the Pacific, and in 1906 was a very remote
place indeed. The Hunts and Maude were to go to the spot as
an advance party. Joshua would in the meantime sound the call
to the faithful, telling them that they would remain away from
Eden at their own peril.

"Peril?" asked Frank Hunt, who was not yet fully apprised
of the powers of a genuine prophet.

"Peril, yes," replied Joshua, and added, "Brother Hunt, I
have called down the wrath of an angry God on these modern
Sodoms of Seattle, of Portland, of San Francisco, of Corvallis
itself. Have no fear, Brother Hunt. My faithful will return to
the fold—all of them. They will leave all behind them—their
scoffing fathers, their brothers, their husbands—and come to
our Eden." And then he uttered an awful curse.

"A curse, Oh God, on San Francisco, on Portland, on Corvallis, on Seattle."

This tremendous curse was loosed on the morning of April 17, 1906, just as the Eden advance party got aboard a train at Seattle on the way to Newport, Oregon, nearest railroad station to the Garden.

Next day, the 18th, Joshua again laid foot on Oregon soil. He avoided Corvallis, where he would have had to change cars, by getting off the train at Airlie and being taken in a livery-stable rig to Wren, 12 miles west of Corvallis, where he boarded the train for Newport. He was met at the depot by his wife and the two Hunts, who were all but speechless and who told him in awed tones of telegraphic dispatches that day reporting the total destruction of San Francisco by earthquake and fire.

Joshua smiled, probably smugly. "I knew it," he said quietly. "I knew that God would respond. The other cities of the plain will be next. We must rouse the faithful before it is too late."

And rouse they did. When a man with a big long beard has friends who can shake a big city to pieces—well, it is time to pay heed. And Joshua had sent the word through the mails to Corvallis. Within 24 hours trainmen on the Corvallis and Eastern Railroad wondered at the amount of traffic, all of it female, heading for the end of the line at Newport. There were middle-aged women with babies, middle-aged women with grown daughters, middle-aged women alone and young girls who, it turned out, had run away from home. Most of all, trainmen were struck with and remembered the slim beauty of fair-haired Esther Mitchell, soon to be in headlines throughout the West.

There were two trains daily out of Corvallis, and for the next several days every train brought a few more girls and women. All had to be ferried across Yaquina Bay, thence on foot or by buggy to the Garden of Joshua.

The cynical folk around Waldport put no stock in the prophet, not even after the terrifying results of his great curse became known. Waldport was openly hostile. But 90 miles east, back in troubled Corvallis, Joshua's trumpet call had sounded loud and clear. Young girls in their teens started for school and disappeared. Husbands returned home in the evening to find their wives gone, at least one of them carrying a six-week-old babe with her. Still another husband found a note pinned to a pillow in his home. It told him his wife had heard the call.[4]

Down in the Garden, Joshua was receiving more revelations. One message told that Corvallis itself was to be the next sinful city to be destroyed. Another directed all members of the cult to burn their clothing and to wear a sort of holy wrapper. A big fire was set going, and into it screaming, moaning women and girls heaved all their vile finery, forthwith dressing themselves in the wrappers that Joshua provided.[5] And the prophet's search for the second Mother went on wonderfully well. . . . Praise Joshua and great day in the morning!

Living conditions in the Garden were pretty bad. Lean-to and wigwam huts were made. Everyone slept on the ground. Food was cooked over open fires and was plain. Between 40 and 50 girls and women and the two men made up the colony.

By April 26 at least one man in Corvallis had learned the whereabouts of Joshua. This man's young daughter had disappeared, and investigation showed she had walked most of the way to Newport, then down the coast road to the Garden. The youngster, all alone, had done more than 80 miles of the trip on foot. Her father, one of Corvallis's highly respected citizens, set out to find her.

---

[4] This note, which survives, is a fair example of how strong was Joshua's call: "I don't want to leave in the daytime because the children will see me and cry to go with me. I must leave while they are asleep. I have taken $2.50 of your money. This will not pay all my fare and I will still have to walk 90 miles or more to where I want to go." Walk she did, and alone, over the Coast Range mountains, where bear and cougar stalked the road.—S.H.H.

[5] Considerable research has failed to reveal where or how Joshua got these wrappers, but one who saw them at close range tells me they were like heavy cotton bathrobes.—S.H.H.

This man meant business. At Newport he paused long enough to purchase a 32-caliber revolver and a box of cartridges. Going down to the waterfront to get transportation across Yaquina Bay, he barely missed the ferry which was just pulling away from the dock. On the ferry he could see the bearded prophet amid a group of wrappered females. Without more ado this man pulled his gun and aimed it at Joshua, while the women screamed. But the gun only clicked—five times in a row.

Out on the ferry Joshua smiled gently at the puny attempts of a mere man to kill him. "See?" he told his women. "You see? No man can kill Joshua." And the women were certain they had witnessed another example of the prophet's power.

Not so the man on the dock. "It was the goddam fool who sold me them cartridges and gun," he complained to friends. "The gun is center-fire, and the cartridges rim-fire. That's why that —— is still alive."

But the men of seething Corvallis, now thoroughly aroused, were getting ready to lay the prophet low. Singly and in twos and threes they took trains to Newport. Armed with rifles and revolvers, they crossed on the ferry and went to Waldport. Here they learned that Joshua must have been forewarned. He had last been seen heading for Newport, alone, and had no doubt hidden in the woods to let the several posses pass.

This information was hurriedly telephoned to Corvallis. In that town was George Mitchell, 21-year-old brother of Esther. Taking a revolver, he went to Albany, thinking he might catch the prophet there waiting for a train to Portland. Mitchell learned he was too late; the prophet was already gone. With him was his wife Maude, and the two had bought tickets to Seattle. Young Mitchell had to remain overnight in Albany for another train. He arrived in Seattle on the morning of May 7, 1906.

Whether or not Mitchell knew where in Seattle to look for

the prophet has never been clear. What is clear as daylight is this:

About eight o'clock on this May morning Joshua Creffield and his wife, now both dressed in orthodox fashion, but the prophet in full beard, left the cheap rooming house where they had taken lodgings and walked down Second Avenue. At Cherry Street they turned and walked to First Avenue. In front of Quick's Drugstore was a weighing machine. The prophet's wife stepped onto the machine, while Joshua stood looking into the store window.

Young Mitchell had sighted the couple. He stepped quickly up behind the man, placed the muzzle of his revolver at the prophet's left ear and fired. Joshua the Second slumped quietly down to the sidewalk.

The small and wiry woman turned and screamed. She flew at Mitchell like a cat and tried to take the gun from his hands. Mitchell retained the gun, but made no attempt to escape. In a moment Maude left him and bent over her husband, whose blood was now running in a stream across the sidewalk. The prophet had died without moving, without even a shudder.

Mitchell stood idly, holding the gun in his hands. Without a word he handed it to a policeman who had hurried from a nearby corner.

Mrs. Creffield at first was frantic, but she calmed. "This man," she told the surprised cop, pointing to the figure on the sidewalk, "this man is my husband, Joshua the prophet. He will arise in three days and walk."

"Sure, sure," said the officer, who was used to all kinds of people. He called the wagon and an ambulance.

At the police station George Mitchell was calm, even happy. He asked for a telegraph blank and sent a message to O. P. Hunt at Corvallis, who, it will be remembered, was again the prophet's father-in-law. "I got my man," read the wire, "and I am in jail here."

In spite of the protests of the widow and of Mr. and Mrs. Frank Hunt, who had hurried from Eden to Seattle, the body of the late prophet was turned over to the Bonney-Watson undertakers. These kindly men stuffed cotton into the hole in the prophet's ear and laid him away tenderly in Lakeview Cemetery on May 9. Only the widow and Bonney-Watson employees were at the grave. No services were held.

That was how they laid Joshua the Second away in the ground. But his work was far from done.

As King County (Seattle) prepared to prosecute George Mitchell for the murder of Edmund Creffield, all eyes turned to the Puget Sound city where the trial would be held, and the late prophet's Garden of Eden, 300 miles to the south, was forgotten. Things were going badly there. On May 15, a week after the shooting, George Hodges, timber cruiser of Salado, Oregon, had been looking over some fine old Douglas fir not far from Waldport on the coast. It was a cold, windy day. When he emerged from the timber onto the beach he saw something that liked to have caused him to swallow the chewing tobacco he was working on.

Hodges couldn't know, of course, that he was in Garden of Eden country, and he brushed his eyes when he saw five women and young girls, one of them with a baby in arms and all dressed in outlandish wrappers, camped on the beach. One look told him they were starving. Their cheeks were pinched, and some were too weak to stand. They were grouped around a frayed and torn old tent and they told the startled timber cruiser that they were followers of Joshua, the prophet who recently had destroyed San Francisco.

Hodges was a man who read the papers. He began to get the drift of what he had stumbled into. And where was this Joshua, he asked. The women said that Joshua had gone north to Queen Charlotte Islands, off the north coast of British Columbia, where he was seeking out a new Garden of Eden for his followers.

"But this prophet of yours, he is dead," Hodges told the women. "He was shot and killed in Seattle a week ago."

The women laughed crazily at that one. Joshua dead? He could not be killed. They had seen a man try it with a revolver. You couldn't kill Joshua.

Convinced that the bedraggled women were completely out of their heads, and learning that they had had nothing to eat in two weeks except for a few crabs and mussels, Hodges left them what provisions he carried in his pack and went to Newport. He then telephoned authorities at Corvallis, giving them, in true land-looker style, the line, range and section of the Garden of Eden. Expeditions of brothers, husbands and fathers set out at once to bring their womenfolk home.

Up in Seattle the trial of George Mitchell was getting underway. William D. Gardner, superintendent of the Oregon Boys and Girls Aid Society, testified that "a large number of young girls" had been sent to his institution from Corvallis by their parents; that most of these girls had confessed to "criminal relations" with the prophet that they insisted were really not criminal at all because the prophet was searching for the mother of a second Christ. Certain practices of the prophet had been particularly revolting and would have made a chapter or two for Herr Doktor Krafft-Ebing.

"Creffield was a degenerate of the worst sort," said John Manning, district attorney of Portland, in a letter to Kenneth MacKintosh, who was prosecuting Mitchell—and added, "He practiced unspeakable brutalities on ignorant and unsophisticated girls."

A Corvallis citizen testified that Esther Mitchell, sister of the defendant, had been sent to the Boys and Girls Aid home to get her away from Joshua. When released, she immediately took up with the prophet again. "She is obsessed," concluded the witness.

Esther herself attended the trial of her brother. Day after day she sat there, and spectators remarked on her lack of emotion—or was it something else?—as she watched and listened with a dead-calm face.

Evidence to be given on several days of the trial was such that the court was cleared of spectators.

George Mitchell conducted himself with quiet dignity. He was the hero throughout the trial. A large delegation came from Corvallis, including Mr. O. P. Hunt, the late prophet's father-in-law, who attempted to put up bail for Mitchell and who was a staunch supporter of the youth during the trial. Women heaped flowers on the defendant every day until the judge ordered that this should stop, so far as the courtroom was concerned.

Mitchell's statement was simple. "I came here to kill this man because he ruined my two sisters. I have completed my work." He seemed the happiest person in the room.

From the first it was clear that the Messrs. Silas M. Shipley and W. H. Morris, counsel for Mitchell, were attempting to indicate justifiable homicide as well as temporary insanity, the latter which was just then coming into popularity as a defense in criminal trials. Nobody, one could guess, was surprised when the jury, out an hour, returned a verdict of not guilty. George Mitchell was all but mobbed by friends and well-wishers. It was noticed, though, that his handsome, sad-faced sister Esther left the courtroom without going near him.

The trial ended on July 10. Two days later George Mitchell and brothers Fred and Perry went to Seattle's King Street station to take the four-thirty afternoon train to Oregon. The waiting room was crowded with summer tourists. It was a jolly gathering.

Fred Mitchell spied Esther standing near a pillar in the big depot, nonchalant and aloof. Her skirt was a bit short, coming almost to the tops of her shoes. Around her throat was a white satin ribbon, done in a big bow, its ends streaming down over a white shirtwaist. She carried a light coat over one arm.

Fred left his two brothers and went to Esther, asking her if she wasn't going to bid good-bye to George. The slim girl assented with a nod. She and Fred joined the others. She took George by the hand, but did not respond to his greeting, and the four Mitchells walked toward the gate of the train shed. The station announcer was now calling the train for Portland and way points.

And now the silent girl moved quickly as a panther. Reaching her right hand under the coat on her arm, she brought out a small pearl-handled revolver—just the sort a woman would buy. In a move so quick that Fred Mitchell had no time to think or act, she placed the gun's muzzle behind George's left ear and pulled the trigger. George sank to the marble floor without a word.

In the noisy, crowded station the gunshot made little impression, but Patrolman John T. Mason had seen the move. He took the smoking gun from Esther and placed her under arrest. The man on the floor was already dead.

At the Seattle police station Esther remained calm and dry-eyed. She said the killing had been a matter of course. Her brother had killed God in the form of Joshua Creffield, hadn't he? Well, that is why she had killed her brother. Shot him in the same place he had shot Joshua, she pointed out.

It took no questioning at all by police to learn that Esther and Maude Creffield, the prophet's widow, had planned to kill George Mitchell should he be freed by the court. Detectives

were sent to bring Maude to the station. The stories of the two
women agreed in everything: Maude had bought the gun; it
was decided after some discussion that Esther should do the
killing. She loaded the gun herself and put it in the bosom of
her shirtwaist. Maude had objected, saying that perspiration
might prevent the gun from firing. Esther then wrapped the
gun in a handkerchief and put it in her waist. She would have
done the shooting on the day the trial ended, she said, but no
opportunity had presented itself. It was the same on the day
after the trial. She knew her brothers were to leave town on
the following day. She was at the station, waiting.

This new sensation rocked both Seattle and distant Corvallis.
When a girl who has been chosen to be the Mother of a Second
Christ picks a crowded railroad station to kill her own
brother—well, the Harry Thaw case was moved off page one
for a few days.

Both Esther and Mrs. Creffield were held. Tried on a charge
of murder, Esther was found not guilty because of unsound
mind. She was committed to the Washington State Asylum.[6]
Maude Creffield was being held in the county jail for disposition,
but she took care of the matter herself. One morning the
matron, a Mrs. Kelly, found the young woman stiff in her
bunk, quite dead. An autopsy revealed much strychnine in her
stomach.

Three years later Esther Mitchell was released from the
asylum. Two days afterward a thin and tragically beautiful girl
came into the editorial offices of the *Morning Oregonian* at
Portland and asked Miss Amanda Otto, secretary to editor
Harvey Scott, if she knew where George Mitchell was buried.
Miss Otto immediately recognized the girl as Esther Mitchell

---

[6] Colonel A. E. Clark of Portland, Oregon, defended Esther Mitchell
without charge. He remembers her as "a girl of fine appearance and of
high intelligence, except for her one tragic delusion."—S.H.H.

and replied she would see if she could find the information. She left the room a moment. When she returned, Esther was gone.

Some weeks later the unfortunate girl—she was only 20 years old—died at the home of friends not far from Waldport, scene of the late Joshua's erstwhile Garden of Eden.

VIII

Greek Tragedy

Renée Huggett and Paul Berry

Love affairs are one thing. Family affairs are another. When the two become entangled, the result can be disastrous. In the case of Mrs. Christofi and her son and daughter-in-law, the disaster took the form of a tragedy that could have been performed in the amphitheaters alongside the works of Aeschylus and Sophocles.

THE trial of Mrs. Christofi might have been expected to arouse a great deal more interest and controversy than it did. It came at a time when the question of abolishing the death penalty was coming into the limelight. It threw into relief the unsatisfactory state of our insanity laws. It was a "family" murder, which arouses different and deeper emotions than the murder of a stranger.

A hundred years ago Mrs. Christofi would have been a tartar of a mother who never allowed her children to marry; 200 years ago she would have been burned at the stake as a witch; 2000 years ago she could have been a Roman empress, and before that her story would have formed the basis of a tragedy for her Greek ancestors.

Today, inured to violence, we can see no difference between her crime and that of any other murderer. Yet the circumstances form a rare, sinister story that abounds in psychological interest. Here was no murder for money, or intrigue, or petty gain. Here was a full-blooded slaughter for mother love, vengeance, hatred. It was as simple and primitive as Oedipus, and as cruel.

It was almost as tragic.

The Christofis family lived in a flat in a tall, gaunt Victorian terrace house in Hampstead.

Stavros Christofis, one of the sons of Styllou Christofi, was Greek by birth and had been brought up in Cyprus. His family were peasant people, and the mother was the matriarch; she ruled her family; she loved them; her family was her entire life. When he was a little boy, Stavros heard strange rumors about his mother; but the rumors were hushed up; he never quite knew what the closely guarded secret was.

In 1937 he decided to go to England, and four years later he met a German girl, Hella Bleicher. They were married in 1942. She was a tall, attractive brunette, and their marriage was perfectly happy. He gave her a ring engraved with his name, and she wore it till the day of her death.

They settled in the Hampstead flat, and Stavros worked as a wine waiter and insurance agent. By 1953 they had three children—Nicholas, Peter and Stella. Mr. and Mrs. Christofis were well liked by their neighbors, who thought that they were "extremely nice people" and described Mr. Christofis as "the kindest father you could wish to meet." Hella came from a good home and was a methodical and scrupulously clean housekeeper.

Upon this happy household descended in July 1953 the Matriarch. Her arrival is like the voice of Creon foretelling doom, bringing to a tragic end the happy marriage of Jocasta and Oedipus. Here again is the Clytemnestra of the 20th Century who brings suffering upon the son she loves.

In the old Greek story, Agamemnon is murdered by his wife Clytemnestra when he returns from the Trojan Wars. It is left to their son Orestes to avenge his father, but to do so he must murder his mother.

The story revolves around this two-fold tragedy—the family rent in two, the son's love for his father, his opposing feelings for his mother.

But a murder demands vengeance. Clytemnestra pays with her own life. It is the state which demands retribution, but the suffering does not end there; Orestes must live on, absolve his own conscience.

The Matriarch did not murder her husband in Hampstead, but her daughter-in-law; and as in the Oresteia it is around the son that the tragedy revolved.

When she arrived from Cyprus she had been separated from her son for many years. She had missed him, and now that she was with him again, she decided to stay. She told her son and daughter-in-law that she wanted to save some money so that she could buy a plot of land in Cyprus.

Hella could speak only a few words of Greek, the Matriarch could speak only a few words of English, so with the best intentions in the world, they could not get to know each other very well. But to the Matriarch all that mattered was her son— and her son's children.

She was put in the back bedroom with the two little boys. Hella and Stavros slept in the front bedroom with their small daughter.

The days passed, the weeks lengthened into months, and still the mother-in-law remained. Inevitably, slowly, the two women found they could not get on together beneath the same roof, and for a while the Matriarch went to live elsewhere. But once more she returned; her son was still her son, his children were her grandchildren, and she began to feel critical about the way in which Hella was bringing them up. Hella was not a peasant woman; she had never taken her children to work in the fields. In fact Hella had a job; she wore nice clothes. But in her heart the Matriarch could not understand why Stavros loved her, as he obviously did.

Slowly disapproval was replaced by jealousy; she resented her pretty daughter-in-law, she resented the way they talked in a language she could not understand.

Hella began to feel an increasing tension. She felt the criticism that could never be spoken and she became nervous and depressed. It was decided that she should go to Germany to her parents for a holiday and take the children with her. They had a talk with the Matriarch; she could remain with her son while Hella was in Germany, but when Hella returned she must go back to Cyprus. They explained that the winter was coming on, and it would be better for her health if she returned.

The Matriarch accepted this. "If you feel that way, I will go back," she told her son.

But to her it must have seemed like a death warrant. Cyprus was far away; she would never have the money to come again to see her son. They would be separated forever.

At about eight-thirty in the evening of July 28, just a year after the Matriarch came to England, Stavros set off for work. His wife and children came to the door to say good-bye to him. The Matriarch was standing just outside the kitchen door in the passage, watching them. Perhaps for her the tragedy was crystallized in that moment: a son with his own family; herself a mother who no longer had any right to be there.

The children went to bed, and Hella and her mother-in-law washed up. Some visitors called to see Hella and stayed only a few minutes. Hella went to the front door to see them off, and we see her for the last time in the twilight, this smiling, friendly mother, with the shadows of the sinister Greek woman falling across her shoulders.

Then Hella decided to take a bath, and the Matriarch went up to bed. She must have returned almost immediately, because her bed was later found untouched and Hella was found still undressed.

In the pattern of all Greek tragedy, the avenger struck. The sinister portents, the animosity and jealousy found their fulfillment in Hella's terrible fate.

She was hit on the head with an ashpan taken from the kitchen stove, causing her to lose consciousness. Then she was strangled with a scarf. Finally, she was burned.[1]

[1] Mrs. Christofi is the only murderer in this country [England] since Alfred Rouse in 1931 who has tried to dispose of the victim's body by burning it. Rouse burned the body of an unknown man in his car on a lonely Northamptonshire road to make it appear that he himself had died.—R.H. and P.B.

At about eleven-thirty that night, a neighbor took his dog into the garden and he noticed that the whole of the back of the house next door was aglow.

He called out, but received no reply, and his wife came and looked as well. Crossing the garden, he peered into the back-yard and saw what he thought must be a wax model lying on a bonfire. He could not see the head because it was surrounded by a circle of flames. The arms seemed to be raised and bent at the elbows. He could smell paraffin and wax, and looking through the French windows into the kitchen he saw a figure there come around the table and out into the yard, evidently about to stir the fire. It was the Matriarch.

An hour later a restaurant keeper was driving near Hampstead Heath station with his wife when he heard a woman shouting, "Taxi." The Matriarch was standing on the pavement, waving her arms. She ran towards the car and said breathlessly, "Please come. Fire burning, children sleeping."

The driver asked her to get into the car, but already she had run on. He turned and followed her.

"Where's the fire?" he asked, probably somewhat astonished when she replied, "Shush, babies sleeping."

She took them through the house and opened the door into the yard, and there they saw the body, its head covered with blood.

As they solemnly awaited the police on the doorstep of the house, Mrs. Christofi summed up the story of her crime, acting as her own Greek chorus.

"Me smell burning, me come down, me pour water, but she be died. My son married Germany girl he like, plenty clothes, plenty shoes, babies going to Germany."

That last sentence summed up all her feelings and motives.

Now, following the crime, must come retribution, not for herself alone, but for her son, her son's children.

Returning in the early hours of the morning, Stavros Christofis learned of his wife's death. But in Greek tragedy, no horror comes alone; it carries with it terrible implications, further and greater disaster. The murder of Agamemnon was a disaster, but the real tragedy was that the murderer was his wife.

Even as he listened, the son must have realized the full meaning of his wife's death—"a strange death, full of fear."

As the chorus chant to Clytemnestra says:

> "Woman, what evil tree,
> What poison grown of the ground
> Or draught of the drifting sea
> Way to thy lips hath found,
> Making thee clothe thy heart
> In rage, yea, in curses burning
> When thine own people pray?
> Thou hast hewn, thou hast cast away;
> And a thing cast away thou art,
> A thing of hate and a spurning!"

What terrible feelings of misery and anger and remorse must have torn him as he took the children from their beds in the early dawn to stay with friends, then acted as interpreter between his mother and the police, maintaining in the circumstances a more than heroic restraint. Like Orestes, he was the interpreter of his mother's fate; unlike Orestes, he did not take the vengeance which was so justly his. Revenge, once embarked upon, can be limitless.

Hella's wedding ring was found hidden in the Matriarch's bedroom, the final and symbolic act of a woman who believed she had finally and irrevocably separated her son from the woman he loved.

At her trial the Matriarch pleaded "not guilty." Every word had to be translated for her. She listened coldly to the evidence, and when in the witness box she told, through an interpreter, how she saw two men outside the house when she was awakened by the smell of burning at 1:00 A.M.

But at 11:30 she had been seen in the backyard, watching the fire. It was probably felt that she fetched help after the crime in order to establish her concern—and innocence. It is equally likely that she lost her head when she saw the flames rising and really did fear that the children might be burned.

The jury of ten men and two women were taken one night by motor coach to the house. They saw the kitchen and the gruesome backyard; they looked through the French windows to the room lit by a naked electric light bulb. Before they entered the house, police had carried into the now bare kitchen a table and chairs, scenery for the drama.

They decided that Mrs. Styllou Christofi was guilty. She asked if she could say something from the witness box, but she had already given evidence, and Mr. Justice Devlin, without comment, sentenced her to death in a language she could not understand.

Her son was not in court when sentence was passed.

Neither had he been in Cyprus in 1925 at another murder trial, when his mother had been acquitted of murdering *her* mother-in-law by ramming a burning torch down her throat.

Those were the rumors he had heard. That was the secret.

Mrs. Christofi was sentenced on October 28. On December 28 an interpreter told her that there would be no reprieve.

During the weeks set aside for repentance, which is presumably the reason for the delay in carrying out the death sentence, the Matriarch did not repent. Her letters written from prison are poetic in their passion and ferocity. Already retribution has turned upon her; love is turning to hate; her triumph of revenge will be canceled out by her punishment.

Again we imagine the chorus in the background:

> Oh, doom shall have yet her day,
> The last friend cast away,
> When lie doth answer lie
> And a stab for a stab returneth!

Her son Stavros visited her in prison, torn between despair at the fate of his wife and horror at the fate of his mother.

> How shall I weep, what words shall I say?
> Caught in the web of this spider thing.
> In foul death gasping thy life away!
> Woe's me, woe's me, for this slavish lying,
> The doom of craft and the lonely dying,
> The iron two-edged and the hands that slay!

In the old Greek tragedy Orestes is faced with the same problem: The murder of his father must be avenged; but if he takes revenge on the murderer, his own mother, he transgresses other, deep-rooted laws of nature.

The Matriarch, true to her nature, turned upon her son in prison, reviling him, hating him now that Hella was gone, blaming him for marrying her, accusing him of betraying his mother.

To him, the word *mother* had become a mockery. Her final letter is a pathetic mixture of hatred and affection; in her final hours she was torn with memories of that other life she had hoped to recreate.

I hope you are all right as well as your children. I hope that you will always be well with God's help.

It doesn't matter what is going to happen to me. You have tried too hard to hang me, in order to put around my neck the noose, so that you may rest.

I am not obliging you to come and see me, my son.

She wrote of the days when the whole family was together in Cyprus; when she made bread; and of how they worked together in the fields, the Matriarch, the father and their five children.

She said that she had come to England because she loved him; she could not bear to be apart from him.

It was undoubtedly true. Her jealousy must have become so strong, her fear of losing her son so overwhelming, that in the end it became stronger than herself, an evil fate of which she herself was also the victim.

The day before her execution, a medical report on Mrs. Christofi made by the principal medical officer of Holloway Prison found its way into the papers. He had had Mrs. Christofi under observation for months. In his opinion—and he had obviously had a better chance of forming one than anyone else —the Matriarch was insane.

Furthermore, even before the trial he had reported that she was suffering from a mental disease which prevented her from knowing that she was doing wrong when she murdered her daughter-in-law. It was not, therefore, a last-minute decision at which he arrived; it was dated October 5.

According to Dr. Christie, "The fear that her grandchildren would not be brought up properly induced a defect of reason . . . whereby however much she may have been capable of appreciating the nature and quality of the acts she was doing, at the time of the acts, the defect of reason was such that she was incapable of knowing that what she was doing was wrong."

One wonders immediately why, if she was insane, it was not pleaded at the trial. The answer is that the Matriarch furiously resisted the suggestion of an insanity plea.

"I am a poor woman, of no education, but I am not a madwoman. Never, never, never."

The home secretary had made his own inquiries and come to his own conclusions. He considered the report of an independent panel of doctors, set up after Mrs. Christofi was sentenced, and he found no reason, apparently, to doubt her sanity.

There were three Queen's Counsels amongst those who tried on the last day to save her life. They asked to see the home secretary; they tried for 48 hours to get an interview with him, without success. He had made his decision.

His action led to a Socialist motion in the House of Commons demanding a statement of government policy on the report of the Royal Commission on Capital Punishment.

Weeks later the statement came, but by then it was too late for Mrs. Christofi. In any case, she had known nothing of that final effort to save her life.

The prosecution had described it as "a stupid murder by a stupid woman of the illiterate peasant type," as though illiteracy were a disease to be despised. Even if she was responsible for her wickedness, one might feel she could hardly be blamed for being an "illiterate peasant woman."

Tragedy is not dismissed by abuse. Mrs. Christofi was as much encircled by tragedy as Hella, Stavros and the three children.

Her last letter almost ends the story. The chorus takes up the tragedy, proclaims that as one sin is avenged, another takes its place. The death of Hella leads to the death of the Matriarch.

For my fortunes, there are my family in the streets of Cyprus, crying for me.
If you saw their letters, you would be moved and cry as we do.
My brothers say that if the sea were earth, they would come on foot to see me.
Kiss the children for me.

To the end it is her family, her children and her children's children. And yet . . .

> . . . the wrongs she wrought,
> Wrought upon us, upon us, she and none other?

Oh, fawn and smile; but the wrongs shall soften not,
Wrongs with a wolfish heart, by a wolf begot:
They see no smile, they reck not the name of
    Mother!

Then, at dawn, the priest lit an altar candle in her cell. She had left her family behind.

For Stavros, his wife's death was expiated; only the horror remained.

Many years later, after Orestes had wandered the world with the burden of his mother's death on his mind, he was ordered by Apollo to submit himself to the court at Athens where he was acquitted, to return to Argos and ascend the throne.

The Matriarch's son had no such guilt. It was the state which demanded revenge. And it was taken.

IX

Willie's Legs

Edmund Pearson

One of the big problems of a love affair and a murder is that they do not necessarily equal the sum of their parts. This was especially true in Willie's case. But in the curious triangle between the barber, the midwife and the masseuse, a lucky duck simply waddled right into the solution.

THERE was a man who had a duck—a white duck. He lived in Woodside, that not over-fashionable suburb of New York, on Long Island. One summer evening—it was around the Fourth of July in 1897—the duck came tottering home in a condition which amazed her owner, and made him rub his eyes. Could this be the sunset glow, or had it something to do with the approach of Independence Day? For the ordinarily white and stainless breast of Julia, his well-behaved duck, was crimson, incarnadined, red, with blood.

The man examined her closely: there was no mistake. All through the summer night he pondered, until a thought came to him. In the morning, when he liberated Julia to her diversions, he followed her on tiptoe. In a few moments she was quacking merrily as she entered a small pool, and a mystery had been solved—a mystery which had been giving the great Mr. William Randolph Hearst chronic insomnia. For "The Murder House" had been discovered; Mr. Hearst's men and the New York police came piling over to Woodside, and everyone achieved fame—everyone except Julia and her owner.

For a week they had been assembling, at the Morgue in New York, the fragments of a man. On a Saturday, two boys in swimming at the foot of East 11th Street found a bundle which contained shoulders, arms and chest. There was no head, and the chest had been partly flayed. On Sunday, other boys, exploring Ogden's Woods near East 176th Street, found another bundle—wrapped like the first in red and gold oilcloth—containing the lower part of a torso.

And a few days later, sailors on the U.S.S. *Vermont,* at the

Brooklyn Navy Yard, recovered the legs that belonged with this body. But since the head remained elusive, the reporters of New York got no sleep. Who was this dismembered person? The people must know, and in the meantime the people's curiosity must continually be flogged.

Late one night a reporter was drinking a glass of beer in a Third Avenue saloon. He overheard a conversation between two men whom he recognized as "rubbers" in the Murray Hill Turkish Baths. Said one of them:

"Willie hasn't been to work today."

"No," said the other, "and not since Friday."

The astute reporter was soon at the Baths, inquiring for Willie.

"Oh," said the superintendent, "Willie Guldensuppe? Yes, he works here. I don't understand where he is."

The reporter mentioned the "headless mystery."

"It would be easy to identify Willie," remarked one of the *masseurs,* "he had the head of a woman tattooed on his chest."

"And a scar on one of his forefingers," said another.

"Where does he live?" pursued the reporter.

The boss consulted his address book.

"At 439 Ninth Avenue."

"With a lady named Nack," added the helpful one.

In the morning the *masseurs* were at the Morgue, engaged in the mournful business of identifying Willie. And in a day or two more Mrs. Augusta Nack was undergoing a long questioning at police headquarters. A shopkeeper from Astoria had recognized her as the purchaser of six yards of red and gold oilcloth.

Mrs. Nack was calm and dignified. At the end of the interview, the police captain tried an old gag of the kind which used to be thought infallible. He led her out the back door of his office, and let her almost stumble over the severed legs which had been fished out of the East River.

"Are those Willie's legs?" he yelled.

But he didn't know Mrs. Nack. She had no lorgnette with her, but there were lorgnettes in her manner and in her voice, as she surveyed the fragments and then turned to the captain. She would show him she was both lady and logician. First, the lady:

"How should I know? I have never seen Willie's bare legs."

Next the logician:

"And moreover, since he is alive, they can't be his legs."

Unluckily, she had taken a partner in crime, whose heroism was not of this cast. He was a barber and he couldn't keep his silly mouth shut. Born in Posen, and called Martin Torzewski, he had shortened this to Martin Thorn. To his fellow barbers at Conrad Vogel's place, on Sixth Avenue, he had loudly announced that he intended to kill Guldensuppe—with a revolver, with a poison dagger, and by six or seven other methods. After he *had* killed Guldensuppe, like the thirsty woman in the sleeping car, he still must dwell on the subject. So he talked to a barber named Gotha—invited him to tea, to discuss the assassination in minutest detail—and Gotha told the police.

All of this butchery was for the love of a lady—for big, beefy, forty-year-old Augusta Nack, a German midwife. She practiced, without a license, the profession of helping people into this world. And at least once, and equally without license, she practiced the profession of helping them out of it. For years, she had beamed upon the gentlemen and they found her not to be resisted.

Herman Nack she had married in their native Germany. They came to New York, where he set up on Tenth Avenue as a dealer in Bologna sausages. Business interfered with his pleasure, which was drinking beer, and one day he readily sold out his shop, for the price of several kegs, and applied himself to his heart's desire.

By the summer of 1897, Mr. Nack had faded into the background, and was driving a wagon somewhere. His regret at the death of his rival, Guldensuppe, was so sincere that the police could not suspect him of any part in the slaughter. His only wish had been that Guldensuppe should go on living with 'Gusta. It served him right.

But Willie Guldensuppe, the triumphant adulterer, was in turn supplanted by Martin Thorn. To the end, Mrs. Nack persisted that she had not really cared for Thorn—at any rate, not greatly.

"I never loved him," said she, "only since the time when he choked me."

This display of tenderness softened her heart. Besides, Thorn had money, while Willie the rubber got only $10 a week, and commenced to borrow from Mrs. Nack. There was trouble in the *ménage à trois* on Ninth Avenue.

Martin threatened Willie with a revolver. Willie uttered a loud "Ho, ho!" of Teutonic merriment; took the gun away from the barber, and proceeded to beat him up. He knocked him down—right in Mrs. Nack's parlor—picked him up again, gave him two black eyes, a bloody nose and a lame jaw. Then he knocked him down twice more, kicked him in the ribs, and finally—his imagination failing—threw him downstairs.

It was a mistake. Thorn was offended. He began to assemble his weapons, and talk of revenge. There must have been in Thorn a strain of the Dyaks of North Borneo, for he announced again and again, that he would have Willie's head.

The horrified judge, who listened to this recital in court, when Augusta turned State's evidence, interrupted hastily.

"Said he would have *what?*" he asked.

"His head," repeated the placid lady, with a respectful bow.

The last straw for Mrs. Nack was that she caught Willie philandering. So she joined forces with Thorn, and they took a little villa at Woodside. Willie was persuaded to go out there to inspect the property, where, so said Augusta, she was going to start a baby farm. Augusta waited in the side yard, while Willie went puffing through the house.

In a closet, upstairs, waited Martin Thorn, with a gun and a dagger and a bottle of poison—and maybe a noose and a blackjack and a Malayan creese.

He shot Willie and he stabbed him and he cut off his head with a razor. Mrs. Nack went over to Astoria to buy red oilcloth. Thorn put in a long, hard day, wrapping up bits of Willie in bundles, and the two of them made several trips to distribute these bundles. The head—the only part of Willie that Thorn really wanted—he encased in plaster of Paris and sank in the river. The other parts all returned to plague him.

Thorn was defended by Big Bill Howe, who used to wear a yachting cap and diamonds. Mr. Howe blustered and said that his client would be acquitted. Instead, Thorn was executed.

Mrs. Nack was defended by Emanuel ("Manny") Friend, who was quieter about it and more successful. He said his client should not be electrocuted. And she was not. She got nine years for manslaughter.

I must not forget Julia, the duck. You see Thorn had done most of his dissection in the bathtub. Then he left the tap running for a day or two. Something like 40,000 gallons of water flowed down the pipes. And the blood of Willie Guldensuppe. Thorn believed this was all going into the sewers. But there were no sewers in that region, and a pool was formed near the cottage. And to this pool came Julia.

But, as usual, Mr. William Randolph Hearst got all the glory.

X

First Night Murder

Bruce Sanders

Evelyn Nesbit was called "the most beautiful woman in the world." Born in poverty, she celebrated her teen-age years in a sybarite's playground of sensuality—the pampered mistress of the infamous millionaire architect Stanford White. But, when she met the equally infamous and incalculably wealthier Harry K. Thaw, she forsook White's red-velvet swing for a trip to the altar. It was a mistake for Evelyn, a disaster for Thaw—and the beginning of a tragic end for all the luminaries in America's most notorious *affaire cèlèbre.*

Like so many lovely women whose names become inseparably associated with violence and tragedy, Evelyn Nesbit was not born to riches. At 15 she almost starved to death in a tenement area of New York.

She had come, with her brother and mother, from Pennsylvania. New York was to be the golden city that brought fame and fortune. In those grim months when the Nesbits went without comfort and food and worried about where the next week's rent was to come from, the city seemed more of a prison camp. There were times when the family considered a retreat tactical and strategic. But to move out of New York would have cost more than to continue living on their debts and some scraps of extended credit.

So the Nesbits stayed. And Dame Fortune learned to smile for them.

Evelyn's mother believed her daughter to be beautiful. "You're just like a picture, Evelyn," she would say, and the girl studied her face in a shabby mirror and believed her mother's assertion.

"Perhaps I can become a model," she said. "For artists and photographers."

Mrs. Nesbit was very dubious. New York was full of pretty young women. But Evelyn was young enough not to perceive difficulties or to spend too long considering objections. She began haunting agents' offices. The dollars were slow in coming, but she did some work and even procured an offer to join the chorus of the successful musical *Floradora,* the New York smash hit. In the chorus she showed her legs, tossed her head and bustle, and became friendly with a girl named Edna Goodrich.

Edna was one of those young women who knew her way around town. Especially after dark. One day she introduced Evelyn to a big-framed, red-haired man in evening dress, with a very bright eye and the smile of a professional voluptuary. Stanford White was a connoisseur of the fashionable standards of feminine pulchritude pertaining at the beginning of the 20th Century. He was an artist, a dreamer, a creator of good architecture, a man of vision, and a fool and a villain where women were concerned.

Although he was rich and famous and a lion in his own set, he had an unenviable reputation throughout New York. He had one major hobby—indulging his senses. It was to this assured and practiced sensualist that a dimple-faced Evelyn Nesbit gave her hand one evening after the show.

The dove was shaking hands with the jackal. But at least this dove was willing, as she showed when Stanford White paid her attention, took her to swank restaurants and invited her to his rather exotic bachelor apartment; she was to have her photograph taken. Mother was told and was smilingly acquiescent. Evelyn had justified the mother's belief in her daughter's good looks. Now she had an admirer who was a man of the world.

What neither mother nor daughter realized was that Stanford White's world was rather restrictive at times. Evelyn went to the lush apartment to have her face captured on a camera's plate; she stayed to become Stanford White's mistress. The sensualist had suddenly found someone young and enchanting who could recapture for him a lost wonder. He was enslaved by his own conception of this girl from the *Floradora* chorus. He could be the Prince Charming who made dreams come true for both of them.

It was the kind of delightful fancy with which middle-aged artists are occasionally prone to indulge themselves. With one major difference—Evelyn Nesbit was far from being a figure of fancy. She was young and near-perfect in Stanford White's jaded eyes. In the not too distant future a newspaper reporter was to provide a pen portrait of her:

She is petite. Her figure is well formed and its natural curves need no artifice to accentuate them. Her hair is indeed her crowning glory—black, thick, long, and heavy. She is of the distinctly brunette type, though her eyes are deep blue, unusually large, with heavy brows arching over them. Her chin is small and, she has been told, might be a copy of the Venus de Milo's.

This was the young woman for whom Stanford White, America's foremost architect in his day, prepared a sybarite's love nest. He took her to it, installed her with kisses and champagne and gave her the key.

It had one special room, with soft lights and many mirrors round the walls and another in the ceiling. In the center hung a red-velvet swing, and the atmosphere of that room was made languorous with a subtle perfume.

The starry-eyed girl, about to become the toast of New York and a byword among its sophisticates and habitués of the brightly lit flesh-pots, entered her adolescent's dream of a woman's seventh heaven through her own private door, her feet muffled in a carpet with a pile deep enough to brush her ankles. Stanford White had awakened her to a terrible truth: She had a face and figure to make men dream, and through her eyes shone a spirit to make those dreams restive. Perhaps Stanford White had been self-indulgent too long, and habit had weakened his mature will. Perhaps the man of many parts, with a mind to conceive and fashion creations in brick and stone and cement, had been tricked by his own senses into becoming a slave to the witchery of youth. But it is very certain he enjoyed his silken bonds and indulged to excess those whims of his young mistress which he artfully and assiduously encouraged.

"Stanford White," said a prominent American art critic, "is changing the face of the country's great cities."

His work in stone was described as exquisite and daring, and his talent and capabilities had made for him a host of influential friends and a wife who worshiped him almost to idolatry.

The girl who moved into the love nest he had created for her had no talent, only beauty. Her intelligence was limited, though she was to develop a natural shrewdness, as she revealed when she stood in a New York courtroom with a world spotlight glaring over her day after day. She had an older woman's passion for the soft things of life and she wanted her share of the glittering prizes.

Stanford White, the middle-aged architect with a large bank balance, made a fairy tale come true for the girl who had her personal reasons for hating poverty. She had seen her mother change after her father's death. She had seen a sheriff's officer in Philadelphia nail a foreclosure notice on the door of their home. She had heard her mother, without any real hope of obtaining employment, crying herself to sleep at night. Mrs. Nesbit had been a dress designer. This fact had encouraged the move to New York. But the sweatshops of the East Side didn't want her skill. She tried elsewhere and found that lack of experience in Paris was a crippling handicap. Seemingly there were rules to becoming stylish. Flair and hard work were not enough.

These were the daily conditions that shaped Evelyn Nesbit's girlish mind. Seventeen dollars a week from her modeling had to support the family. When she joined the chorus of *Floradora* she was given $15 a week for kicking up her heels and wiggling her bustle—a total of a little over $30 a week.

Her face and figure, at 16, had helped her to emerge above the poverty line, so they obviously had a price. It was not a matter of morals, but of economics.

Stanford White was crazy about her. Those were the days when crazes of any kind were fashionable, and crazes paid off in cash for those who fostered them. She fostered the architect's craze for her. She took gifts and an allowance, a home and parties. She even took Stanford White himself into her heart when she forgave him for teaching her how she was expected to repay his lavishing of money and dresses and jewels and rich goods and wines on her.

The bewitched sensualist put a substantial sum to her credit in a New York bank. It was drawn on freely by Evelyn and her mother. Mrs. Nesbit remained a shadowy figure thereafter in the darker background of the fairy-tale years. There is no record of what she thought of the red-velvet swing or the mirrors.

Stanford White, in these same years, was a man living in two different worlds. In one he was a family man with family problems and a son at Harvard. In the other he was a libertine refusing to believe that years could take their toll on flesh and spirit. He gave Evelyn Nesbit everything she wanted except the one thing she grew passionately to desire above all else— marriage.

But then fairy tales usually end short of marriage.

She was drifting through a state of enchantment that was becoming a gilded boredom when she met America's most notorious playboy, Harry K. Thaw, moody, demanding, extravagant and in his way every whit as self-indulgent as Stanford White. No woman had succeeded in leading Thaw and his fortune of $40 million to the altar; for Harry Thaw there was always a fairer bloom to be plucked from another bush. He paraded down a path strewn with the blooms he had discarded. Not unnaturally Harry Thaw was a cynic. He was $40 million worth of cynic.

Until he met Evelyn Nesbit.

Then, like Stanford White, he found himself gazing on a beauty that held something special for him. Here, he knew, was a bloom that he would not discard. The problem was how to pluck it.

Stanford White owned the bush, and not even Harry Thaw would get close enough to touch it with his fingers unless he changed his erstwhile tactics.

But he decided he wanted her, and $40 million reminded him there was a good reason for supposing he could get her. He told himself he would even be prepared to marry her if he couldn't get her any other way. He couldn't believe that any woman could resist $40 million even if she had to take Harry Thaw with them.

There was more than a little irony in the situation developing in New York after Harry Thaw had convinced himself he was in love. Both Evelyn Nesbit and he came from the same state, the girl from a Philadelphia slum and the man from a Pittsburgh mansion crawling with flunkies. Evelyn Nesbit, in the realistic phrase of the day, came from nothing. The Thaws were New World aristos. What this really meant can be judged when it is recalled that one of Harry Thaw's sisters had married an English earl, and another had shared her wedding day with a Carnegie. Not without some reason, they considered themselves a family of American bluebloods. True, the blue was patchy in places, and at most times of stress was inclined to become quickly overheated, most unbecomingly so. But the fact remains that at the time Harry K. Thaw met Evelyn Nesbit and assured himself he had fallen in love with Stanford White's mistress the scion of the Thaws was one of the biggest social catches in America.

Evelyn did nothing to avoid catching him. But she did play hard to get. And she had to gamble to win after she had made up her calculating little mind that a Thaw weighed more heavily in a bank's balance than a Stanford White.

Harry Thaw quickly tired of getting nowhere with Evelyn in Manhattan. He put everything into a capsule proposition and made it sound like a romantic plighting of a troth.

"Come with me to Europe, honey, and I'll marry you when we get back."

Evelyn considered the proposition with clear, hard, young eyes and decided that although she saw strings attached, the marriage would have to wait until she had been to Europe.

Well, Europe sounded romantic and remote and well-nigh irresistible when it led toward $40 million. Besides, although her mother might not have reached Paris to get some top-grade training as a dress designer, there seemed no valid reason why her daughter shouldn't arrive and allow the haute couturiers to show what they could do for her.

So Evelyn gambled for the second time. She stepped out of the velvet swing and left it dangling amid the mirrors. Stanford White had been the finicky kind of middle-aged lover who sends his mistress to school. The last of the Pennsylvania slum grime had been polished off Evelyn in an expensive private school. That suited Harry Thaw. Evelyn, after a couple of years' grooming, had a workaday veneer of culture that wouldn't crack in Paris.

Evelyn decided her mother should come along as chaperon. Bags were packed, and she walked out the door of her plush love nest without a backward glance. She was driven to the gangplank of an Atlantic liner and entered the finest stateroom in the vessel. Inside were flowers from Harry Thaw.

Most circumspectly, he was following a week later. Evelyn had clipped through a few of the strings attached to the wedding offer.

The trip to the Old World broadened her outlook and extended her youthful horizon. She saw what her beauty could do to men of other nationalities and allowed a delighted Harry Thaw to dazzle her with new concepts of luxury and ease. She matured rapidly, like a rosebud in midsummer heat.

In Paris the overall plan seems to have come apart at the seams, so far as Harry Thaw was concerned. Mrs. Nesbit left with her daughter and returned to New York after staying for some time in London. Harry Thaw gave Evelyn a letter to his lawyers. On the sealed envelope he scrawled: "Secret."

The letter in the envelope read as though penned by a lunatic. It was incoherent, instructed his lawyers to phone Mrs. Nesbit and put down the phone when she replied.

When Harry Thaw arrived back in New York the lovely Evelyn was enthroned in a suite at the Hotel Navarre. She decided not to keep herself out of the public eye and had no difficulty in obtaining a part in a play called *The Girl from Dixie*. She had been hearing stories about Harry Thaw's treatment of women who had been indulged by him. There was a sadistic note to most of the stories. One girl had been tied to the posts of a bed and beaten with a horsewhip. Another had had scalding water poured over her when naked in a bath.

Evelyn had plenty to think about. Maybe her second gamble had been a mistake.

Harry Thaw pursued her. He took to sitting beside her when she ate in the Café des Beaux Arts on Sixth Avenue. He asked what she had heard about him and told her not to believe the stories; they were malicious gossip.

On Christmas Eve, 1903, Harry Thaw stepped into Evelyn's dressing room at the Madison Square Garden Theater. It was a triumphant Christmas for the girl from Pennsylvania's hinterland. She had returned from Europe to find New York quite ready to be stampeded by her newfound charm and heightened beauty. Society columnists raved about her. They even agreed on a caption they could tie to her photo: *The Most Beautiful Woman in the World*. John Barrymore, heading toward fame, was supposed to have fallen in love with her.

Harry Thaw clinked his millions. Stanford White looked

over his shoulder, pained but full of memories. All New York stared and speculated.

Evelyn let Harry Thaw lead her to the altar as though she were a queen. Hers was the most lavish wedding New York had gaped at in a decade. When the last champagne toast to the bride had been drunk, the fairy tale was over.

But that was a well-kept secret for 14 months.

Almost from the moment they had accepted each other as husband and wife and swore to honor and obey before the straining eyes and ears of New York's awestruck café society, Harry Thaw's attitude toward the prize he had captured from Stanford White underwent a grim change. At first subtly, then more noticeably.

By some strange mental quirk he sought compensation for having chased his bride in now misusing her. He chose to believe that he had been cheated and had received damaged goods. He was not shy of mentioning the price he had been forced to pay.

He took his bride to the Thaw family's palatial home in Pittsburgh, and Evelyn was back in her home state, where the Thaws of several generations had created and amassed great wealth from sales of coal and coke. Some of the black dust seemed to settle almost at once on Evelyn's life and darken it. After days of futile pleading with a man growing estranged from her, it was not hard to believe she was living in her own private hell.

The most beautiful woman in the world was barely out of her teens. And she was suddenly very lonely. She had climbed well-nigh unaided to the topmost rung of the social ladder. There was no longer any way up. Only down. When she contemplated it she grew sick with fear, and that secret numbing fear grew as her husband's manner became week by week more strange and even terrifying to his young wife.

Moreover, she found no favor in the hard stares of her husband's family. She felt they barely tolerated her for his sake. Her mother-in-law, a rich widow with a passion for travel, afforded her only arch smiles and stony glances tinged with unmasked contempt.

Harry Thaw took to talking at length and frequently on the unrewarding subject of the man who had preceded him in his wife's love and life. There were times when the subject of Stanford White made him physically ill. Hatred of the other became a passion and an obsession. The well-trained servants in the Thaw mansion went their soft-footed ways with eyes averted and ears stopped.

Life on the top rung became very bleak and scary.

Then one day Harry Thaw bought a pistol and stood in front of a mirror in his dressing room, watching his reflection point the weapon at arm's length.

He had been married a little more than a year.

It was about this time that his widowed mother decided to embark once more on her travels. Her son and daughter-in-law accompanied her to New York, ostensibly to see her off once more to Europe. It was mid-June, and summer heat shimmered in the New York streets and baked the sidewalks as though they were cement pancakes on a griddle.

The 25th was a scorching day. Harry Thaw spent the afternoon in the cool lounge of the New York Whist Club. It was one of the few comfortable oases in the city in those days before air conditioning. He played cards with some friends and cronies of his wilder bachelor days and made arrangements to dine with his wife and two friends at the fashionable Café Martin. One of these friends was Truxton Beale, formerly United States ambassador to Persia; the other was a California author, Thomas McCaleb.

Just before the Thaw party arrived for dinner at the Café Martin, three earlier diners left. They were Stanford White, his son Lawrence and Leroy King, Lawrence White's classmate at Harvard.

Destiny was weaving a close pattern that June night.

A new and sparkling musical comedy with the promising title of *Mam'zelle Champagne* was opening that evening in the roof-garden theater of Madison Square Garden. Harry Thaw had booked seats. However, when he and his party arrived he found a friend seated in one of the seats he had reserved. When the mistake was explained the friend quickly jumped to his feet with an apology and a warm smile towards the dazzling Mrs. Harry Thaw. But her husband was feeling most unusually magnanimous. He tapped the pocket of his well-fitting evening coat.

"I insist you remain," he told his friend. "I shouldn't think of disturbing you."

He gave a brief nod, waved a hand and walked towards the rear of the roof-garden auditorium. There he ran into James Clinch Smith, Stanford White's brother-in-law, and remained chatting with him most amicably. He laughed at a joke, talked about the heat and the play they were to see. He behaved like a normal man with nothing special on his mind.

He was still making easy conversation with Smith when Stanford White arrived. The architect began making his way through the assembly. He was alone; his son and Leroy King had gone to another theater, possibly feeling that the parent of one cramped the style of both. Anyway, they had professed to prefer entertainment that wasn't a "leg show."

The show was late starting, and it was ten minutes to eleven when the chorus danced on stage in fancy costumes and waving foils for a special fencing ensemble. They went through a number entitled "I Challenge You to a Duel."

The cue was perfect; no murder story in real life ever had a better one, or one more neatly contrived—except that the duel was to be very one-sided.

As the chorus danced back, heels flashing, the male lead came forward, showing his teeth to the audience. He went right into a new number, "There Was a Maid."

Cue number two.

He hadn't gotten far into the song when from the shadows at the back of the roof garden moved a lone figure, weaving between the tables at which the audience sat, until he came to one at which a man sat alone.

The man who had moved from the back lifted his right hand, which gripped a revolver. Above the sound of the orchestra's strings and the singer's voice crashed a pistol shot—a second —a third.

The conductor's baton remained in midair, in a frozen posture. The orchestra's strings cascaded down the scale in a tuneless cadence, and the singer stood in a rain of white light with his mouth open and no sound coming from it.

For terrifying seconds there was an eerie, dreadful silence. Then the solitary figure seated at the table started to slide towards the floor, and the nearer members of the audience saw blood on the snowy tablecloth and made out the glittering shape of the pistol in the hand of the man standing posed like a statue.

A woman screamed. The sound trailed around the auditorium like a trapped echo.

Someone thought to switch on the lights, and gasps came from scores of throats. A millionaire, the audience saw, had just been slain by another millionaire. The first-night audience that had come to see a light-hearted musical comedy had been unknowingly present for a stark tragedy in one brief act.

Attendants ran up, seized the man holding the smoking pistol, and Harry Thaw unfroze to smile. He offered no resistance. His face grew animated. He was like a man forcibly shrugging off the effects of a powerful drug and not wholly succeeding. He stared down at the man he had slain.

"I'm glad I killed him," he said in a voice that carried across the tables. "He ruined my wife."

It was the voice of a man whose mind had become twisted by its own obsession. Harry Thaw, however, looked sane enough, which did not do him justice; for years he had been teetering on a mental seesaw.

Now he had fallen, with a resounding thud. His $40 million would be considerably dented to save his life.

The police arrived, and he was taken into custody. A few hours later New York newspapers carried banner headlines announcing the first-night murder. "Pittsburgh Idler Kills Architect," read one. The killer of Stanford White was in for a bad press.

His first meeting with New York's district attorney did not help him. He described the scene when he recognized Stanford White seated alone at a table.

"I saw him sitting there," he said, "big, fat and healthy, and I thought of Evelyn, poor delicate little thing, all trembling and nervous."

His notorious hypocrisy had reached a new low. Expensive lawyers hurriedly proclaimed their client insane. This enraged him so much that he almost justified the claim in his cell. He was only pacified by the arrival of his English butler, as imperturbable as his stage counterpart, carrying a suitcase containing a shirt and clean undergarments, socks and a freshly pressed gray suit.

A turbulent and booing crowd waited outside police headquarters on Center Street when the handcuffed millionaire arrived to be photographed and fingerprinted before being officially arraigned in the magistrate's court. He was held on a charge of first-degree murder, and was taken to a cell in the notorious "Tombs."

He couldn't have much done about the cold walls of the prison cell, but he could about the prison diet; his meals were sent in daily from Delmonico's, New York's most fashionable and expensive restaurant of the period. He summoned the prison doctor and so bemused him that the man of medicine prescribed a pint of champagne daily for the State of New York's prisoner.

In the first hectic days following the killing, Harry Thaw could make a headline by just holding his breath. His case became internationally famous when the ship on which his mother had sailed to Europe docked in England. Reporters were waiting for her, and she gave a hurried press conference as soon as her Parisian shoes stepped on British soil. She told the pressmen, "My son is innocent," which might explain the feelings of a mother's heart but was scarcely in accord with the facts. She added a more newsy item: "If it takes the fortune of my entire family to clear him, every dollar we possess will be used to help Harry regain his freedom."

The Thaw family, as of habit, was closing its ranks.

The vast majority of Americans remained unimpressed by the reminder of the dollars reposing in the Thaw coffers. Back in the citadel of Thaw wealth, Pittsburgh, cynical bookies offered four to one that Harry Thaw would end up in Sing Sing's electric chair.

When the trial opened eventually, on a biting January day in 1907, the dominant personality behind the scenes was the prisoner's mother. Upheld by her stern Presbyterian convictions, she was convinced the Almighty would see that justice triumphed—her way. She drove lawyers as though they were beasts of burden, and she did have her measure of triumph. When all the arguments had been made for and against, when every stitch of Evelyn's dirty linen had been soaked and washed and rinsed and then muddied again before the public gaze, the dog-tired jury finally retired.

They took three days of bickering to come to a decision, and then they agreed to disagree. Seven stubbornly voted for first-degree murder, and five just as stubbornly maintained Thaw was innocent because he was insane.

That jury was dismissed. It had produced an anticlimax at a cost to the taxpayers of the State of New York of $100,000. The Thaw family coffers were lighter by some $500,000.

The second trial began almost a year later. It lasted a month, and this time the jury was out for 27 hours. The unanimous verdict was "Not guilty because of insanity at the time of the act."

The big drama seemed over, and so it was—for a time.

Harry Thaw disappeared inside the somber walls of the New York State Asylum for the Criminally Insane. His loyal family had won a Pyrrhic victory on his behalf.

Nearly seven years later he escaped and reached Canada. After heated legal exchanges at the international level, he made a dash for New Hampshire, where he was arrested and declared sane. He was a free man and very bitter. One of his first acts was to divorce his wife, who had been left nearly penniless by his family.

A brief year of freedom brought more trouble. He horse-whipped a teen-ager to whom he took an intense dislike, and as a result he was forced to become an inmate in another asylum. He left it, again judged sane, in 1924.

Evelyn Nesbit was then appearing in an Atlantic City night club. He went and stared at the show, but left before it was finished. He hadn't been able to recognize the woman who had been his wife. Twenty-three years later, in 1947, he died in Miami of coronary thrombosis. He was 76 and forgotten, a man who had never been able to come to terms with his own past.

XI

The Picnic

Stuart Palmer

Harold Wesson's mother had ordered him to stay away from girls. When he joined the staff of a private girls' school, that wasn't easy. His problems compounded as he grew attracted to a lovely young teacher, who unfortunately was also the object of the assistant headmistress's affections. Harold didn't understand these things. His courtship wasn't the usual kind—no words of love were spoken, no overtures of passion were made, and he remained, always, controlled and constrained, the model gentleman. Then one day he planned a picnic. It was to be an innocent and fun affair, replete with party games. One little trick incorporated a small wad of cotton. That was unfortunate, because when it came into play, poor Harold came all unstuck.

HAROLD WESSON was brought up on a farm in Maine. The farm was a poor one, and to make ends meet, Harold's father operated a small grocery store in the nearby town. The father spent long hours at the store, and Harold saw little of him. What he remembers of his father is that he was a quiet man who never seemed to get upset about anything. It was Harold's mother who ruled the household, and in a quiet forceful way she dominated everyone around her.

Harold was the baby of the family; there were two older sisters. His earliest memories, at age four, are of his mother telling him not to do this or that because he would get hurt. She would not let him play with other children and kept him close to her. She had been a schoolteacher, and when he was four she began teaching him to read and write, add and subtract. By the time he was seven he could do these things quite well. She had kept him out of school the first year, saying that there was no need for him to go—he knew everything they would teach him in the first grade. So, at seven, he started school in the second grade.

Now, in his seventies, Harold Wesson vividly recalls that first day. As he sat through the morning's classes he began to sense that the other students, and the teacher as well, resented his starting in the second grade. At eleven-thirty the bell rang. Harold picked up his lunchbox and started out of the classroom, heading for home. He thought school was over for the day; his mother had not explained to him that he was to eat the contents of the lunchbox at school.

The other children began to laugh. He heard one say, "He's not smart enough to start in the second grade."

Harold was thoroughly humiliated. Looking back on the incident, after more than 60 years, he says, "I felt as small as an ant. I could have crawled into the floor. It took me several years to get over it."

As he went through the early grammar-school grades, Harold's mother made him come home directly after school every day. She seldom set him to doing any chores; she just wanted him with her. She was an intensely moral woman and she spent long periods telling him what were the right and wrong ways to act in life.

There in the prison, when I was interviewing Harold Wesson, I asked him, "How did your mother act when you didn't do what she wanted you to do? Did she punish you?"

An old man wearing a hearing aid, fat, but with quick piercing eyes, he looked up abruptly. "That was the trouble," he said. "She never punished me. No reason to. I always did what she said. I wouldn't have dared to do anything else."

He sat in thought for a moment, breathing slowly, heavily. Then he said, "I never did anything wrong in my whole life. Never. Except that one time when I—when I did what got me in here."

When Harold was nine his mother developed cancer. She was in bed continuously for the next eight years and underwent nine operations. During those years she insisted that Harold be with her almost constantly except for the hours when he was in school or sleeping. She never asked him to do very much; she just wanted him near her. She was always afraid he'd get hurt if he were out somewhere. When he was in high school she wouldn't let him play on any of the athletic teams. He never had a date; his mother told him young men did not go out with girls until they were engaged. He never thought to do other than what she told him. His main interest during those years was reading. He read widely, most of Shakespeare, Dickens, Tolstoy, Poe.

And then, in June of 1904, in the same month that he graduated from high school, Harold's mother died. He felt very bad, but, also, free for the first time in his life. He had done well in school and although he had little money he decided to attend a nearby state university. That summer his father died.

Harold entered the university in the fall. He found a job stoking a furnace nightly in one of the large buildings on the campus, and since he slept in the building, he had enough money to get by. During his first two years of college he studied very little; he felt emancipated and he spent most of his days simply idling. He read what appealed to him; he went for long walks; he joined a fraternity, took an interest in athletics and began to play on the fraternity tennis and basketball teams.

His grades during his freshman year were adequate, but in his sophomore year his lack of study took effect and they slipped badly. He began to apply himself, and from that point on his grades were extraordinarily high. Harold Wesson was, and is, an extremely intelligent man. His overall I.Q., as measured by the prison psychologists, is 142, higher than more than 99 percent of the United States population.

"Did you make any friendships with female students when you were in college?" I asked him.

"No. No. There weren't many of them there. Ten or fifteen, that's all. It wasn't like it is now. But then, too, it was my mother's influence, I suppose, even though she had died. As I said, she'd always told me never to go out with girls until I was engaged to one. And I always tried to do just what she told me. Except that one time. When I lost control of myself."

After graduating from college, Harold had no clear idea of what profession he wanted to follow. He took a job in a brokerage house. He did not particularly like the work, but nothing else appealed to him more. He read plays, studied them and occasionally on weekends went to New York to the theater.

After he had been in the brokerage house nearly three years it occurred to Harold that teaching might interest him. He applied to a teacher's agency and soon found a position as an English teacher at the Greymount School for Girls.

At that time Harold Wesson was an exceedingly handsome young man. He was small, about five foot six, and weighed only 120 pounds, but he had deep brown eyes, regular features and a most ingratiating smile. He was the type of young man who appears to be a highly sensitive person, yet not effeminate. Dr. James Taggart, headmaster at Greymount, was pleased to have him on the staff.

Practically all of the teaching staff were women, and Harold soon made good friends among them. One was a Miss Ruth Johnson, about 40, the assistant headmistress of Greymount. A second was Miss Francis, a history teacher in her late twenties. A third was Miss Sheehan. Patricia Sheehan, like Harold, was new at Greymount. This gave them a common bond, and they became particularly good friends.

This little group of four—Ruth Johnson, Miss Francis, Patricia Sheehan and Harold—were often together. They went to meals, to dances and to various community activities together. And usually, within the four, Patricia Sheehan and Harold were more or less paired off.

Twenty-eight years later, in prison, Harold Wesson wrote a brief autobiography. In it he explained his relationship to Patricia Sheehan. The following is a paraphrase of what he wrote:

Miss Sheehan and I were good friends from the beginning. There was never any sort of romantic attachment between us at all. I never even put my arm around her. And I never once called her Patricia. Always Miss Sheehan. I thought she might have had some romantic inclination toward me although I could never be sure. Sometimes she used to suggest things that made me wonder a little but I acted as if I didn't notice. For example, one evening we had been to a church supper and I think she said as we started home something such as: Why don't we walk back through the woods, it's so nice there now, and the others will never miss us? I said immediately: No, I think we'd better not. People might begin to talk, Miss Sheehan.

During the spring of his second year at Greymount, Harold received a letter from Patricia Sheehan that surprised him greatly. In it she said: "Please stop forcing yourself on me. I want to feel free to go with whomever I like. So please leave me alone."

Harold was extremely hurt that Patricia Sheehan should feel he had been forcing himself on her. The next day he caught up with her as she was returning to her room from breakfast.

"Miss Sheehan, that was an awfully mean thing to do, to write me that letter."

Patricia Sheehan looked around to be sure no one was in sight, and then she put the tips of her fingers on his left forearm and said, "I'm sorry, Harold. I couldn't help it. Miss Johnson made me write that letter. She said there had to be a stop put to our seeing each other so much."

"Then we're still good friends? You're not angry at me?"

"No, of course not. Only we mustn't see so much of each other for a while."

Harold felt much better. That afternoon he went to the office of Miss Johnson, the assistant headmistress. He said, "Miss Johnson, I think that was a terrible thing to do, make Miss Sheehan write that letter."

"What letter?"

"Saying that I should stop forcing myself on her."

"I did no such thing!" Miss Johnson stood up, her face red. "Though you *have* been seeing entirely too much of her. And if you ask me, I think you *have* been forcing yourself on her. In fact, you've been forcing yourself on all of us."

"I'm sorry. I didn't realize I had been," Harold said, shocked. Miss Johnson did not answer. "But you didn't make Miss Sheehan write that letter to me?" Harold asked.

"Of course not. I knew nothing about it."

Harold left Miss Johnson's office not knowing what to think. And very upset. He remembers that he felt strongly like committing suicide. But he did nothing except to avoid Patricia Sheehan and Miss Johnson for several weeks.

About a month later there was a community dance. Harold went by himself. Patricia Sheehan and Miss Johnson were there. He looked over at them, and they smiled at him. He asked Patricia Sheehan if he might dance with her, and she said yes. It was the first time they had talked together since that morning when he had asked her about the letter. Now she seemed quite friendly. At the end of the dance there was an intermission. Harold remembers that he asked Patricia if he might have the next dance, and she said she would like that. He then returned her to where she had been sitting with Ruth Johnson.

When the next dance began, Harold looked for Patricia, but could not find her. Finally he saw her. She and Ruth Johnson were dancing together. Harold could not understand it. When the dance ended he went up to them and said to Patricia, "Miss Sheehan, you agreed that this dance was to be with me."

Patricia Sheehan glanced quickly at Ruth Johnson and answered, "I did not say that!"

"But—"

"I thought we made it clear to you once before," Ruth Johnson interrupted, "that we do not like you forcing yourself on us."

Harold turned, walked away and left the dance. He later wrote much as follows in his autobiography:

I didn't know what to believe and I was extremely upset. That night I decided that the only thing for me to do was to go and see Miss Sheehan's mother, who lived in New York. I thought that I would leave a note for Miss Sheehan explaining about my visit. I wanted to give her a present with the note so I bought her a kind of thermos jug in a leather case which I was able to get her initials stamped on in gold.

I left the thermos jug and the note in her room and took the train to New York and when I arrived I telephoned Mrs. Sheehan and she agreed to see me.

We had a most pleasant conversation (we had tea), and I explained to her that my intentions toward her daughter were entirely honorable, that I had never even called her Patricia, and that I had never meant to force myself on her. Mrs. Sheehan said that she understood and that it was perfectly all right with her for me to go on seeing her daughter as long as I did not continue to give her expensive presents. (I didn't tell her about the thermos jug.)

When Harold returned to the Greymount School he found the jug in its leather case in his room, returned by Patricia Sheehan.

The next morning he asked Miss Johnson if she knew why Patricia Sheehan had returned the jug.

"I certainly do," said Ruth Johnson. "Miss Sheehan is angry with you because you went to see her mother without even talking it over with her first."

"I left her a note." Miss Johnson did not answer. "Do you think she'll speak to me?" Harold asked.

"No, I don't," Miss Johnson said, and walked on.

During the next weeks Harold stayed by himself much of the time and brooded about the disintegration of his friendship with Patricia Sheehan and Ruth Johnson.

Finally he asked Miss Francis, the young history teacher, if she would try to help him regain the friendship of Patricia Sheehan and Miss Johnson. She said she would. Harold suggested that they all have a picnic at a cabin beside a nearby lake owned by the school. Miss Francis agreed to invite Patricia

Sheehan and Miss Johnson. They said they would come. This was in the early summer of the year 1914.

Harold planned the picnic carefully. The girls were to meet him at the cabin at four-thirty in the afternoon. He would bring the necessary food. They would all fish, and cook the catch for dinner.

Harold was there at four o'clock, getting everything ready. Four-thirty came, but the girls did not appear. He waited and grew restless. He was afraid they would not come. Five-thirty came, and still there was no sign of them. At six they arrived. Harold was very upset, but he tried not to show it. The girls seemed unconcerned about their tardiness. He mentioned something to the effect that it was getting pretty late to fish. The girls agreed. Harold said he had brought some canned meat along and they could have that for dinner.

Then Harold asked the girls if they would like to play some games before dinner. They said they would. He had been in charge of entertainment in his fraternity and apparently he had in mind some of the milder games used at initiations. One of these was to see who could most quickly push a penny the length of a tabletop with his nose. Another involved a person putting some cotton in his mouth, then blowing it up into the air for a second person to catch in his mouth. He explained the games to the girls and said that Miss Francis and Patricia Sheehan should play the game where one pushed the penny with the nose. He asked them to go outside for a few minutes while he and Miss Johnson prepared for the other game. They thought this odd, but did as he asked.

Harold took a wad of cotton from the carrying pack he had brought and began to place it in Ruth Johnson's mouth. She bit down hard on his forefinger and yelled, "What kind of funny business do you think you're—"

Harold hit her on the side of the face with his fist. He went berserk. He grabbed her throat with his left hand and forced the cotton into her mouth, choking her. He picked up a stick that was leaning against a wall of the cabin and hit her over the head with great force five or six times.

Patricia Sheehan and Miss Francis ran in. Harold hit Miss Francis with the stick several times, knocking her unconscious. Then he hit Patricia Sheehan with his fist, dragged her into the bedroom, threw her on the bed and bound her hands and feet to the bedposts. He ran out, bound Miss Francis's hands. He ran to the kitchen, picked up a carving knife, went back to the bedroom, and wildly cut the clothing from Patricia Sheehan. Then he threw himself on her and raped her.

Finally he went outside and sat down on a rock beside the lake. It was very still. There were no sounds except the occasional notes of a bird in the woods.

After some time, Harold, in a trance-like state, got into a canoe and paddled mechanically down the lake to the town. He went into a drugstore and telephoned Dr. Taggart, headmaster of the Greymount School.

"Dr. Taggart, this is Harold Wesson. I wish you'd go up to the camp immediately. Something terrible has happened."

"What? What has happened?"

Harold hung up and walked out of the drugstore. He went over to the police station. Police Chief Giles was at his desk.

"What can I do for you, Harold? What's the matter? You don't look so good."

"You'd better lock me up, Mr. Giles," Harold said. "I think I've done something wrong."

Harold was examined by several doctors and found to be legally sane. Supposedly, the prosecuting attorney visited Harold in his cell and said he would make a deal with him. If Harold would plead guilty, it would save the state considerable expense and save the prosecutor's office much time. The prosecutor would see that Harold got life imprisonment rather than the death penalty. But Harold would have to promise never to request a pardon. If he did not agree to this, he would certainly get the death sentence.

Harold, in a severe depression, is supposed to have agreed. He pleaded guilty and waived trial by jury. He was sentenced to life imprisonment without possibility of parole.

Some 40 years later Harold Wesson told me his version of the crime. We sat in what amounted to his "apartment" in the prison. He had more seniority than any other inmate, was in effect head of the prison school and had never caused any trouble, so he was allowed special privileges. He had four rooms in the old cellblock which was otherwise unused now. We sat in a room the size of a large living room. This was his office. There was a desk with a typewriter and "In" and "Out" baskets. There was a workbench with various carpenter's tools on it. There were bookcases, one containing copies of *National Geographic* magazine dating back to 1920. Separated from this main room by barred but unlocked doors were three small rooms: Harold's bedroom, a room with a hot plate and cooking supplies, and a storage room.

Harold wore a white shirt and trousers, unlike the blue denim of most of the other inmates. His stomach strained against his shirt front and hung over his belt. He looked like an old man who has gone to seed, except for his eyes, which glanced about sharply, never missing anything.

"I don't believe half of those things that came out in the papers at the time of the trial," he said. "Not half of it. I hit her, I know that. Ruth Johnson, I mean. But I never choked her, and I never hit her with a stick. And I never raped Patricia Sheehan. I'll tell you about that. But about my killing Ruth Johnson. When she bit my finger like that and implied that I was trying some funny business with her, I saw red. I just went out of my head. And I remember taking my fist and hitting her and going on hitting her, and then she fell down and I realized what I'd done and I picked her up and propped her against the wall. She wasn't dead then, but I killed her—she must have hit her head when I knocked her down—and I admitted it."

"And then what happened?" I asked.

"What?" The ear his hearing aid was on was turned away from me.

"What happened then?"

"Well, I've never been able to remember clearly. My memory blacked out on me partly. Like being in a room and switching the light on and off. That's what it's like. I remember some things and not others."

"What's the next thing you remember?"

"Well, the other two girls came in. I told them I'd hit Ruth Johnson. But none of us thought she was dead. Then Patricia Sheehan asked me to come into the bedroom with her for a minute. And they said I raped her. Nonsense, I say. You know what happened? She asked me if I wanted her to undress and she said I could do anything I liked with her. Well, I was extremely upset emotionally after having hit Ruth Johnson and after all I was human and I guess I helped her undress. You can believe this or not, but I'd never had intercourse with a woman before. I'd never even thought about it, because my mother had always made such a point of the fact that people didn't even kiss outside of marriage. And I'd never seen a woman naked before.

"So I helped her undress and I remember I tried to take her shoes off for her and she said, 'Silly, untie the laces first.' We had intercourse once and that was all. I went outside and I felt terrible, worse than I ever had in my life. I sat down on the

bank by the stream, and then after a while I got in the canoe
and I paddled down the lake to the town. That was the hardest
thing I ever did in my life."

"Which made you feel worse, having killed Miss Johnson
or having had intercourse with Miss Sheehan?"

"The intercourse," Harold Wesson answered immediately.

"Why was that?"

"Why? Well, when I hit Ruth Johnson I'd lost control of
myself. I didn't know what I was doing. Of course I shouldn't
have done it, but I couldn't control myself. With the intercourse, that was different. I was upset, but I knew what I
was doing and I went ahead anyway."

"Do you think it's ever right for people to have sexual relationships outside of marriage?"

"No, I do not," he answered. "My mother always taught
me that. She was too strict about a lot of things, but about that
she was right.

"I tell you, this country has gone sex-mad. You can't pick
up a magazine, you can't pick up a book but what it isn't sex,
sex, sex." He groped through the papers and magazines on his
desk in order to find something to illustrate his point, but then
he let the matter go.

The most significant fact in Harold Wesson's early life which
bears on his crime is the extreme degree to which his mother
dominated him. He was so dependent on her that he never
dared to do other than that which she dictated. But acceding
to her every demand was necessarily highly frustrating to him
time and time again. His own desires went unfulfilled, and he
kept the pain of their unfulfillment within him. He could not
help unconsciously developing an enormous resentment, tremendous feelings of aggression, against her. And since to him
she represented all females, this submerged aggression gen-
eralized, unknown to him, to include all women.

At the same time, as a developing child, Harold was unable to learn adequately the male role he would later be expected to play. Never allowed to take part in athletics, never allowed to argue or even express his views, he had no opportunity to acquire the competitiveness and self-assertiveness demanded of the male by our society. He developed, instead, as a weak image of his mother—basically feminine, but without her strength of purpose and confidence. Thus, Harold as a young man was a highly sensitive, seemingly passive, quiet, nice lad who was actually more feminine than masculine in his approach to life. As Dr. Taggart, the headmaster at the Greymount School, said: "I think Harold always got along so well with the young ladies on the staff because when he was with them he seemed to forget that he was a man."

But at the same time Harold had a normal sexual urge. This could not be fulfilled because of the dead hand of his mother upon him, saying in effect, "Sex is not nice. Sex is wrong." Together with this unfulfilled sexual urge, he had that tremendous, submerged aggression against women.

He was, then, a young man in severe conflict. On the one hand, associating with females almost as if he himself were a female; on the other hand, unconsciously both wanting them as sexual partners in order to prove himself a man and hating them for being women.

Then there arose what was for him the extremely frustrating situation of not knowing where he stood with respect to Patricia Sheehan. This, it would seem, was due largely to the influence of Ruth Johnson. Although it cannot be verified, it would seem that Ruth Johnson had a strong if latent homosexual attachment for Patricia Sheehan. Ruth Johnson recognized Harold as a threat and so she did what she could to place a barrier between him and Patricia Sheehan.

Ruth Johnson thus became Harold's enemy and the focal point of his unconscious aggression toward women. He had been fighting to play his masculine role in society by associating steadily with Patricia Sheehan. And Ruth Johnson kept throwing blocks in the way of this attempt to prove himself a man.

At the same time Harold was also unconsciously aggressive toward Patricia Sheehan as well. She was a woman, and all women were associated with his frustrating mother. Beyond that, Patricia Sheehan had at times indicated a natural enough desire to engage in some degree of physical intimacy. This threw Harold into a specific dilemma, his natural desire and his need to play the masculine role pulling him one way, his mother-induced fear of the immorality of such behavior pulling him the other.

When Ruth Johnson bit Harold's finger and implied that he was making sexual advances toward her, she triggered all this mounting aggression. The sudden pain of the bitten finger, caused by a woman, and the accusation that he was attempting to do what he really wanted to do—make a sexual advance toward a woman—and yet was afraid to do, were too much for him when coupled with the fact that he saw Ruth Johnson as the barrier to his relationship with Patricia Sheehan. He lashed out at her, and once he began feeling the release of aggression he could not stop himself. Then he went on to rape Patricia Sheehan, in a blind attempt to both prove himself a man and to release further his aggression against all women.

But there still remains the question: Why did Harold Wesson lose all control of himself on that fateful day? There are many men who have been dominated by their mothers and who as a consequence have been thrown into conflict in their relationships with women and who also are suddenly frustrated by some one woman as Harold was by Ruth Johnson. Yet these men do not necessarily commit murder and rape.

First, Harold's mother had denied him the usual forms of aggression release—athletics, arguing, sexual activity and the like—under threat of withdrawal of her love. Thus his aggression mounted to unusually high levels. The second factor was the weakness of Harold's conscience. Conscience is partly a learned set of more or less unconscious fears concerning the consequences of committing a socially unacceptable act. If these fears are strong enough, they act as automatic regulators of our behavior. Harold had a conscience, to be sure, but he did not have one sufficiently developed to inhibit his enormous aggression when he was confronted with a greatly frustrating situation.

It would seem logical to think that in Harold's case his conscience would be, if anything, overly strong because of his dominating, highly moral mother. But the point is this: If a parent is too dominating, too militantly moral, the child inwardly rebels. He *appears* to learn what the parent teaches him; he *appears* to be docile, cooperative, firm in moral conscience. However, this is on the surface; underneath there is a strong spark of resentment, kindled over the years by the frustration caused by the parent's excessive demands. The child acquires, that is, a superficial conscience—he never truly internalizes the hated parent's teaching, and at the core of his being there remains a hidden lawless approach to the world. If he is later confronted with extreme pressure, his surface conscience cracks, and his inner, resentful lawlessness drives the compressed aggression outward in one tremendous surge.

Harold Wesson, Ruth Johnson and Patricia Sheehan. They went on a picnic together.

XII

Memphis Serenade

E. D. Radin

When a quiet, silver-haired, 69-year-old bachelor was poisoned, the police were at a loss for a motive—until they discovered the passionate letters and the photographs of dozens of lovely motives, many of whom were depicted in various states of undress. Some were single, some were married, and they ranged from wild young girls to respected matrons. None had been able to resist "Daddy Samples's" extraordinary masculinity, and one had wanted—too desperately—the only thing he seemed incapable of giving.

To his neighbors, Walter Lewis Samples was a simple, unpretentious, silver-haired bachelor of 69 who lived alone in a house much like himself, plain, comfortable, white-painted, on a quiet residential street in Memphis. A retired civil engineer, he was able to live well on his monthly pension plus the rents he received from several small multiple dwellings he owned in South Memphis. Despite his years, he was a vigorous man, drove his own car and was actively interested in the Spanish-American War Veterans' Association of which he was senior commander. He liked to play bridge and was on friendly terms with his neighbors.

Samples died on February 27, 1941, in the Veterans' Administration Hospital several hours after admission. His personal physician was puzzled. Shortly after two o'clock that afternoon he had received an emergency call from Samples and went at once to his home. He found his patient in extreme agony, complaining of violent pains in his stomach and an inability to hold any food. A much younger woman was at his bedside attempting to administer first aid.

The dying man said he had first felt the pains shortly after breakfast two days earlier on the 25th. He had gone about his affairs the rest of that day, but had refrained from eating. Although the pains persisted all during the following day, Samples attributed them to an upset stomach and continued his normal routine. He still failed to seek medical attention on the third morning, but as the pains grew in intensity he returned home and notified his doctor.

From the symptoms described by the patient, the doctor suspected either tainted food or some kind of poison. Samples told him he kept no poison of any kind in the house. The last meal he had eaten had been his breakfast two days earlier which he had prepared himself. It had consisted of his customary bacon and eggs, toast and two glasses of milk. He recalled one unusual occurrence. When he had stepped out on the porch for his morning paper he had found a bottle of milk beside the door. It was not from his regular dairy, and he telephoned his next-door neighbor, who received deliveries from this concern. She told him that the milkman had brought her customary order. Assuming that the driver had left a complimentary bottle in the hope of picking up his business, Samples drank the milk with his breakfast. The milk had seemed fresh to him, but he had a cold and his sense of taste was blunted.

The physician found the bottle of milk in the refrigerator and when he sniffed it, detected the odor of phosphorus. He sealed the bottle, gave it to the young woman with instructions to turn it over to police and arranged to have his patient taken to the hospital.

When Samples died a few hours later, the doctor notified police and told his story to Inspector M. A. Hinds. The inspector checked with the desk sergeant.

"No bottle of milk was turned up here," Hinds told the doctor. "Do you know the woman?"

The doctor shook his head. "She told me she had insisted that Samples telephone for a doctor and she scolded him for not calling me sooner. She may have turned the milk over to one of his relatives."

Detectives checked with the doctors at the hospital who had treated the patient and learned that they, too, felt that Samples's death had been caused by some form of poison. Hospital records showed that he had listed a brother as his next of kin to be notified, and the latter agreed readily to have an autopsy performed. He said he knew of no reason why his brother should take his own life as he had been in excellent health and had not found retirement dull; he had been engaged in frequent real-estate deals and was occupied with his duties in the veterans' organization. As far as the brother knew, Samples had no enemies, but he seldom had discussed any of his personal affairs. The bottle of milk had not been turned over to him.

Late that night the autopsy was completed. "We'll have to wait for the toxicologist's report to make it official," the surgeon reported, "but I can tell you now that he died of poison and I could smell phosphorus." He explained that this particular poison works slowly on the human body, causing severe pains for several days, with the patient dying in agony.

Questioning of milk-company employees ended any theory of accidental death. The milkman denied that he had left a bottle of milk on Samples's porch, and company officials agreed that they did not give away free bottles as a means of getting customers. They also pointed out that it would be impossible for poison to enter just one bottle; milk bottles move on mechanical conveyors directly from the sterilization tanks to the filling machines without being touched by any employees. If poison somehow had entered a batch of milk, then other customers would have been affected, and the milk company had received no complaints, nor were there any reports of similar deaths. Somebody had deliberately inserted the phosphorus into one bottle of milk and just as deliberately left that bottle on the porch. The death of the elderly unassuming man was murder.

Police had not been able that night to trace the woman who had been in the house. The following morning detectives visited neighbors of the murdered man. One woman said she had seen Samples arrive at his home the previous day, his car weaving on the road. He had been bent over almost double as he climbed the steps and entered his house. Shortly after, a young woman arrived in a car and ran up the porch steps. She was followed later by the physician. The neighbor said that Samples once had explained to her that the younger woman, who had been a frequent visitor at his home, assisted him in his work with the veterans' association.

Following this lead, detectives checked at the organization headquarters and obtained the name of the woman. She showed no alarm at the sight of the officers and said she had just learned of Samples's death and was preparing to bring the bottle of milk to headquarters. It was in her refrigerator with the doctor's seal intact. Asked why she had failed to bring the milk bottle in earlier, she replied that it was inconceivable to her that anybody would want to murder Samples. Since the older man had been reluctant to call a doctor, she had not wanted to involve him in anything.

Her story shed no new light on the murder. Samples had telephoned her shortly after noon the previous day to tell her he thought he was dying, and she had hurried over. It was upon her insistence that he reluctantly telephoned for the doctor. She did not think he was trying to hide anything, since he told her the same story about the gift bottle as he later told the doctor.

The woman said she knew very little about Samples's personal affairs. He had known her husband, and when he died the elderly man acted as financial adviser to her. In appreciation of his kindness, she assisted him by working for the veterans' group.

"Then you were very close friends?" she was asked.

"Not close, just friends," was her immediate response. "I liked him because he was so kind, but nothing existed between us, if that's what you mean."

Her questioners hid their smiles and wondered at her vehemence. They had not been seeking romantic implications in the murder of a 69-year-old man, particularly since she was less than half his age, but they were curious to know why Samples had called upon her for assistance when he felt he was dying.

Their smiles faded, however, when a search was made of the murdered man's house. In the bedroom were many framed photographs, all of them of women, and while some appeared to have been taken many years back, there were a great many current snapshots with affectionate inscriptions on them to "Daddy Samples." Hidden in a locked desk drawer were more pictures of women, some of them partly clothed. Quite a few of these photographs appeared to have been taken inside his house. Other drawers in the desk yielded letters from women. These letters were signed with pet names, and almost all the writers referred to Samples as "Daddy," but their tenor left little doubt that it was not filial devotion that had caused them to write; they were love letters from women who had been conducting ardent affairs with a man old enough to be their father or grandfather. Some of the letters were pleas from women begging for a resumption of their lovemaking. Others seemed to be trying to recapture passionate moments with him as they discussed in detail the lovemaking hours they had spent together.

The surprised officers brought their find to Inspector Hinds. Instead of finding one motive, police now were overwhelmed with possible suspects and motives. Officers recognized some of the women in the snapshots as well-known matrons in Memphis. Others were single girls. Any one of the women, desperate to get back her letters or photographs, might have poisoned him. The evidence also provided a motive for an enraged husband, sweetheart or parent of one of the young women.

Poisoning, to Inspector Hinds, was more of a woman's crime, and he directed his men to concentrate on checking on the women. With members of many prominent families among Samples's picture gallery, handpicked detectives, pledged to secrecy, were assigned to question them.

Neighbors of the murdered man knew nothing of the double

life he had been leading. He had lived quietly, spending many evenings sitting on his porch, waving friendly greetings to passersby, or else playing bridge in their homes. Although some neighbors had noticed women callers during the afternoon and occasionally in the evening, they had attached no significance to it.

Police learned that Samples had employed a housekeeper for a time and she had lived in the house with her husband. The couple had left after the husband had quarreled with Samples. They were traced to their new home and questioned separately. Both told the same story: Samples had attempted to fondle the housekeeper, and the indignant woman told her husband; the two men quarreled when the husband gave Samples a tongue-lashing. He denied to officers that they had come to blows, but he and his wife had moved out of the house after that as quickly as they could find new quarters. The couple had been out of town visiting relatives at the time the poisoned milk had been left on the porch.

Chemical analysis of the milk showed that it contained a large concentration of phosphorus crystals and starch, a combination used in making commercial rat poisons. With these products on sale at almost all food and drug stores, police had little hope of being able to trace the purchaser.

A thorough search had turned up no trace of any poison in the house. Samples's personal papers were equally barren of clues. In addition to three houses he owned in Memphis, he also held title to two tracts of farmland in Arkansas which he rented to tenant farmers. He carried a small insurance policy, with his estate named as beneficiary. No will was found in his home or in a safe-deposit box where he kept his real-estate deeds.

There were tearful scenes in many Memphis homes as officers pressed their investigation among the women who had known

Samples. At first many of the women insisted that they had known him only casually. But they changed their stories when shown the pictures; many of them admitted illicit romances with the elderly man and pleaded with the officers to keep their names secret.

"If you didn't kill him, you have nothing to worry about," officers kept assuring them, and then demanded an accounting of their movements on the night the milk bottle had been placed on the porch. The women were also required to furnish a list of the stores they dealt with, and the owners were queried as to whether any of the women had made any recent purchases of rat poison.

Many of the women told similar stories of becoming infatuated with the older man and then finding themselves powerless to break away from him "He was like a drug," one woman explained. "I went out with him before I was married and thought I was cured when I fell in love and was married, but I couldn't stay away from him even after my marriage."

"Whenever he wanted me, I went to him," another young woman told detectives. "Each time I told myself that I would never see him again, but when he called I went."

But while the hardworking officers gathered evidence that Samples had been an extraordinary lover, they had little else to show for their efforts. The list of suspects began to shrink, with police no closer to finding the poisoner.

Attention focused on the possibility that a jealous husband might be the killer when a local merchant revealed that a man had been watching the house several weeks before the murder. He said the man had been in his store and stood watching Samples's home. When he had asked the stranger if he could serve him, the man blurted out that he wondered if his wife might be with Samples and asked the merchant if he could find out for him. The storekeeper remarked that he minded his own business, and the man walked out muttering threats to get Samples. The merchant said he had never seen the man before and described him as tall and husky, weighing about 200 pounds.

One of the women questioned remarked that Samples at one time had been upset about a pending court suit. That was all she knew about it. Lawmen were directed to inspect court records and follow through on the lead.

A businesswoman who had had many transactions with Samples over the years said that she had been a frequent caller at his home and had seen different women there on many occasions. She described these women to police, and they were able to identify all except one, described as a short, slim brunette. "She was there much more often than any of the others," the businesswoman said.

Pressed for further details, she recalled that the brunette had been a steady visitor for several years, and then had stopped coming. Later the brunette resumed her visits, and the businesswoman now noticed that she wore a wedding ring. On one occasion when she dropped in to discuss a real-estate deal with Samples, she found the brunette crying, and from the look on Samples's face she thought they had been quarreling. The businesswoman left hurriedly.

A search was started for the brunette. Meanwhile detectives went through records of the superior and chancery courts without finding Samples's name in the dockets, but they finally located a minor suit in the records of a justice-of-the-peace court. Samples had been a defendant in a suit involving title to a washing machine. A writ of replevin had been sworn out by a man named Harvey Collins, and he had been awarded possession of the washing machine.

Details of the suit showed that Collins had sued to recover the machine because his wife had given it to Samples. Detectives learned that Collins had been the owner of a prosperous trucking concern in Memphis, but had recently sold out his interest in the business, buying a 14,000-acre plantation in adjoining Mississippi, about 150 miles from Memphis. He had moved there with his wife, a petite brunette, some months before the murder.

Mrs. Collins answered the description of the woman caller who had been seen frequently at Samples's home, and information linking Mrs. Collins with the murdered man was soon obtained. Collins's former bookkeeper said he had been checking the trucking firm's books one day when he uncovered a shortage of more than $7000 in cash. Mrs. Collins had taken a job in the office for a while, and the shortage had occurred during that period. When Collins questioned his wife about the money, she admitted taking it and said she had given it to Samples for a real-estate investment.

The bookkeeper said that Collins had quarreled with his wife over her visits to Samples's home and he suggested to police that they question Mrs. Collins's former maid, who still was living in Memphis. The maid confirmed the story about Mrs. Collins giving the $7000 to Samples and said she had been present when her mistress turned the money over to the elderly Lothario. She added that she had seen Mrs. Collins give Samples money on other occasions.

Friends of the couple were queried to find out if either, or both of them, had been in Memphis at the time of the murder. Collins had been in the city five days before the poisoning to attend a meeting of the Interstate Commerce Commission, but hotel records showed that he had stayed in Memphis just one night.

The evidence against the couple was too slight to justify extradition, and officials were afraid to ask them to come to Memphis, since it might only serve to put them on their guard. Inspector Hinds realized that his best chance was to surprise them; one of them might blurt out the truth.

On the morning of April 3, 1941, a telephone call was made

to Collins at his plantation, and he was informed by the caller that he was needed in Memphis in connection with a business matter. The caller further suggested that he bring Mrs. Collins along for the outing. Although Collins was puzzled by the call, he agreed to come.

A patrol car was stationed off the road, not far from the Tennessee-Mississippi state line, on the highway that Collins would use to get to Memphis. About seven o'clock that night his car was spotted as it crossed the state line, and a few minutes later the patrol car forced his machine to the curb and the couple were taken into custody.

When Collins learned that he had been lured to Memphis to be questioned about the murder of Samples, he seemed surprised. "We would have come right in if you had told us you wanted to see us," he assured officials. "We know nothing about his murder and have nothing to hide."

Mrs. Collins tearfully admitted her affair with Samples. She said it had started back in 1925 when she first met him. After her marriage to Collins she had stopped seeing him, but when Samples began telephoning her, she resumed her relations with him, calling during the day at his house.

"I tried to break away from him, but no woman could resist him," she told the officers. She said that Samples had wanted her to divorce Collins and marry him, but she had refused because she loved her husband. Even though she loved her husband she had been unable to break away from the older man, no matter how she tried. At the time the businesswoman had seen her crying, she had been pleading with the elderly man to let her alone; she told him that she was afraid that her husband would leave her unless she stopped seeing him. She had promised Collins that she would end her affair with Samples after he learned about the $7000 she had given his elderly rival, but despite her promise the washing-machine incident had followed, and this had led to a temporary separation and the court suit.

While Mrs. Collins was willing to discuss her romance with Samples, she denied any knowledge of his poison murder. She said she had been at the plantation for several months and had deliberately stayed away from Memphis so she could not see Samples.

Collins likewise denied any knowledge of the murder, adding that he thought Samples had died a natural death. He also denied that he was the man who had lurked in the neighborhood to see if his wife was with Samples and he was able to prove that he had been in Mississippi that night.

Mr. and Mrs. Collins were held on an open charge while Mississippi police were asked to conduct an investigation at the plantation. A deputy sheriff searched the plantation house and reported that he had found no rat poison there, nor had he been able to establish any purchase of the poison by either of them. He did report, though, that there were a large number of milk bottles in the basement, all of them bearing the name of the Memphis dairy.

While this was a link in a chain of circumstantial evidence, it still was far from any proof that Mr. or Mrs. Collins was involved in the murder.

Mrs. Collins was searched by a matron, and a legal document was found hidden in her shoe, a will signed by Samples in which he had left everything he owned to Mrs. Collins as his sole beneficiary.

She was brought back for further questioning. Asked why she had not mentioned the will, she replied that she did not think it was anybody's business but her own. She said Samples had drafted the document himself on his typewriter in his home shortly before she had moved to Mississippi. "He said he wanted me to have everything he owned when he died because I had been so kind about letting him have money when he needed it," she explained.

It was obvious that the will was news to Collins. He said his wife had never mentioned it to him.

The typewriter was brought to headquarters, and experts were asked to compare the type on the document. They reported that the will had not been typed on the machine in Samples's home. Comparisons also were made with the typewriter in the office of the veterans' organization, and this machine also was ruled out.

Although the signature on the will looked genuine, Inspector Hinds sent it to the FBI laboratory for examination by federal experts. He also sent along the typewriter for further study. C. A. Appel, Jr., head of the Identification of Questioned Documents division, reported that the signature on the will was a clever forgery and not Samples's own.

Both suspects were confronted with the information. Collins was silent for a time. Then glancing at his wife, he confessed that he had placed the bottle of poisoned milk on the porch. In his confession he completely cleared his wife and said that she knew nothing about the murder. Inspector Hinds nevertheless ordered the arrest of Mrs. Collins, pointing out that she was the one who had possession of the forged will.

The evidence given here was presented to a grand jury, and both Mr. and Mrs. Collins were indicted for murder. They were placed on trial in June 1941. Collins repudiated his confession and denied the murder. Mrs. Collins, who had never confessed, also testified that she knew nothing about the murder.

After debating for 12 hours, a jury returned with a verdict finding both guilty of murder, but with mitigating circumstances, and punishment of each was fixed at 20 years and one day imprisonment. (The extra day adds substantially to the length of time a prisoner must serve before he can be paroled.)

But the case was not yet over. The convicted couple filed an appeal, and the State Supreme Court ordered a new trial.

Some 18 months dragged by before they again were placed on trial. The first day, January 19, 1943, was occupied with the selection of a jury, and a complete panel had not yet been selected when the court recessed for the day. Spectators noticed that Mrs. Collins appeared to be very nervous, and her husband sought constantly to calm her.

The following morning, while the questioning of the prospective jurors continued, Mrs. Collins was even more agitated than she had been the previous day. Reporters were dozing, waiting for action, when Mrs. Collins suddenly leaped to her feet, ignored the outstretched hand of her husband and ran toward the bench shouting, "I can't stand it any longer. My husband is innocent. I did it alone, and he's been trying to protect me."

The courtroom was hastily cleared, while defense attorneys consulted with Mrs. Collins and then conferred with the prosecutor and the presiding judge.

Mrs. Collins was allowed to confess, describing in detail how she had placed the poison in the bottle and left it on the porch for Samples. She said that her husband had sold out his business in order to help her get away from Samples, but the elderly man still pursued her with telephone calls. Afraid that he might be able to lure her back, she decided to poison him as the only means of breaking the strange hold he seemed to have over her. As his mistress she knew of his habit of drinking milk for breakfast.

Collins admitted that in order to shield his wife he had confessed to a crime he had not committed. He had not known about the murder, but when the will was found in her shoe he feared that she might be involved. He sought to protect her by accepting responsibility and stating that she had nothing to do with it.

When court reconvened, Mrs. Collins pleaded guilty to the murder and again was sentenced to the 20-year term. The indictment was dismissed against Collins, a gallant figure and the real victim of the strange riptides of passion that existed between his wife and the elderly Daddy Samples.

XIII

Murder on Big Moose Lake

George E. Minot

One of the most moving romantic dramas in contemporary fiction, Theodore Dreiser's *An American Tragedy*, was based upon this pathetic tale. It is the story of Grace Brown, an innocent farm girl whose inherent goodness was her downfall, and Chester Gillette, a cunning youth whose selfish desires were his own destruction. It is an open-ended triangle, a love story gone wrong. And the fateful course of events that brought these two together one summer evening on Big Moose Lake is as classic and as inexorable as it is poignant.

NOAH H. GILLETTE was the wealthiest citizen in the little town of Cortland, New York. He owned a factory for making women's skirts, the principal industry there, and he was a deacon in the church. He was a stern, strict man, with cold, fishy eyes and a disposition that inclined him to view everybody with suspicion.

He boasted that he never erred in his judgment of his associates or employees. So when a clerk brought a sleek-haired, weak-faced youth into his office on a fall morning in 1905, a single look seemed to be enough to tell him that here was a person who gave every appearance of having little or no good in his makeup.

When the youth stepped forward confidently, stretched out his hand and addressed the factory owner as "Uncle Noah," the man at the desk showed no sign of pleasure or recognition. Nor did he unbend after the youth had introduced himself. His name, he said, was Chester Gillette, and he was the son of the elder man's brother, a wandering religious fanatic. Chester himself had traveled all over the country with his parents, going from New York to San Francisco, and then had started out on an aimless career of his own. He had been a brakeman on a freight train, a waiter, and had attended college for a time. But now, at the age of 23, he had decided to settle down, he said. He had made up his mind to come to Cortland and learn the skirt-making business. Almost as an afterthought, he asked his uncle for a job.

The elder Gillette could not fight down the feeling that he was making a mistake, but finally, more for the sake of appearances in the town than anything else, he hired the youth as a stock clerk at ten dollars a week.

For a time it appeared as if the uncle's suspicions had been unwarranted. The youth became active in young people's societies in the church. He did his work well. He made friends everywhere, especially among young women. Gillette had no sons of his own, and he took a measure of pride in his nephew's popularity. "That boy is made of better stuff than his father," he said one night to his wife, but when he suggested that he offer the youth a place in their own home, the wife complained that it might make extra work for her, so the matter was dropped.

Then, after Chester Gillette had been there for about a year, Grace Brown came to work in the factory. She received four dollars a week for inspecting the skirts after they were made, but before long she was making twice this amount on piecework. Nobody in the shop was as quick as she. Noah Gillette said she was his best worker.

A homely setting sometimes produces tragedies just as great as those that occur in the so-called higher circles, and such was the case with Grace Brown. There have been thousands of girls, tired of the drab, colorless life of the farm as it appeared to them in early age, who have gone to the city to earn a better living and enjoy themselves more, where they have been swept into a whirlpool of gaiety and excitement and have forgotten the sterner lessons of life.

But Grace Brown was not one of these, and because she was not her tragedy is even greater. It has about it a pathos and a romance that lifts it above the sordid circumstances of most such cases. Hers is an old story, but her inherent purity, her sweetness and her love raised her downfall to a plane far above those of most girls caught in the same net of circumstances. It has formed the basis of a great novel, and a play that ran for weeks on Broadway.

Grace Brown was the darling of a family of seven children. Their farm home in South Otselic, in the northern part of New York State, was large and comfortable. Few families in that town at that time had more of the luxuries of home. But when Grace was 16 the family fortunes changed sharply. There were debts and mortgages and a succession of poor crops. To lighten the burden on her father, she went to live with one of her married sisters in the town of Cortland, 50 or so miles away.

Such were the circumstances under which Grace Brown and Chester Gillette met. She was the prettiest and smartest girl in the factory, sweet, full of life and the joy of living, with brown eyes, a mass of hair of the same color and a smiling mouth of the type often compared with a rosebud.

But she was no match for Gillette, who had seen so much of the world. With her he never mentioned his more questionable experiences—and he had had plenty of them—but talked of the days when he went to college and of the religious work of his father and mother. He didn't mention that they were engaged in this because it was easier than any other work they could think of. Very much impressed, Grace set him on a pedestal.

When her sister moved away from Cortland, Grace stayed because she could not bear to be parted from Gillette. She lived in a rooming house, and where else could she entertain him? The landlady must have been blind, or ignorant, or broadminded. At any rate she did not interrupt his visits, no matter how late they lasted. There is no need to go into Grace Brown's struggle against her love, but it is enough to say that nobody ever put up a stronger fight against odds that were bound to be so overwhelming from the start.

Although they became engaged secretly, Gillette never gave this contract a serious thought. To him Grace was merely for his amusement, to be discarded as soon as some of the more socially prominent girls of the town smiled upon him. And finally, when Grace came to realize this, she tempered her anger and resentfulness with forgiveness because she loved him so much.

In the latter part of March 1906, it became evident to Grace Brown that she was pregnant. She went to Gillette, now begging that he marry her at once, but he was merely annoyed. He was afraid that anything like that would interfere with his plans for good times that summer with young women he considered above Grace. He hoped that eventually he might marry one of these, preferably one with money, and then his future would be assured, and he could leave the factory forever.

So he told Grace to go back to her home in Otselic, and from her farm home she wrote him a series of letters that have since become famous. As a story of a girl's suffering and courage, they have few equals anywhere. They contain such expressions of love, sorrow and sacrifice, brightened here and there by a ray of hope and now and again darkened with despair at its lowest depths, that it is hard to believe that they come from an unsophisticated girl, raised on a farm, without much education and with only a single experience of the world at its worst.

In reply to a letter in which Gillette roughly told her that he could not see her on July 4 because he preferred to be with other girls in Cortland, this 18-year-old country girl penned an answer like this:

I won't interfere with any of your plans. I was ill nearly all yesterday and the veins in my head were frightfully swollen. Mamma bathed them in cologne and they are not so bad today. They were swollen because I cry so much. Chester, I don't suppose you will ever know how I regret being all this trouble to you. I know you hate me and I can't blame you one bit. My whole life is ruined and, in a measure, yours is, too. Of course, it's worse for me than for you, but the world and you, too, may think I am the one to blame, but somehow I can't—just simply can't—think that I am, Chester. I said no so many times, dear. Of course the world will not know that, but it's true just the same. My little sister came up just a minute ago with her hands full of daisies and asked me if I didn't want my fortune told. I told her I guessed it was pretty well told.

Then later came hope, because Gillette wrote and promised to meet her the following weekend to take her away on a trip, on which they would be married. In reply to his letter of these plans, she wrote him:

You would smile if you knew how I am trying to get strong, for I don't care how rough my life is after next Saturday. I think I could carry packs like women peddlers. I shall certainly die if you don't come. Dear, don't make me suffer any more after next Saturday, please. I just can't bear it, and I don't think I deserve it, do you? I don't suppose I shall be home for some time, shall I?

And then, a final letter, perhaps sadder than all the others, in which, after telling how she was planning to go away with him, she added:

I have been bidding good by to some places today. There are so many nooks, dear, and all of them so dear to me. I have lived here nearly all my life. First, I said good by to the spring house with its great masses of green moss, then the apple tree where we had our play-house; then the "bee hive," a cute little house in the orchard, and, of course, all the neighbors that have mended my dresses from a little tot up, to save me from a threshing I really deserved.

All the time Grace Brown was collecting her pitiful trousseau, careful not to arouse the suspicions of her mother.

"If I could only tell Mamma," she wrote Gillette, "but I can't. She has trouble enough as it is, and I couldn't break her heart like that."

But while Grace was planning for her secret wedding trip, Gillette had an entirely different object in view. He was fever-

ishly studying timetables, railroad guides and maps of the
Adirondack region. He was not hunting for a quiet spot where
they could spend their honeymoon. He was searching for a
secluded lake, far back in the mountains, where he could
drown her.

Grace wanted to go to Cortland and meet Gillette, but he
would have none of that. He was afraid that somebody would
see them together, and that would be disastrous. He had made
his plans far in advance and he thought that he had covered
all his footprints.

So they met at a little railroad station somewhere between
Otselic and Cortland on the evening of July 7, and they
traveled to Utica, New York, on different cars of the same
train. Grace could not understand why they did not sit together,
but Gillette said that somebody from Cortland might see them
together, and while Grace still did not understand, she consented because she did not want to let anything come up that
might interfere with their marriage.

At Utica they went to a hotel, where Gillette registered as
Charles Gordon, using a name that would coincide with the
initials on his suitcase. Grace wanted to be married there at
once, but instead of going to a clergyman's house, Gillette
went to a laundry to get himself a clean shirt.

The next day Gillette took the girl miles into the woods—
the same girl who had written him that her illness would prevent a long trip. Tupper Lake sounded good to him, but when
they reached there, the plan was blocked temporarily. A manufacturing plant was located there, and scores of persons were
walking along the shores of the lake. Even more important for
Gillette's purposes, there was no wooded point jutting into the
lake, and he needed just such a point so he could row a boat
behind it.

So they stayed on another night, Gillette using the name of
Carl Graham, again the initials of his own name. Then they

went to Big Moose Lake, and Grace wrote a happy postcard to her mother. She said that she was going to be married, and would write more about it that night.

The card thoroughly frightened Gillette. He decided to kill Grace before that letter could be sent. At dusk that evening, before they had had any dinner, he hired a boat and he and Grace rowed away from the landing and across the pond. On the other side was just the kind of sheltered cove for which Gillette had been looking.

What happened there will never be known; there were no witnesses to the tragedy. But just after sunset a person on shore heard a woman scream, and that was all. The next morning the overturned boat was found, and after further search the body of Grace Brown was located on the bottom of the pond. There was a bruise on her forehead and water in her lungs.

Considering the pains that Gillette had taken to hide his tracks, his arrest came surprisingly fast. The police surmised at once that there had not been a double drowning, and when no second body was found in the lake they started to search for "Carl Graham," and Gillette was taken into custody. At first he denied that he had been on Big Moose Lake and that he and Carl Graham were the same person, but when he saw that he was cornered, he changed his story completely.

He said that he and Grace, planning to be married and supremely happy, had gone for a boat ride, and that while they were discussing their plans on the lake, his hat blew off. In attempting to get it, the boat was overturned and the girl drowned. That convinced nobody, so he changed the story again. He said that during their talk Grace suddenly had exclaimed that she was tired of life and had jumped into the water, upsetting the boat as she did so.

Although he was an expert swimmer and the shore was only a few yards away, he said that he did not save her because she struggled so in the water that he feared he would be pulled under with her. He told various stories to account for the bruise that was found on the forehead of the dead girl.

In November 1906, Gillette went on trial at Herkimer, New York, charged with the murder of Grace Brown. The government contended that he had struck the girl over the head, perhaps with a tennis racket, and had tumbled her unconscious body into the water. The racket had been found behind a tree on the shore of the lake, not far from where the tragedy took place.

The defense, of course, was that Grace had ended her own life, but the fact that Gillette had neither made an outcry for help nor attempted to save her nor reported the incident, leaving her body unrecovered and unlooked for on the bottom of the lake while he hurried to fill social engagements he had made earlier, was too much even for the most credulous.

The trial attracted little attention until Grace Brown's letters were read in court, and then the case swept the country. Gillette's mother "covered" the trial for newspapers to earn money for her son's defense, when his wealthier relatives showed little inclination to hurry to his assistance.

On December 4, 1906, a jury, after deliberating for five hours, returned a verdict of guilty. The first five ballots stood 11 to 1 for conviction.

The usual appeals and discoveries of new evidence followed. The mother "learned" that Grace had been subject to epileptic fits, and argued that she must have been seized with one of these and fallen into the water, but nobody took this contention seriously. There were also despicable attacks on the character of the dead girl.

The governor of New York was Charles Evans Hughes and he was not to be stampeded. On February 18, 1908, the court of appeals unanimously confirmed the verdict, and the governor again and again declined to intervene.

On March 30, 1908, after his mother had vainly held several

rallies in theaters and public halls in his behalf, Chester Gillette died in the electric chair at Auburn, New York.

After his death two clergymen who had become friendly with him in prison gave out this cryptic statement, indicating that he may have confessed:

"Because our relationship with Chester Gillette was privileged, we do not deem it wise to make a detailed statement, and simply wish to say that no legal mistake was made in his electrocution."

XIV

The Wicked Countess

George Dilnot

When one man is not enough for a woman, and two are inconvenient, and three are a bore, and four . . . Well, certainly some have to go. In the inspired love rondel the stunning young Countess Tarnowska played, poisoned daggers, chloroformed cigarettes, and dueling pistols were but a few of the means to the ends she desired— and to the beginnings, too.

Once upon a time there lived a beautiful if wanton countess, and many men loved her. It is proper that I should open this story as a fairy tale, for there are few points in it where I shall be able to avoid fantastic realities of life, which are sometimes even more incredibly imaginative than the wildest resources of fiction.

Take some of the most colorful of these resources—intrigue, suicide, unbridled passion, murder plots, forgery, theft, poisoned daggers, a runaway wedding, chloroformed cigarettes, duels, a murder trial—set them in Venice and St. Petersburg, and you get the elements of the lurid and tragic story of Maria Nicolaievna, Countess Tarnowska.

From a secluded, almost monastic life in the neighborhood of Kiev, this slim, imperious but unsophisticated 19-year-old beauty—who came of good family with some hint of Irish blood in their veins—was snatched, after a runaway wedding before a village priest, to the wildest gaieties of St. Petersburg in the days of the tsarist regime in Russia. But the dashing Lochinvar —Count Vassili Tarnowski—who, in face of parental opposition, had carried her away, speedily proved a poor figure of romance.

The curtain of a new world rolled suddenly up before the eyes of the girl—a world of glamor and disillusion. Stark and bitter truths ate into her soul. There were other women; there were bright lights and red wines. It needed not certain crude brutalities to bring home to her quick and sensitive mind that she was merely an incident in the life of the man she had married. Disillusion was forced upon her.

"My husband," she declared, "took me to restaurants and to

227

café concerts, where gentlemen paid much attention to me. On a certain occasion one of these men made a declaration of love to me, and I in perfect sincerity told everything to my husband. He replied that he was not my keeper and that others might court me if they liked."

In this sordid spirit of cynicism did the education of an adventuress begin. She was not the type calmly to accept humiliation and neglect and insult, and, partly convent bred though she was, she proved an apt pupil in the arts of gallantry. The early years of their married life were largely spent in traveling, with spasmodic visits to their home at Kiev. Children came, but they brought no increase in domestic felicity.

The seared soul of the woman—or rather girl—was in revolt. She was becoming conscious of her fascinations, her power to make men her playthings, to torture them mentally at her caprice, to send them willingly to death almost by a gesture. In the way of her complete domination stood only Count Tarnowski. He was to her no longer a gallant figure of romance, but an incubus and a scandal. She embarked with calculation and subtlety on the task of provoking his jealousy.

I pass over the suicide of young Pietro Tarnowski, her husband's brother, for which, rightly or wrongly, she was blamed. But her responsibility in the affair of Borzewski is very clear.

Borzewski was one of those chance visitors at their home on whom she first chose to exercise her gifts of fascination. Possibly at first she intended merely to make him an instrument of revenge on her husband, whom she hated so coldly and viciously. But she had an easy faculty of falling in love herself.

As Borzewski's infatuation grew, she sought to test her power over him. An occasion arose at a rifle gallery which affords a singular glimpse of the girl's methods and mentality.

"First"—I quote the countess—"he had said that he loved me and I replied that I believed he was joking. He rejoined: 'You will see that it is not a joke.' Then I took a gun and fired at a bottle. He having just put in a bullet, placed his hand over the muzzle. The hand was shattered. Then I understood that he loved me very much."

Matters flamed quickly to a head. The fiery Borzewski made no concealment of his passion. He denounced Tarnowski to his face and challenged him to a duel. For some reason Tarnowski would not fight, and he was assailed with strong taunts of cowardice by his wife. However, the affair apparently passed over.

Then came an evening when the count and countess and Borzewski and another woman had a dinner of reconciliation in a restaurant. As they departed, Borzewski gallantly threw a cloak about the countess, then stooped low and kissed her hand with a fervor that was not lost on the sullen and watching husband.

Suddenly a shot rang out. Borzewski reeled and dropped into the arms of the countess, while blood spurted over her dainty dress and cloak. Count Tarnowski laughed as he stood with the smoking revolver in his hand.

"That's all right," he commented.

It is difficult to disentangle the crosscurrents of passion and intrigue that surged across this girl's life, for they were very often without direct relation to each other. She was never without a lover, and it has been said that she loved each of them— after a fashion and in the absence of the others. Certainly the revelations that were made at the trial of her husband for murder were richly purple. Borzewski, after lingering for some months, died in her arms at a hospital. It was said that the murdered man had declared that he could have married Countess Tarnowska if he had had 500,000 rubles.

She, according to a witness, had expressed the hope that her husband might be deported to Siberia. She was disappointed. It is possible that the plea of the unwritten law prevailed, concerning husbands' rights, for Tarnowski was acquitted. He promptly instituted successful proceedings for divorce. The countess, beautiful butterfly of fashion, was left with expensive tastes and a meager income of about £200 a year. The suspicion cannot be avoided that money was now an imperative necessity for her.

So we come to the entrance of another singular figure in the drama—one Prilukoff, a Moscow lawyer something under 40, of much reputation and ability, with an ardent capacity for work, an income of 25,000 rubles a year, a fortune in the bank and a happy domestic life. Here was the type of hardheaded man of the world one might have thought little likely to fall to the wiles of a siren.

The countess had met him at a casual social dinner some years before and she had called him in to watch her interests in connection with the murder charge against her husband. Later he acted for her in the divorce proceedings. Sheer business, you observe. Yet ere the business association ceased it had become something very much closer. The slim girl had him completely under her spell. The money that she needed was hers without even the asking. He was completely dominated by her.

For two years he remained her abject slave, and then some sense of manhood seems to have returned to him. He attempted to break with her when she summoned him to Kiev one Easter, but his resolution gave way. He went to Moscow and, probably in despair at his failure to break his chains, attempted to poison himself with chloral.

This was the turning point. I quote a fellow lawyer and an intimate of Prilukoff's:

"Tarnowska wanted to see Prilukoff and wished me to fall in with their opinion so that Prilukoff might leave his family and join her. Overtures were even made to Madame Prilukoff. My own impression is that the hydrate of chloral which Prilukoff had taken had tended to make him melancholy, and he became distracted and abnormal in his habits. He drank a great deal and did not go to the courts any more. Instead of this he frequently accompanied Tarnowska to restaurants, and that cost him a great deal of money.

"As to his association with the countess, I think that everything was done at his expense and he did not spend less than £400 or £500 a month. Prilukoff was completely dominated by Tarnowska, who prevented him from attending to business and would never allow him to be alone. She was unwilling that he should be under the influence of anybody but herself, and wished even that the servants should be chosen according to the information which she gave him. In consequence of all this, Prilukoff's business interests went from bad to worse. Tarnowska had forbidden Prilukoff to see his wife or children, and in sending them money he did it unknown to the countess.

"I did not believe that she ever loved the lawyer. It seemed to me that she was much more interested in the gradual submission of Prilukoff to her will than in his sentiments towards her. Sometimes without motive Tarnowska obliged him to do things which made him ridiculous and compromised him. I remember one evening when we were at the theater the lady compelled Prilukoff to jump from the box onto the stage. I tried to hold him back, but he jumped all the same."

Again it must be emphasized that Prilukoff was no callow, impressionable fool. He was very much a man of the world, but his obsession for the girl had mastered him. Everything—wife, family, fortune, friends—was sacrificed on the altar of his infatuation. At last he scraped together some thousands of pounds—money belonging to his clients—and joined her in Vienna. There in church before a holy image she made him swear that he would follow her. The months passed in travel—Berlin, Paris, Marseilles, Algiers. Now and again they separated, but always there was a stream of letters and telegrams between them.

Obviously this was not altogether an idyllic romance. The lady had other strings to her bow, and Prilukoff's money could not last forever. Sometimes in her feverish rushes about Europe other men were with her. But he seemed more or less content—this was a queer trait observable in many of her lovers—to accept his share of her affections without open jealousy. Her whims, her caprices were absolute.

Among the admirers of the countess was the Count Paul Kamarowski, a wealthy Russian nobleman—"a great bore," she declared—whom she permitted a lover's privileges. This man's wife died in 1907, and she determined that he should marry her. They became engaged.

This was her state of mind when Prilukoff, alarmed at a silence which had lasted for some time, was once more drawn to her side in Berlin. She clung to him passionately and demanded an assurance of his continued love. To his fervent protestations she replied with the request that he should kill himself. It would smooth her path for her, she said. Her maid and friend, Elise Perrier drew the lawyer aside and pleaded with him to do the countess this last favor.

"Die for her," she exclaimed, "and she will love you more in death than in life. She will venerate you morn, noon and night as a blessed saint."

But with the morning, reflection came. The immolation of Prilukoff was waived. Instead it was decided that Kamarowski should be the victim. His death could be made more profitable than the destruction of the lawyer. Kamarowski would be insured for half a million francs—then about £50,000—in favor of Tarnowska, and he would die. But how? Prilukoff and the countess went into executive session.

It is difficult to decide who originally conceived the plot. Certainly Prilukoff threw himself into it with a melodramatic fertility of desire. "Free me the face of the earth from this man," she had urged. He swore to do it. She told him not to use a revolver but some other weapon.

They departed together for Vienna, where Prilukoff assiduously studied books on anatomy, seeking some subtle device for the killing. His mind dwelt upon the idea of a poisoned dagger, and he made experiments which apparently did not satisfy him. As I hinted at the beginning of this story, there was a certain crude and astonishing *naïveté* in the machinations of these people. Thus he even made inquiries of the head of a private detective bureau, who in the best spirit of melodrama recommended chloroformed cigarettes. Whether the suggestion was as artless as it seems I do not know, but anyway Prilukoff was unable to obtain any.

A much more subtle scheme, however, ultimately presented itself. There was still another lover in this complex drama—a Dr. Naumoff, son of the governor of a Russian province. A high-strung, weak young man, he had fallen victim to the countess (she was eclectic in her loves) and had given proof that there was nothing to which her vivid personality could not sway him. Why not use him as a tool for the removal of Kamarowski?

Naumoff, little more than a youth, had always been her willing slave. One of her little habits was to extinguish her cigarettes on his lips and hands. He bore on his arms the scars of a dagger with which she had attempted to carve her initials, afterwards washing the wounds with cologne.

Now her coldness was driving him to despair. He had seen her with yet another lover at Vienna and wrote:

I was and am and would have liked always to be thy slave. Thou hast deceived me. All is now finished and thou hast opened an abyss before me because I am deceived and my life has become impossible. I shall arrange so that nobody can imagine the motive of what I am going to do. Adieu, my joy; adieu, my happiness, my sweet dove, my darling, adieu.

Then there was another letter in which, after sending her a "last kiss," he said, "There will be my road."

The countess went to the young man. She chided him as a mere boy who could not be trusted. She took away his revolver, then spoke of Kamarowski, already known to him as one of her intimates. Very adroitly she instilled hatred in the boy for the man she was anxious to have removed.

No incident could be more fantastically unreal than the one in which the woman and Naumoff went to the cemetery at Kiev where an earlier lover, who had killed himself for love of her, was buried. At his grave she showed the young man a telegram addressed to her and signed "Kamarowski," but really dispatched by Prilukoff, which reviled Naumoff and herself in the most offensive terms.

"See how this man repays our friendship," she remarked. "He will ruin my reputation." Then, after a dramatic pause, "The man buried here would have known how to revenge me."

It was enough. She placed round his neck a chain and locket with her portrait, and he responded to her mood in an exaltation of vengeance. He would seek Kamarowski out, and the other would pay. Then the way would be free for his own wedding with Tarnowska.

The projected crime was discussed down to the last detail. As Naumoff and the countess traveled about Russia, she gave him his instructions. She privately received telegrams and letters of advice from Prilukoff, who was anxious to have the matter carried through. Naumoff's suggestion of a duel was vetoed by the countess on the grounds that it might compromise her. It had to be murder.

"At first," said Naumoff, "she said I ought to kill him with a dagger, afterwards with a revolver. In order that suspicion might not fall upon her, Tarnowska made me write a letter in which I took all the responsibility upon myself. Then she made me cut off my moustache and leave behind a walking-stick by which I could have been identified. She also said that if I were arrested I should never make use of her name."

She instructed him that after carrying out the crime he was to go to Zurich, but if he could not get away he was to say that he had committed the murder because he was wildly jealous of Kamarowski and could not bear his presence. He was to tear up his Russian passport directly he reached the frontier, lest his courage fail him. She took her portrait from him. Finally she gave him Kamarowski's address at Venice where he was then staying.

She bade the young man good-bye. Her arms folded round his neck, she wished him good luck. She told him that he loved her now better than all the others and that she loved him more than anyone else.

His mission of death was marked by two telegrams from the countess. "Beloved, I am always with thee. I embrace thee daily." Then again: "My thoughts are with thee, my adored love. A thousand caresses."

Yet at this moment the woman was meditating a supreme act of treachery. With Kamarowski dead, Naumoff would expect the reward for his crime, a reward that she had held out as the final inducement—his marriage of her. But whomever she really loved, she certainly had no intention of marrying Naumoff. Prilukoff also intended to see to that.

Two Vienna private detectives were called in, on the pretext that the countess suspected Naumoff of some hostile designs against Kamarowski, and with Prilukoff they went to Venice to watch. As soon as the crime had been committed Naumoff was to be handed over to the Italian police.

Thus, from Prilukoff's point of view, two dangerous rivals would be gotten out of the way at one swoop. The countess would have the insurance money, two embarrassing lovers would be disposed of, and she and Prilukoff could marry—if, indeed, she had any intention of marrying a man whom, financially, she had sucked as dry as an orange.

Dr. Naumoff lost no time on his arrival at Venice. Immediately he arrived he went to Kamarowski's home, but, irresolute and faint, he turned away without taking any further step toward his purpose. The following day he steeled himself with vodka and went again to seek his rival.

From an inn facing Kamarowski's house, three men watched the infatuated man enter. They were Prilukoff and his detectives. None stirred to prevent him.

Meanwhile Kamarowski, fresh from bed and in his dressing gown, was facing his visitor. He threw out his arms for the customary embrace, and before he could realize what was happening, a steel-blue revolver came to a level in a shaking hand, and he dropped at the first shot. Four more bullets followed in rapid succession as he feebly tried to escape from the room. The stricken man moaned.

"My God, friend, why have you treated me thus?"

"Lest you should marry the Countess Tarnowska," retorted his assailant.

"Don't you know that I have a motherless boy who will now be without a father?"

The assailant, now in a state bordering on hysteria, dropped on his knees and implored forgiveness. The wounded man advised him to at once take flight. Naumoff turned the weapon on himself, but the sixth cartridge misfired. He hurled it passionately to a corner of the room. Leaning from the window he called for help, then he fled, tears streaming down his face, calling aloud, "Mamma, Mamma."

In this state of hysteria he reached his gondola and was rowed to the railway station, the gondoliers apparently being under the impression that he had merely been a witness to some tragedy of which they knew nothing. For some reason which is obscure, neither Prilukoff nor the private detectives made any attempt to carry out the scheme of handing him over to the authorities.

Kamarowski, seriously wounded, was taken to a hospital,

where his first thought was to telegraph the countess to come to his side. "Come, for the love of Heaven," he wired. But the woman paid no heed to this frantic appeal. She in turn wired Prilukoff for advice on what she should do, and he, replying from Trieste, asked her to meet him at Vienna.

Thither she went. But the murder trail had not been as cleverly covered as the conspirators thought. There were telegrams and other documentary evidence found at Kamarowski's house, and the Italian police were quick to move. Naumoff had been arrested in a few hours at Verona, and Prilukoff, the countess and Elise Perrier, her maid, were roped in at Vienna.

While they were in prison, Kamarowski, badly treated by one of the doctors attending him, died. It had been thought he was well on the way to recovery.

Italian law moved slowly. Although the murder occurred in September 1907, it was March 1910 before the accused were brought before the Court of Assize in Venice for trial. Naumoff was accused of murder, the countess and Prilukoff of having instigated the crime, and Perrier of complicity. At the preliminary investigations all had made varying statements. The two men swore that they were acting under the hypnotic influence of the woman, while the countess threw the greater part of the blame on the shoulders of Prilukoff. Only Elise Perrier remained faithful—to her mistress, whom she tried to shield by every means in her power.

Prilukoff, while awaiting trial, several times attempted suicide by strangulation, by poison, by opening his veins. Only the vigilance of the warders preserved his life. Many plots for the escape of the countess were frustrated, and bribery was tried in vain.

For nearly three months the trial proceeded, with days of fierce drama and hours of tense emotion. It became something of a fashionable spectacle, and even Italian royalty attended.

Accusations were hurled by the prisoners against each other, and they vigorously gave each other the lie. In the end, by the light of the sentence inflicted, Prilukoff was adjudged to be the villain of the piece. He was sent to ten years' solitary confinement. Tarnowska, beautiful, fascinating butterfly, was sent to eat her heart out in prison for eight years and four months. Naumoff, the poor infatuated dupe, got three years and one month. The maid, Perrier, was given a minor sentence.

And with the clang of the prison doors ended the career of perhaps the most astonishing adventuress of modern times.

XV

Rattenbury and Stoner

F. Tennyson Jesse

When a lady of standing has healthy female desires and her gentleman husband has but money and memories, then certain discreet marital arrangements can be made. In the case of the Rattenburys, the adjustment was an anxious young chauffeur-handyman on the brink of sexual awakening. But few things are as serious—and even sacred—to youth as sexual initiation. For Stoner, the young man, sex quickly became love, and love soon became a matter of life and death.

ON September 25, 1934, the following advertisement appeared in the *Bournemouth Daily Echo:* "Daily willing lad, 14–18, for housework. Scout-trained preferred."

This advertisement had been inserted by a Mrs. Rattenbury, of Villa Madeira, Manor Park Road, and was answered by a youth named George Percy Stoner. Since he was old enough to drive a car and his previous employment had been in a garage, he was engaged as chauffeur-handyman.

On Monday, May 27, 1935, Alma Victoria Rattenbury and George Percy Stoner were charged at the central criminal court with the murder of the woman's husband, Francis Mawson Rattenbury. Both the accused pleaded not guilty. Mrs. Rattenbury was 38 years old, and Stoner had attained the age of 18 in November 1934. Mrs. Rattenbury and Stoner had become lovers soon after Stoner was taken into Mr. Rattenbury's employ.

Both Mr. and Mrs. Rattenbury had been previously married; he once, and she twice. Mr. Rattenbury had a grown son, and Mrs. Rattenbury a little boy named Christopher, born in 1922. The marriage of Francis Rattenbury and Alma Victoria took place about 1928, and a boy, John, was born a year later. Since the birth of this child, Mr. and Mrs. Rattenbury had not lived together as husband and wife. Mr. Rattenbury was 67 years old and not young for his age. He was an architect of distinction and had lived most of his working life in Canada, but when he retired in 1928, he and his wife came to live in England. Eventually they took a little white house called Villa Madeira in Bournemouth on a pleasant suburban road near the sea, shaded by pines. A companion-helper, Miss Irene Riggs, came to live with them. Little John went to school, but came home every weekend, and Christopher, the child of Mrs. Rattenbury's second marriage, spent his holidays at Villa Madeira.

When Stoner was first employed at Villa Madeira he lived at home and went to his work by day, but in November he took up his residence in the house. He had become Mrs. Rattenbury's lover before that.

On the night of Sunday, March 24, 1935, Mr. Rattenbury was attacked from behind as he sat sleeping in an armchair in the drawing room. It was never in dispute that the weapon employed was a carpenter's mallet, which Stoner had fetched from his grandfather's house that afternoon.

The events that night, as they first were made known, were as follows:

Mrs. Rattenbury declared that at about ten-thirty, after she had gone to bed, she heard a groan from the room below; that she went downstairs and found her husband in the easy chair, unconscious, with blood flowing from his head. She called Irene Riggs, her companion-maid, and told her to telephone for Dr. O'Donnell, who was her doctor. Dr. O'Donnell arrived and found Mrs. Rattenbury very drunk and Mr. Rattenbury unconscious and bleeding, as Mrs. Rattenbury had described. Mrs. Rattenbury said, "Look at him—look at the blood—someone has finished him."

Dr. O'Donnell telephoned for a well-known surgeon, who, when he arrived, found it impossible to examine the patient as Mrs. Rattenbury was very drunk and excitable and kept getting in his way. The patient was removed to Strathallen Nursing Home by ambulance. After Mr. Rattenbury's head had been shaved in the operating theater, the surgeon and Dr. O'Donnell saw three serious wounds that could not have been self-inflicted and accordingly they communicated with the police.

The surgeon operated on Mr. Rattenbury, and Dr. O'Donnell, between 3:30 and 4:00 A.M., returned to Villa Madeira. He found Mrs. Rattenbury running about extremely intoxicated, four or five police officers in the house (some of whom she was trying to kiss), the radio-gramophone playing and all the lights on. He gave Mrs. Rattenbury half a grain of morphia and put her to bed. During the hours of progressive drunkenness Mrs. Rattenbury had kept on making statements to the effect that she had killed her husband. The next morning she repeated her assertions in a slightly varied form and she was taken to the Bournemouth Police Station and charged with doing grievous bodily harm with intent to murder. When she was charged Mrs. Rattenbury said, "That is right—I did it deliberately, and would do it again."

In most criminal trials the pattern is set at the beginning and merely strengthens as the trial progresses. In the Rattenbury case the evidence—which seemed so damning on the first day—completely altered in character, and the whole complex pattern shifted and changed, much as the pattern of sand changes when it is shaken. Like sand, it slipped away between the fingers, leaving a residue of grains of truth very different from the pile the prosecution had originally built up. But still, that worst of all Anglo-Saxon attitudes, a contemptuous condemnation of the man and woman (but more particularly the woman) unfortunate enough to be found out in sexual delinquency, never had finer scope than was provided by the Rattenbury case.

Mrs. Rattenbury, was born Alma Victoria Clark in British Columbia, was extremely talented musically and a fine pianist. She grew to young womanhood just before World War I, already well known in western Canada as a musician, and although she was not pretty in the usual sense, she was very attractive to men. She had a pale face with a beautiful egglike line of the jaw, dark-gray eyes and a mouth with a very full lower lip. She was a *femme aux hommes*—that is, although she had women friends and was a generous, easy, kindly, sentimental creature, she was first and foremost a woman to attract men and be attracted by them. She first married a young Englishman named Caledon Dolly, who joined the Canadian forces at the outbreak of war and was transferred to England. She followed him and obtained employment in Whitehall. She was very devoted to her husband, but he was killed in action. This was the only completely happy relationship with a man which Alma was ever to know. She joined a Scottish nursing unit, became a transport driver and worked hard throughout the war. After the armistice she married for the second time. She married this second husband—whose wife divorced him, citing Alma Victoria Dolly—in 1921, and the child of that union was born the following year. The marriage was unhappy, and she returned to the house of an aunt in Victoria. There she met Mr. Rattenbury. Mr. Rattenbury was married himself at the time, but fell very much in love with Alma Victoria, and his wife divorced him, citing her. At this time Mr. Rattenbury was about 60 years of age, and Mrs. Rattenbury 31. They went to England to settle in Bournemouth.

Mrs. Rattenbury was a highly sexed woman, and six years of being deprived of sexual satisfaction had weighed on her heavily. But in spite of the urgency of her desires, which must have tormented her, she had not, as far as is known, had a lover since the birth of little John. She certainly had had none the four years she had lived in Bournemouth, and she had no abnormal tendencies. She was fond of her husband in a friendly fashion and he was devoted to her, very interested in her song writing and anxious for her to succeed. Miss Riggs, one of my informants, also said that Mrs. Rattenbury was very kind to her husband, that she was, indeed, kind to everyone.

The household was not an unhappy one, but neither was it

happy. For one thing, Mrs. Rattenbury was a gregarious creature, and her husband was of an unsociable frame of mind.
He knew hardly anyone of his own station in life, except Dr.
O'Donnell and Mr. Jenks, a retired barrister who had an estate
at Bridport. But Mrs. Rattenbury was different than her husband; she had that lavish, easy friendliness which one associates
with music-hall artists, and she could not live without affection.
When she made a friend of Irene Riggs, she did so because it
was her nature to be friendly with people who surrounded her.
Irene Riggs, on her side, was devoted to her employer, in spite
of the latter's impatient temper. Any little outing to London,
any treat, such as going to the theater, Mrs. Rattenbury shared
with Irene Riggs, and the girl remained attached to the woman
who remained in her memory as the kindest person she ever
met, who helped anyone in need that she came across. But
the chief devotion of Mrs. Rattenbury's life was for her children. She was a good and loving mother who thought nothing
too good for her children. There was nothing she would not
have done for them; she was forever occupying herself in practical ways for their welfare.

The Rattenburys lived peaceably as a rule, but sometimes
they had quarrels. These were about money; Mr. Rattenbury,
like a great many men, was generous in big matters, but difficult in small ones. Mrs. Rattenbury had very little money sense,
and her husband had every reason to fear her lavish spending.
He was frequently very depressed about financial matters and
he was apt, during his moods of depression, to threaten to
commit suicide. One day, in July 1934, he harped on this threat
at greater length than usual, and his wife lost her temper and
told him it was a pity that he did not do it instead of always talking about it. Mr. Rattenbury in his turn then lost his temper and
hit his wife, giving her a black eye. She sent for Dr. O'Donnell,
who found her very agitated and upset. Her husband had left
the house, and she feared that he really had gone to kill him-

self. Mr. Rattenbury did not, in fact, return till about two in the morning. Mrs. Rattenbury was by then so ill that Dr. O'Donnell injected a quarter of a grain of morphia, and she slept for 12 hours. After that, life went on as usual with the Rattenburys. She bore her husband no grudge for having struck her. She was a person of quick temper herself, but generous in making up. This was the only serious quarrel between the Rattenburys in four years.

Life might have gone on forever in the usual pedestrian fashion at Villa Madeira, but George Percy Stoner joined the household, and Mrs. Rattenbury fell in love with him. Stoner, except for his virility, was not a particularly interesting or attractive person. Indeed, lack of taste is one of the chief charges against Mrs. Rattenbury, both in her work and in her life. She was very uncontrolled emotionally. Her song lyrics were appalling. She was subject to drinking bouts, which added to her natural excitability. She had not scrupled, twice, to take other women's husbands away from them and she seems to have been, to use a slang phrase, a natural-born bad picker.

Yet, if love had meant for her nothing more than simple physical satisfaction, it would have deserted her when she stood in peril of her life. It did not, and neither did Stoner's love for her. Stoner refused to go into the witness box and told his counsel he did not deny having attacked Mr. Rattenbury. The woman for weeks insisted to her solicitor and counsel that she wished to take the blame in order to save Stoner. Her solicitor made it clear to her that if she lied her story would not stand the test of the witness box; that she would only hang herself without saving Stoner. But not till her son Christopher was sent to her in prison to plead with her to tell the truth did she give way. And afterward, in the witness box, she said as little against her lover as possible. Indeed, one of the most interesting points in this case is that it is the only one, as far as I am aware, where two people have been charged together in a capital offense and neither has abandoned the other in a scramble for safety. Milson and Fowler, Field and Gray, Gabrielle Bompard and Eyrand, Mr. and Mrs. Manning, Ruth Snyder and Judd Gray, to remember only a few at random, all tried to throw the blame on the partner in crime. Mrs. Rattenbury was willing and anxious to take the whole blame and would have hanged without a tremor if by so doing she could have saved Stoner.

Stoner had always been a quiet boy who did not make friends, but his quiet appearance concealed stormy adolescent yearnings. He had the dramatic instincts natural to the young, and, unfortunately, circumstances thrust him into real drama before he could tell the difference between what was real and what was make-believe. Physically he was very passionate, and nothing in his mental training had equipped him to cope with the extraordinary life to which it had pleased Mrs. Rattenbury to call him.

Francis Rattenbury, that outwardly quiet man, is a pathetic figure in retrospect. Mr. Justice Humphreys referred to him as being "that very unpleasant character for which, I think, we have no suitable expression, but which the French call a *mari complaisant.* A man who knew that his wife was committing adultery, and had no objection to it." He was completely incurious. He lived not in the present but in regrets for the past and anxieties for the future. He was a man brilliant in his profession, with many excellent qualities, a quiet pleasant man whose finances worried him and whose emotional relationships had disappointed him. Every night he drank the best part of a bottle of whiskey. A man in his condition and of his age is apt to forget the power that the natural inclinations of the flesh had over him in youth and middle age and he may fail to realize that it is still a factor in the life of anyone else. As far as Mr. Rattenbury knew, he was a good husband to his wife. He admired her, was genuinely fond of her. In regard to his wife, his chief anxieties were financial, and after he started to take his prolonged nightcap each evening, the rest of the world existed very little for him. The passions, the jealousies of a decade earlier had ceased, not only in the present but even as a memory of the past. The chief tragedy in life is not what we are but what we have ceased to be. It is easy to say that a man who knows his wife is committing adultery and has no objection is not a nice character. But it is not necessarily the truth. It is possible for a man who no longer leads a normal life with his wife, to think of her not as his property but as a human being who belongs to herself and has a right to a normal life.

The learned judge, counsel on both sides and the British public assumed that because of her greater age Mrs. Rattenbury dominated her young lover. The actual truth is that there is no woman so under the domination of her lover as the older mistress of a very much younger man. The great Benjamin Franklin knew this, and there is extant a letter of advice written by him to a young man, which is a model of clear thinking. In it he writes:

But if you will not take this counsel [to marry] and persist in thinking a commerce with the sex inevitable, then I repeat my former advice, that in your amours you should prefer OLD WOMEN to YOUNG ONES. You call this a paradox, and demand reasons. They are these:

FIRST. Because they have more knowledge of the World . . . their conversation is more improving and more lastingly agreeable.

SECOND. Because when women cease to be handsome, they study to be good. . . . learn to do a thousand services, small and great, and are the most tender and useful of all friends . . . .

THIRD. . . . there is no hazard of children . . . .

FOURTH. Because, through more experience, they are more prudent and discreet in conducting an intrigue to prevent suspicion. . . .

FIFTH. Because . . . the face first grows lank and wrinkled, then the neck, then the breast and arms—the lower parts continuing to the last as plump as ever; so that, covering all above with a basket, and regarding only what is below the girdle, it is impossible of two women, to know an old from a young . . . and the pleasure of corporal enjoyment with an old woman is at least equal and frequently superior; every knack being, by practice, capable of improvement.

SIXTH. Because the sin is less. . . . debauching a virgin may make her life unhappy.

SEVEN. . . . having made a young girl miserable may give you frequent bitter reflections, none of which can attend the making an Old woman Happy.

EIGHTH and LASTLY. They are so grateful.

Once Stoner had become Mrs. Rattenbury's lover she worshiped him. It was before the consummation of her desire that she was the dominating character, and to that extent she was responsible for the whole tragedy, but to that extent only. She felt this responsibility deeply, and it was remorse as well as love that made her eager and willing to save Stoner even at the cost of her own life. She could not have known that Stoner would be wild with jealousy, but she should have known, had she paused to think, that a lad of Stoner's age and antecedents would lose all sense of values when he became the lover of his social superior, who dazzled him with a whole new mode of life.

Mrs. Rattenbury was a good witness, and in nothing more notably so than in her simple acceptance of the values of life as she knew it.

"You have told us that on Sunday night Stoner came into your bedroom and got into bed with you. Was that something that happened frequently?" asked Mr. Croom-Johnson.

"Oh, yes," replied Mrs. Rattenbury simply.

And later on: "Did it occur to you that if you went to Bridport, Mr. Rattenbury might want to treat you as his wife?"

"No, if I had thought it was going to happen like that I would never have suggested going."

"It never occurred to you?"

"No."

"You know what I mean by saying 'treat you as his wife'?"

"Yes, exactly," replied Mrs. Rattenbury, as though mildly surprised that there could be any mistake about it.

Irene Riggs was not as happy after Stoner's arrival as she had been before. Mrs. Rattenbury told her about the liaison, and Irene was too fond of her to blame her, but nevertheless she felt uneasy about the affair. Though Miss Riggs and Stoner did not like each other, they got on together well enough. Miss Riggs stayed behind when on March 19 Mrs. Rattenbury arranged to take Stoner with her on a trip to London, because Stoner was very jealous of any third person. Thus the charm of the little friendly expeditions that had been the highlights in Irene Rigg's life before the coming of Stoner was gone. In London Mrs. Rattenbury and Stoner stayed at the Royal Palace Hotel, Kensington, and spent their days shopping and going about London. Mrs. Rattenbury explained the trip to her husband by saying she was going to have an operation (she had had several minor operations in the preceding years), and he gave her the generous sum of £250 for this purpose. Mrs. Rattenbury used a large part of this sum to pay outstanding housekeeping bills; the rest she spent wildly upon the London trip and presents for Stoner. The importance of the expedition to London lies in the fact that for four or five days Stoner was accepted by the little world about him as Mrs. Rattenbury's social equal. He did not go to the Royal Palace Hotel as her chauffeur but as her brother. He had free access to his mistress. He was called "Sir" by the servants, and every day Mrs. Rattenbury bought him presents which to his simple mind must have appeared equivalent to Danae's golden shower. Crepe-de-chine pajamas and a made-to-measure suit must have seemed to the young man, who was a laborer's son, most exciting luxuries.

Mrs. Rattenbury affected no superiority with anyone in humbler circumstances of life than her own, and Mr. Rattenbury had lived for years of his life in the democratic country where Mrs. Rattenbury was born. Stoner often played cards with him in the evening, and Mr. Rattenbury, Stoner and Miss Riggs took their meals together. Therefore, merely to have returned to Villa Madeira, to continue its pleasant, easy life, would not necessarily have upset Stoner. But this was not exactly what happened. The lovers arrived back late on Friday evening. Mr. Rattenbury, already having imbibed his nightcap, asked no questions. Even next day, according to Mrs. Rattenbury, he never inquired about the operation his wife had ostensibly been to London to undergo. Saturday found him in one of his worst fits of depression. A scheme for building some flats, of which he was to have been the architect, was being held up, and Mrs. Rattenbury tried in vain to cheer him up.

On Sunday Mr. Rattenbury was still more depressed. In the morning Mrs. Rattenbury took him for a drive. After lunch he slept. They had tea together, little John with them. Mr. Rattenbury had been reading a book, a novel in which there was a perfect holocaust of suicides, and according to Mrs. Rattenbury he expressed his admiration for anyone who had the courage to put an end to himself. Mrs. Rattenbury suggested that she should ring up their friend Mr. Jenks at Bridport and ask whether they could go over on Monday. She did indeed telephone, and Mr. Jenks said he would be pleased to see them and asked them to spend the night, an invitation which they accepted. The telephone was in Mr. Rattenbury's bedroom, which opened off the drawing room, but Stoner came into the bedroom and overheard the arrangements Mrs. Rattenbury was making. He was frightfully angry and threatened her with an air pistol. He told her that he would kill her if she and her husband went to Bridport. He accused her of having had sexual relations with her husband that afternoon—an accusation entirely baseless—and said that if the Bridport plan were carried out he would refuse to drive. Stoner said that at

Mr. Jenks's house the Rattenburys would have to share a bedroom, but Mrs. Rattenbury assured him that would not be so, that Mr. Jenks had two guest rooms. Stoner, though he appeared pacified, continued to brood over the matter. At about eight o'clock that evening he went to the house of his grandparents, and sat and chatted, apparently normally, with his grandmother for some time. It was then that he borrowed the carpenter's mallet.

That same evening Mrs. Rattenbury sat and played cards with her husband, kissed him good-night and went upstairs. It was Irene's evening out, and Mrs. Rattenbury passed the time by getting together her things for Bridport. Irene came in at about ten-fifteen and went straight to her room. Some ten minutes later she went out to go to the lavatory and found Stoner leaning over the banister at the head of the stairs, looking down. She said, "What is the matter?" He replied, "Nothing, I was looking to see if the lights were out." Half an hour after that Stoner came and slipped into Mrs. Rattenbury's bed. He seemed very agitated and upset. She said, "What is the matter, darling?" He replied that he was in trouble, but that he could not tell her what it was about. She replied that he must tell her, that she was strong enough to bear anything, and he then said, "You won't be going to Bridport tomorrow." He went on to say that he had hurt "Ratz." He said that he had hit him over the head with a mallet, which he had since hidden in the garden. "I thought," Mrs. Rattenbury said in court, "he was frightened at what he had done, because he had hurt Mr. Rattenbury. . . . I thought he'd just hurt him badly enough to prevent him going to Bridport, and when I said 'I'll go and see him,' he said, 'No, you must not; the sight will upset you,' and I thought all I had to do was to fix Ratz up, and that would put him all right."

It may be that this was the only idea in Stoner's unbalanced and ill-educated mind, but that he found it impossible to stop after the first blow. Or it may be that in his disturbed and jealous state he would have done anything sooner than allow the Bridport trip to take place. Whichever, directly the sense of what Stoner was telling her penetrated to Mrs. Rattenbury's mind, she jumped out of bed and ran downstairs. A minute later Irene Riggs, who had not yet fallen asleep, heard her mistress shrieking for her. Miss Riggs ran downstairs and found Mr. Rattenbury leaning back in an armchair, as though he were asleep. There was a large pool of blood on the floor, and one of his eyes was very swollen and discolored. Mrs. Rattenbury asked Irene to telephone for the doctor at once, telling her to hurry and, to use Miss Riggs's own expression, went "raving about the house." "Oh! Poor Ratz. Poor Ratz!" she kept repeating. "Can't somebody do something?" Mrs. Rattenbury drank some whiskey; she was violently sick, and drank more whiskey. She kept on telling Miss Riggs to wipe up the blood because, she said, little John must not see any blood. Her first thought was for her husband, her second for little John. Her third was for Stoner, and this thought persisted, and deepened in intensity, during the hours that followed.

Dr. O'Donnell arrived at Villa Madeira at about 11:45, in answer to the telephone call. Mrs. Rattenbury was already very drunk. The surgeon arrived about five minutes after midnight. They took Mr. Rattenbury to the nursing home, shaved his head and discovered the three wounds, which were obviously the result of external violence and of three separate blows. Dr. O'Donnell telephoned the police.

It was half an hour before the constable arrived. The constable then said he must get an inspector, and at about 3:15 A.M. Inspector Mills, who had already been at Villa Madeira, arrived. At 3:30 Inspector Mills, the surgeon and Dr. O'Donnell left the nursing home. Stoner was sleeping peacefully outside in the Rattenbury car and he drove Dr. O'Donnell back to Villa Madeira following the police car.

When Dr. O'Donnell got out of the car he was struck by the fact that every light in Villa Madeira was on, the door was open, and the radio-gramophone was playing. There were four police officers in the house. Mrs. Rattenbury was by now extremely drunk. A constable, who had arrived at 3:00, had observed then that Mrs. Rattenbury was under the influence of alcohol.

At 3:30, according to Dr. O'Donnell, Mrs. Rattenbury was past knowing what she was thinking or saying. Dr. O'Donnell, very shocked, turned off the radio-gramophone and tried to explain to Mrs. Rattenbury the gravity of her husband's condition, but she could not take in what he was saying. Inspector Mills said to her, "Your husband has been seriously injured and is now in the nursing home." To which Mrs. Rattenbury replied, "Will that be against me?" Then she made a statement: "I did it. He has lived too long. I will tell you in the morning where the mallet is. Have you told the coroner yet? I shall make a better job of it next time. Irene does not know. I have made a proper muddle of it. I thought I was strong enough."

Dr. O'Donnell, who considered that Mrs. Rattenbury was unable to understand what was said to her, or to know what she was saying, pointed out that she was in no fit condition to be asked anything and took her up to bed. He administered half a grain of morphia—a large dose—and went downstairs again. After a few minutes he went into the sitting room and found that Mrs. Rattenbury had managed to get downstairs again and was again being questioned by the police. Inspector Mills said to her, "Do you suspect anyone?" and she replied, "Yes. I think so. His son."

Dr. O'Donnell, who was aware that Mr. Rattenbury's son was abroad, knew that Mrs. Rattenbury had no idea of what she was saying and he said to the inspector, "Look at her condition—she is full of whiskey, and I have just given her a large dose of morphia. She is in no condition to make any statement." He then took her by the arm and helped her upstairs again. Then (it was by now after 4:00 A.M.), Dr. O'Donnell went home.

Another police official, Inspector Carter, decided that Mrs. Rattenbury—who had been drinking steadily from about 11:00 P.M. till 3:30 A.M. (quite undeterred by the police), and who had then been given half a grain of morphia—was competent to make a statement by 8:15 in the morning! He wrote her words in his notebook:

"About nine P.M. on the 24th March I was playing cards with my husband when he dared me to kill him, as he wanted to die. I picked up a mallet and he then said: 'You have not the guts to do it!' I then hit him with the mallet. I hid the mallet outside. I would have shot him if I had had a gun."

Inspector Carter deposed that Mrs. Rattenbury had read the statement over aloud and clearly and had then signed it. He then took her to Bournemouth Police Station, where she was charged. Before she left the house she had a moment alone with Miss Riggs and said, "You must get Stoner to give me the mallet." Even in her befogged condition there was one thread of continuity—a desire to help Stoner and to get hold of the mallet with which he told her he had hit Mr. Rattenbury, and which he had then hidden in the garden.

Mrs. Rattenbury was not used to drugs; she had, indeed, a horror of them, and the only time previously in her life that any had been administered to her was when Dr. O'Donnell in July 1934 had administered a quarter of a grain of morphia, when she was ill and excited. On that occasion she was allowed to sleep it off, and she had indeed slept for some 12 hours. When the stronger dose of half a grain of morphia was given to her on the night of Sunday, March 24, she had no chance of sleep. Villa Madeira is a tiny house, and Stoner and the police were up and down and about it all night long. Anyone who has had to have morphia knows that if he is not allowed to sleep off the effects his condition will be far worse than if the drug had never been administered. This was the case with Mrs. Rattenbury, and according to medical testimony she still was suffering from the effects of the morphia three days later. Many people felt that even if Mrs. Rattenbury did not know what she was saying when she was drunk and when she was drugged, what she said came from her subconscious self and hence was true. This is an error, as any doctor knows. What does come through all her statements, if they are carefully analyzed, is her anxiety for Stoner and her wish to take the blame. Another strong point for the defense, besides the undoubted one that Mrs. Rattenbury was quite unfit to make statements, was the complete blank in her memory when she emerged from her drugged state into ordinary consciousness at Holloway Prison. Mrs. Rattenbury remembered nothing from the time when she began to drink after discovering her wounded husband until March 28 at Holloway Prison. The result of the morphia's effect being thwarted was that she stayed "out" for a very long time. She knew nothing about the interrogations, nothing about the injection of morphia, nothing about the police matron who tended her. She did not remember being taken away from Villa Madeira by the police. The only things that swam up at all in her recollection were Stoner's farewell kiss in her room and the face of little John at her door. It is natural for the layman to feel that loss of memory is a convenient defense, but Mrs. Rattenbury could not have deceived the highly trained and astute medical experts who examined her.

Stoner and Miss Riggs were left in the house at Manor Road, but Miss Riggs had no intention of being left alone with Stoner. She knew that Mrs. Rattenbury was innocent: One of Mrs. Rattenbury's most striking characteristics was her horror of cruelty; she could not have hurt anything. Therefore, Irene Riggs thought that either a burglar had broken in, or that

Stoner must have been Mr. Rattenbury's assailant. Her mother and brother moved into Villa Madeira to stay with her.

Irene Riggs still felt herself the custodian of Mrs. Rattenbury's secret love affair and she never discussed it, even with her relations. Although not a Catholic, she went to see a priest, because she knew that what she told a priest would be safe. She came back at about ten-thirty Wednesday night, and her mother opened the door to her. Mrs. Riggs told her that Stoner was very drunk, that he had been going up and down the road shouting, "Mrs. Rattenbury is in jail, and I've put her there." He had been brought back by two taxi drivers. Irene Riggs telephoned the police, and two plainclothes men arrived. Stoner was in bed and seemed very drunk, which was unusual for him; he not only never drank himself, but objected to Mrs. Rattenbury drinking and had had a good influence on her in this respect.

On the morning of Thursday, March 28, Dr. O'Donnell called at Villa Madeira. Irene Riggs opened the door. Up to then it had always been Stoner who had opened it. Dr. O'Donnell asked where Stoner was, and she told him that he had gone to Holloway to see Mrs. Rattenbury. Dr. O'Donnell then said that Mrs. Rattenbury was the best mistress that Miss Riggs had ever had, or that she was ever likely to have, and if there was anything she could tell the police, it was her duty to do so. Poor Miss Riggs, still loyal to her employer, said she could not let Mrs. Rattenbury's secret out, but Dr. O'Donnell, who, you will recall, knew of the affair, very sensibly said that a secret was nothing when a life was at stake. He asked Miss Riggs whether she thought Mrs. Rattenbury had murdered her husband, and Irene Riggs replied, "I know she did not do it." Dr. O'Donnell asked her how she knew, and she replied that Stoner had confessed it to her. He had also told her that there would be no fingerprints on the mallet, as he had worn gloves. Dr. O'Don-

nell rang up the Bournemouth Police Station and said that Miss
Riggs wished to make a statement and that Stoner had confessed to her. Dr. O'Donnell added that Stoner had left for
London and that no time should be lost in taking Irene Riggs's
statement. At two-thirty the police arrived, and Irene Riggs
told them what she knew. Stoner was arrested at the station
on his return to Bournemouth that evening, and this time the
charge was murder, for Mr. Rattenbury had died.

The very fact that both Stoner and Mrs. Rattenbury refused
to implicate each other was a source of great difficulty to their
defenders. During the trial Stoner sat unmoving in his corner
of the dock, with his elbow on the ledge and his cheek on his
hand. His eyes were downcast and his face remained immovable. Mrs. Rattenbury also was perfectly calm, but it was a
frozen, not an apathetic, calm. Her physical aspect changed
in a curious manner. By Friday she looked 20 years older than
she had on Monday. On the last day even her hands changed
color and were a livid greenish-white. She was an excellent witness. Her voice was low and rich. She gave a great impression
of truthfulness and she was astonishingly self-controlled. Only
a nervous tic in the side of her face, which jerked perpetually,
betrayed the tension of her mind. R. Lewis-Manning, her solicitor, was certain that she was not pretending when for several
weeks she insisted that she would not implicate Stoner, pre-
ferring to hang rather than see him come to any harm. She had
immense courage. It was the thought of her children, of what a
fearful heritage would be theirs if she were found guilty, that
eventually made her tell the truth.

Mrs. Rattenbury's counsel told the court: "I am not here to
condone, still less to commend, her conduct. I am not here to
cast one stone against that wretched boy whose position there
in the dock may be due to folly and self-indulgence on her part,
to which he fell a victim. . . ." He went on to say of Stoner,
"Can you doubt seduced; raised out of his sphere; taken away

to London; given a very high time there; a lad who was melodramatic and went about with a dagger, violent sometimes, impulsive, jealous, his first love; a lad whose antecedents had been
quiet, whose associations had been prosaic; never mixed with
girls; flung into the vortex of this illicit love. You may as moral
men and women, as citizens, condemn her in your souls for the
part she has played in raising this position. She will bear to her
grave the brand of reprobation, and men and women will know
how she has acted. That will be her sorrow and her disgrace
so long as she lives. You may think of Mrs. Rattenbury as a
woman, self-indulgent and willful, who by her own acts and
folly had erected in this poor young man a Frankenstein of
jealousy which she could not control."

Consider these people as we know them through the medium
of the trial. Mrs. Rattenbury had a kind husband who allowed
her to live her own life. She had a young and ardent lover who
satisfied her emotionally and physically. She had two children
to whom she was passionately devoted. She was being supported well. She was, as she rather pathetically said in evidence,
"happy then." For her husband she had a maternal affection—
it must be remembered that in all her loves Mrs. Rattenbury
was essentially maternal. She spoiled and protected Stoner; she
adored her children; she comforted her husband; she tried to
give Irene Riggs as good a life as possible; she was kind to
every stranger who came within her gates. The one thing that
would have been impossible to Mrs. Rattenbury, passionate as
she was, would have been to have taken part in harming
another human being.

The unfortunate Stoner, with a much simpler experience of
life and with that adolescent urge to heroics, could not see that
there was no need for any drama of jealousy at all. The boun-
dary line between drama and reality was obscure for him, and
living entirely in an unintelligent world of crude emotion, he

hit out almost blindly. And this gesture, conceived in an unreal world, materialized in a world of actual facts.

The jury was out for 47 minutes and they returned the only possible verdict: They found Mrs. Rattenbury not guilty and Stoner guilty, adding a recommendation for mercy. Mrs. Rattenbury stood immovable while the verdict of not guilty was returned, but when the foreman of the jury pronounced the word *guilty* in respect to Stoner, she gave a little moan and put out her hand. She was led away, and Stoner received his sentence—a judgment of death—without flinching. [This was later commuted to penal servitude.] He was then taken below, and Mrs. Rattenbury was brought back to plead to the accusation of being an accessory after the fact. She could not speak; her mouth moved a little without sound, and that was all. The clerk of the court informed the jury that the prisoner had pleaded not guilty. The prosecution said that they proposed to offer no evidence, and Mr. Justice Humphreys instructed the jury to return a verdict of not guilty, which they did. Mrs. Rattenbury was discharged.

Unfortunately there is a self-righteous custom in the courts to animadvert upon the moral qualities, or lack of them, in a person accused of a crime. I am, of course, using the word *moral* merely in the only sense Anglo-Saxons seem to use it, with reference to sexual morality. Mrs. Rattenbury, at the time the learned judge was making his remarks about her moral character, was a woman at the extreme edge of what it was possible to bear and go on living. But she had to listen to the dread voice of the judge as he said, "Members of the jury, having heard her learned counsel, having regard to the facts of this case, it may be that you will say that you cannot possibly feel any sympathy for that woman; you cannot have any feeling except disgust for her."

We are often told that a criminal court is not a court of

morals, but in this trial apparently it was. Mrs. Rattenbury was
in some ways a vulgar and silly woman, but she was a generous,
kindly, lavish creature, capable of great self-sacrifice. She was
innocent of the crime of which, entirely on the strength of her
own drunken maunderings, she was accused, but her life was
handed back to her in such a shape that it was of no use to
her. That out of such sad and unpromising material Alma
Rattenbury had created something that to her was beautiful
and made her happy was unforgivable to the people of England.
People—that dread judgment bar of daily life—would always
say, "Of course she told him to do it. And anyway she was a
dreadful woman."

Such was the judgment of society on Mrs. Rattenbury, and
she knew it.

Her husband's relatives took her away, but the press be-
sieged the flat where they gave her refuge. The doctor who had
been called in to attend her removed her to a nursing home,
pursued by newspapermen. She was by now very ill, physically
and mentally, and in her fear and grief for Stoner, in her
misery for her children, in her remorse and shame, she wanted
to be alone. She left the nursing home, and what she did during
the nightmare hours that followed we only know from the
tragedy that followed. She must have bought a knife and taken
a train down to that part of the world where she had been
happy in what was stigmatized as an "adulterous intercourse."
And there, beside the placid waters of a little stream, she sat
and wrote, feverishly and passionately, on the backs of enve-
lopes and odd bits of paper. She referred to the assumption
that she dominated Stoner and declared that no one could
dominate him; that whatever he wanted to do he always did.
She repeated that if she had not been made to tell the truth
she would never have given Stoner away. She complained
about the press dogging her footsteps and she wrote of the
scathing attack on her character. How, indeed, was it possible

for her ever to make a home for her little boys, to watch them at play, to invite other children to play with them?

She must have known it would be worse for her children if she lived than if she died. Her writing finished, she thrust the knife six times into her breast. The blade penetrated her heart thrice, and she fell forward into the water, dead.

When an ancient Roman killed himself, he inserted the tip of the sword between two ribs, and fell upon it; he called it "falling upon the sword." He knew that the shrinking of the flesh was such that it was almost impossible to drive a knife steadily into the breast.

Mrs. Rattenbury drove it in six times.

XVI

A Slight Case of Frigidity

Dorothy Kilgallen

Dr. Bernard Finch said that he had a frigid wife. A man named Billy Hoover said that *he* had a frigid wife, too. Masters and Johnson aside, both these men were wrong; Billy Hoover's wife Carole, as it turned out, was far from frigid with Dr. Finch, and Finch's wife Barbara was fiery hot to prove it. In the end Barbara did prove it—to a judge, to a jury, to the nation. But, unfortunately, Barbara's proof was in the premature ejaculation of her husband's gun, and her victory was, regrettably, posthumous.

O<small>N</small> February 26, 1961, Carole Tregoff received a letter from Dr. Bernard Finch. In it he told her of his undying love, his thoughts about their future together, of how he considered her the most wonderful girl he had ever known. It was an anniversary letter, he said, for it celebrated the very first time they had lunched four years before.

Both Dr. Finch and Carole Tregoff were serving life sentences in California penitentiaries.

Carole had been introduced to Finch three weeks after she was hired as a receptionist at the West Covina Medical Center in Los Angeles. Finch and his brother-in-law were partners in the Center and had borrowed a quarter of a million dollars to set it up. When Finch met Carole he said hello and that was that for about seven months.

Carole, 18 when the employment agency sent her to be interviewed, was tall, redheaded, extremely pretty, with an outstanding figure. She was married to Billy Hoover, whom she had first dated in high school. The marriage wasn't working.

Dr. Finch at 40 had a lucrative surgical practice, was a ranking tennis amateur and had a winning way with the ladies. The home in which he and his wife lived, with their small son and her young daughter by a previous marriage, was quite elegant. They each had a car—he a Cadillac, she a Chrysler. They had a dog. And they had a lovely young Swedish girl to take care of the two children and help around the house.

After seven months as a receptionist, Carole became secretary to Dr. Finch. From time to time members of the staff would lunch together, but it wasn't until another seven months had passed that Finch asked Carole to lunch with him. By then Carole could more than sense the mutual attraction between them. She was in love with the doctor.

The luncheon, on February 26, 1957, led to dinner later in the week. The dinner led to six hours of agreeable conversation, which led to Carole's arrival at home at 4:15 A.M., which led to a battle with her husband. At that point, Carole said later, she stopped all sexual relations with Billy Hoover, which was no more than any right-thinking, virtuous wife would do.

During the next few weeks Carole and the doctor found the blips on their personal radar screen clearly on a collision course. Neither wanted to avoid it. For a while they lunched and dined most decorously. Finch was an old hand at this game, so there were no cramped clutches in the back of an automobile, no furtive slinking in and out of motels. They both were tenderly teasing each other; she with a show of shyness, he with a semblance of manly gentleness and patience.

In due time Dr. Finch suggested, quite reasonably, that if they found a little apartment they could be together more frequently and in greater comfort. Even then, after an apartment had been rented in the name of Mr. and Mrs. George Evans, a month went by—if you can believe Carole—before they surrendered to the inevitable. Après that, le déluge!

During their trial Dr. Finch testified that for a year and a half, in that apartment and in another to which they later moved, he and Carole met at lunchtime daily, and very often early in the morning and at cocktail time as well! One had only to look at luscious Carole to realize that the doctor's spectacular performance owed something to her inspiration.

All this time, or at least whenever they had a chance to catch their breaths, they talked over plans for the future. It was decided that each would seek a divorce. Finch would have to wait a little, because he felt a divorce at that time would create problems with the financing of the Medical Center, affect his practice and, above all, require him at a most awkward moment to share his fortune with Barbara under California's community-property laws.

He had long since explained to Carole his version of the arrangement under which he and Barbara maintained a front to their broken marriage. They continued to live under one roof, sharing everything except conjugal rights. Barbara, he said, had been sexually frigid since the birth of their son a few years before. They had agreed that their private lives could be lived as each saw fit, as long as one did nothing to embarrass the other.

Not long after Finch had rented the first love nest in Monterey Park, his wife, driving by, had seen him emerge from a store with a bag of groceries cradled in one arm and Carole draped on the other. They waved at each other. When Finch got home he said he'd only been performing a neighborly good deed, helping Carole with her shopping.

On September 9, 1958, Barbara telephoned Billy Hoover and blew the whistle on Carole. Billy was stunned. The idea that Carole might be unfaithful to him had never entered his mind. Her coldness, he believed (unwittingly echoing Dr. Finch), was the result of sexual frigidity. All he could say to Barbara Finch, he later testified, was to ask why she didn't divorce the doctor. Her answer was brief and to the point. When she was ready she could, under the law, get a better than 50-percent property settlement if she could prove adultery.

When Carole got home that day Billy broke the news to her with a slap in the mouth. This destroyed Carole's faith in the sanctity of marriage, and she moved out the next day, never to return. Her father and his wife made room for her, at least for the time she wasn't with Dr. Finch.

A few days went by, and then Billy Hoover showed up at the Medical Center to see Dr. Finch. Finch denied that there was any substance to Barbara's accusations. But Carole filed for divorce.

Finch feathered another little nest for his love, and they moved there soon after the confrontation with Billy Hoover.

In January 1959 Barbara Finch began talking to an attorney, Joseph Forno, about a divorce. She also employed private detectives to follow the doctor and Carole to collect evidence of adultery. Finch became aware of this in April.

On May 16 Barbara called the lawyer and told him that the doctor had struck her with a pistol the night before, opening a wound over her eye that required several stitches. (The stitching was done by Finch at his hospital. He claimed she had fallen against a table.) Barbara went to Forno's office, where the wound was photographed. Barbara frequently said that she was in mortal fear of Bernie Finch.

On May 20 divorce papers were filed against Finch, including a petition for division of community property, alimony, and support for six-year-old Raymond Bernard Finch, Jr. Barbara's private eyes hadn't gotten enough evidence of adultery against the doctor; the divorce action merely cited "extreme cruelty."

The next day, May 21, Barbara also sought a restraining order that would forbid the doctor to molest her in any way, directly or indirectly. It also prevented him from withdrawing or disposing of any funds or property. She included in the request a statement that on May 15 the doctor had done her bodily harm and had threatened her life. To Finch, who was reputed to be worth about three-quarters of a million dollars, it meant that he couldn't touch a penny without Barbara's consent. At the same time Finch was ordered to pay $2000 in counsel fees, $500 in court costs and $200-a-month alimony.

Back at the love nest, there had been a change in plans. After Dr. Finch had been served with the papers, Carole decided that perhaps it might be wiser if she removed herself from the scene until the dust of battle had settled. On May 26 she moved to Las Vegas, staying first with friends and then moving to an apartment that she and Finch located and for which he paid the rent. To occupy her time she got a job as a cocktail waitress. When Finch wasn't busy, he visited Carole.

On the evening of July 18 Finch and Carole drove Carole's car to the country club near the Finch home and parked. They walked to the house, which was on a rise just above the home of Finch's father. The garage was empty. They waited. About 11:15 Barbara drove up and into the garage. Finch went in after her. Barbara began screaming for help. The young Swedish maid ran out of the house and into the garage. There was a shot. Then Barbara came dashing out of the garage and down the incline toward her father-in-law's house. Finch ran after her. There was another shot. Barbara started down some wooden steps, then fell in a heap at the bottom. The maid by that time had run to the house and called the police.

The police found Barbara dead, shot in the back. Neither Finch nor Carole were anywhere to be seen, although Carole swore she was actually hiding in the shrubbery during the time the police, detectives and doctors were all over the place. Finch had taken off immediately after the shooting, stolen one car and then another and made his way to Las Vegas, where he went to bed in Carole's apartment. Carole drove herself back after everyone had left the Finch home.

Finch was arrested next day in Las Vegas. He coolly explained that he could not have murdered his wife because he was in Las Vegas at the time of the killing. To prove it he showed the police his car, which he said had been parked in the Los Angeles airport parking lot since Friday, the day before the murder. Employees there said the car had not been moved.

But Carole guilelessly placed Finch at the scene. She and the doctor, she said, drove to West Covina that night in her car. "We left it in the parking lot at the country club, because we thought if Barbara saw the car she would not come out and talk to us."

They wanted to talk to Barbara about the divorce, Carole said, although precisely what they hoped to gain was never made clear. She had no explanation for Dr. Finch's brown leather attaché case found on the lawn by the police, which contained two pairs of rubber gloves, some rope, a butcher knife, sedatives, a hypodermic, some .38-caliber ammunition and a flashlight—a collection the police later dubbed "the do-it-yourself murder kit."

When Barbara drove into the garage, as Carole told it, the irate wife refused to talk to Finch and threatened them with a gun. Carole fled to a clump of bushes and hid. From the bushes she heard a commotion and some shots. She remained cowering behind the bushes for five or six hours, then picked up her car and returned to Las Vegas.

Dr. Finch and Carole Tregoff were undoubtedly the most awkward pair of amateurs ever to do murder. If half of what the prosecution outlined was true, the Finch-Tregoff case must have been the most preposterously prepared and elaborately bungled murder in the annals of modern crime.

The trial began with Assistant District Attorney Whichello's opening statement for the prosecution, pointing to Marie Anne Lindholm, the Finch maid, as the state's key witness. A slight, slender girl, she sat quietly in the packed courtroom as Whichello gave the prosecution's version of the slaying and her part in it as a witness.

She had been Mrs. Finch's confidante, had heard her fears of the doctor, had seen the signs of the beating he had given his wife, had witnessed his breaking into the house after he had moved out and the locks had been changed. Mrs. Finch had told her of a hired killer from Las Vegas. Then came the night of July 18. She had been home with the two children and heard her employer drive into the garage and, a few minutes later, her cry for help. The maid, who was putting her hair up in curlers, ran to the garage and found Mrs. Finch lying on the floor and Dr. Finch standing over her, holding a gun.

The doctor, in a fury, had seized Marie Anne and banged her head against the garage wall, stunning her and breaking a hole in the plaster. Then he fired a shot at nothing in particular, ordered both the maid and Mrs. Finch into the car and got in himself behind the wheel. Marie Anne docilely got into the back seat, but Mrs. Finch, although showing evidence of a brutal beating, got out and began to run down the driveway. The doctor followed, and there was another shot. The girl rushed into the house and called the police.

Whichello charged that Finch, with the help of the "murder kit," planned to put his wife in a car and drive it down the hillside to a curve and over a cliff, making the death appear an accident. The plan went awry, Whichello said, when Marie Anne burst into the garage. Finch then tried to put both women in the car and carry out his scheme, but the entire plot collapsed when Barbara broke and ran.

The doctor's 12-year-old stepdaughter backed up the eyewitness story of the Finch maid.

A movie actor, Mark Stevens, testified that he had urged Barbara to defend herself with a jack handle if Finch ever attacked her. He gave her this advice after Barbara told him of Finch's threats. (The police found the jack handle next to Barbara's bed.)

Don Williams, 21, a University of Nevada honor student and a childhood friend of Carole's, stated that Carole had asked him to find "a couple of tough guys" to kill Mrs. Finch. Later he claimed she only wanted someone to "rough up" the doctor's wife. An acquaintance of Williams's recommended as a prospective killer John Patrick Cody, age 29. Police traced Cody, a small-time crook, to Minneapolis, where he was in jail for forgery.

Cody fingered Carole Tregoff. He credited her with going to quite a bit of trouble to "discover" him in Las Vegas, lining him up as Mrs. Finch's assassin, then introducing him to her lover. Dr. Finch, who was paying for the job, made a few suggestions about the manner in which it might best be carried out.

Cody maintained from the beginning that he never had any intention of doing the job; he just saw an irresistible chance to play a couple of suckers (ultimately he cost the lovers $1300), so he kidded them along.

Carole gave him a map of the Finch place, warned him that the garage door might stick and told him not to worry about the Finch dog, which looked ferocious but actually was harmless. She also gave him a picture of his intended victim. According to Cody, Carole gave him a $350 down payment and a plane ticket to Los Angeles. After lying low for a few days, he said, he went to Carole, told her Mrs. Finch had been murdered and received the remaining $850.

When Finch returned to Las Vegas, Carole and Cody told him his wife had been eliminated. "You must be nuts," the doctor was quoted as saying. "I called my home this morning and talked to my wife."

Cody said: "Well, I killed some woman. I put the body in the trunk of an old automobile standing on the street near the Hollywood Hills Motel."

"My God," Cody reported the doctor as saying, "that is a terrible tragedy. Some poor innocent woman got killed."

The doctor's remorse, however, did not prevent him from insisting that Cody go through with his end of the bargain.

"The doctor told me I could use the shotgun he always carried in the trunk of his Cadillac," Cody continued. "But I told him I didn't like to use a shotgun because it was too messy, so he said he guessed I was right." (Police later did find a shotgun in Finch's car.)

Finch and Carole put Cody on a plane for Los Angeles. Once again he reneged, took a bus back to Las Vegas and blew the rest of the money gambling.

This time Finch became enraged and declared, "Okay, we'll have to do it ourselves."

Cody also testified that he had once asked Dr. Finch if he knew what he was doing, if he really loved Carole and if she really loved him. Dr. Finch said indeed they adored each other. Reflecting on this, Cody told the other man: "I'm only twenty-nine years of age, but I been around, and to start out killing your wife just for money doesn't add up. Let her have every cent if that's the way she's got you boxed in. Go up on top of a mountain and live off the wild, and if this girl loves you she is going to stay with you. This is from my own experience."

Regretfully, Cody told the court, Dr. Finch did not agree with him. The doctor said his wife had him bottled up and was "no good."

Then Cody, who had already taken $1200 or more to do the job, attempted to reason with Carole in Mad-Hatter-tea-party fashion. He begged her not to ask him to do what he told the court he wouldn't have dreamed of doing anyway. But she ignored his friendly advice. Mrs. Finch had been causing her trouble, was giving her a bad time, much grief. She had to go. "I was pretty disgusted with Carole," Cody told the court.

Under cross-examination there were contradictions in Cody's cockeyed tale, but he stuck to his story that Carole had bargained with him over the price, briefed him with addresses of places where Mrs. Finch might be found, checked him on Mrs. Finch's description, drawn maps of the terrain around the Finch home and the Hollywood apartment where the wife might be staying with a friend, given him money as a down payment, paid for his airplane ticket, chauffeured him to the airport and eventually paid him the balance due—a little brown envelope stuffed with crisp hundred-dollar bills.

Admittedly amoral, larcenous, given to living off ladies whose sources of income were not precisely defined, Cody still presented a giant problem to the defense.

Grant Cooper, for the defense, in cross-examination indicated that Dr. Finch, supported by the girl he wanted to marry, would testify that they hired Cody only to catch Mrs. Finch in a compromising situation—or, possibly, to get her into one himself.

Their explanation of how they expected this dreary-looking semiliterate to penetrate Mrs. Finch's social circle—or Mrs. Finch herself—had to be a beaut. If this man was not hired to murder Mrs. Finch, what was he hired to do? And even more pertinent, how was he supposed to do it? Ring her doorbell and pretend he was lost, then turn on the charm with such rapidity that she would beg him to come in and stay for a cocktail or something? Had he planned to get a friend to break into her bedroom and tear off her clothes while he snapped pictures with his camera? The jurors didn't know Barbara Jean Finch when she was alive, but they knew she moved in a world of comfortably fixed, well-bred suburbanites. It would be interesting to hear Dr. Finch explain how Cody was supposed to manage a social—let alone amorous—relationship with Mrs. Finch. The thought of him with his padded shoulders, his white-satin ties and his scrambled tenses picking her up anywhere was laughable. The prosecution drew attention to the disappearance of Barbara's white purse, which like the gun, was never found. What the jury thought on this point was vital. Cody had testified that when Carole engaged him to kill Mrs. Finch she described the jewelry Barbara probably would be wearing. She told him to be sure to remove rings and wristwatch from the body and to take the purse, to make the whole thing look like a robbery. The prosecution implied that when Cody failed to carry out orders the lovers did the job themselves and, before they fled the scene, remembered to fake the "robbery."

Defense counsel Cooper offered an explanation for the injuries Mrs. Finch said she suffered in squabbles with Dr. Finch: "She was creating false incidents and making false accusations in an attempt to further her divorce action."

As for the dangerous testimony of Jack Cody, Cooper said that Dr. Finch first hired a private detective for $50 a day, plus mileage and expenses, to tail Mrs. Finch in traffic. Dr. Finch then tried to hire a Los Angeles police officer to do the job, but was unable to make satisfactory arrangements.

"Dr. Finch said that if someone did tail his wife they'd find out, because of abstinence between them for some period of time, that she was seeing some man—although he didn't have any particular man in mind." So he decided to look around Las Vegas for someone to try to get evidence of adultery.

Barbara Jean, who hadn't much to do but sit around the tennis courts or sip cocktails in the country-club bar or go to the beauty parlor, harassed Finch in every way, Cooper told the court. She plotted a divorce action behind his back, withdrew all the money from their joint account and notified him of the fact with a taunting "By the way, Charlie, don't try to cash any checks." She also lied about him to her lawyer and her servant and her friends, made uncalled-for scenes and even tried to get him in trouble with the police.

When Dr. Finch took the stand he reinforced the tale of persecution at Barbara's hands. He described the day he drove back to return the Cadillac he had borrowed. His wife was not at home but Marie Anne was. She showed him how Mrs. Finch had changed the locks on all the doors of the house and had bolts and chains inside. The doctor obviously hated that memory. "She had no reason to be afraid of me," he cried. "She knew that!"

The doctor described how he and Cody spent an afternoon sitting in the cocktail lounge of the Sands Hotel in Las Vegas, discussing how Cody could get a date with Barbara Jean Finch. He testified that Cody told him he would give him a full report in 30 days but not to keep bothering him for details.

" 'I wouldn't tell you how to perform an appendicitis operation,' " the doctor quoted the hoodlum. " 'Women are my business.' "

The handsome surgeon had dozens of details to explain, and he was not speaking only for himself; as he testified, he had to talk the way a tightrope walker walks, for the fate of his co-defendant, his mistress and his love was also involved. He had to proceed with caution to keep from contradicting anything she had said on the record.

Dr. Finch wept when he told how he shot his wife. But many of his statements were puzzling. One concerned the struggle in the garage when he was trying to wrest the gun from his wife so nobody would get hurt.

"I was behind her, trying to pull the gun up and away from her. Then I heard someone running toward the garage. I stepped around in front, yanked the gun from her—and I hit her with it."

Cooper asked, "Why did you do that?" and Dr. Finch replied, "Help was coming for *her*—not me."

Think that one over. "Help was coming for *her*—not me." So he slugged her with the .38.

He said he assumed it was the housemaid—he had no vision of a burly boy friend who might slug it out with him—and he was right. It was Marie Anne Lindholm.

Dr. Finch told the jury he thought Marie Anne might have a shotgun with her—one of his shotguns that he had once taught her how to use. Marie Anne was unarmed, but he charged at her and banged her head against the garage wall to stun her. Then, so he said, he managed to wrest the gun from Barbara and drop it on the convertible top of the car. Barbara, although wounded from the blow Finch had struck, suddenly picked herself up, according to the doctor, grabbed the gun from the car top and ran outside. Finch ran after her, because, he said, Carole was out there somewhere and he was afraid Barbara might try to shoot her.

Finch did not see Carole, but at length he saw his wife in her white summer dress at the top of a flight of earthen steps leading to his father's house on a lower level of the hillside. In his own words:

"I kept charging right straight into her. . . . I grabbed her left wrist and at the same time pounded the gun out of her hand." The gun fell to the ground. Dr. Finch did not leave it on the ground. He picked it up. "I was going to throw the gun so nobody would get shot and we'd have no struggle," he said. As he raised it to throw it away a terrible thing happened. It went off—"flashed right in my eyes," he said—and drilled a fatal little hole in Barbara's back.

Some time elapsed before it crossed the doctor's mind that the accidental bullet had hit his wife. He saw her continue to run down the steps. He went to the edge of the little cliff, and as he watched her she "sort of crumpled down."

Naturally, he dashed to assist her. He had heard the shot, he had seen the white fire right in front of his eyes, but he thought Barbara had broken her leg as she stumbled. It never occurred to him that she had been shot.

As he knelt beside her he said, "What happened, Barb? Where are you hurt?"

"Shot . . . in . . . chest."

"Don't try to talk, Barb. You stay here real quiet. Don't move a thing. I've got to get you to an ambulance and get you to the hospital."

"Wait . . ." She moved her hand.

He took it in his.

"I'm sorry . . . I should have listened," she said softly.

"Barb, don't talk about it now. I've got to get you to a hospital."

"Don't leave me . . . Take . . . care . . . of . . . the kids," she murmured.

Finch felt for her pulse, could find none. She was dead.

"I stayed there for a few minutes," Finch, tears drenching his face, continued. "I sobbed. I was all upset. I don't remember things too clearly. It was like a nightmare. I remember walking into the garage and sitting down in the open door of the car, just sort of on the floor. I was just sitting there crying. . . . I saw Barbara's purse on the floor right at my feet . . . the contents strewn on the floor. I was sitting there picking things up and putting them in the purse. . . ."

"What did you do next?" asked Mr. Cooper.

"I panicked. The next thing I knew I was running as fast as I could across the golf course. I remember falling down. . . . I dropped everything I had. I think that maybe I had her purse. . . . I may have had the gun. I'm not sure. I fell down twice more."

He said he had no recollection of taking a Ford station wagon from a neighbor, nor did he recall exchanging the station wagon for a shiny new Cadillac.

"I remember sort of becoming aware that I was driving a car," he continued. "It wasn't a car I knew—it wasn't any of my cars."

He arrived in Las Vegas, he said, shortly after he regained his senses. He parked the car at a distance from Carole's apartment.

He said he went to bed. The next thing he remembered was that Carole had her arms around him and was saying, "I'm so glad you're here. I'm so glad you're safe." She was crying.

Later, he said, "All of a sudden I was aware there were a lot of lights in my face and people were standing there pointing guns at me."

He said the police told him he was under arrest and not to say anything because it could be used against him.

"So I didn't say anything," he said.

In mild tones and with a pleasant manner, Assistant District Attorney Whichello opened the cross-examination. He went first into Dr. Finch's financial status and California's community-property law.

Dr. Finch acknowledged that he was aware that all assets gained after a marriage were considered community property.

The surgeon was asked to estimate roughly his total wealth. He said he could not place any accurate value on it but he considered it far below the $750,000 figure set by his wife.

Under cross-examination Dr. Finch told the jury that he felt his wife had given him permission to commit adultery with Carole Tregoff. He had no feeling of guilt about his relationship with the sultry young redhead.

Whichello asked, "When you were sharing an apartment with Carole, did you ever give any thought to adultery and the fact that it might be wrong and that you should exercise self-control until both of you were divorced and free to marry?"

"No, sir," Dr. Finch answered.

"Would you say you were so much in love it didn't matter?" pursued the prosecutor.

"I'd say we didn't think about it. Barbara had agreed that I was free to do as I pleased, and so it was all right."

Mr. Whichello peered at the defendant on the stand. "Is it your opinion, Doctor, that a wife is free to give her husband permission to commit adultery, and that makes it all right?"

"Yes, sir," the doctor replied promptly.

Dr. Finch testified that his trysts with Carole took place at a rented apartment not far from his clinic almost every day at noon, sometimes early in the morning and frequently around the cocktail hour.

Q. You sometimes went there at noon?

A. Yes. We had lunch there almost every day.

Q. Oh, you had lunch there, too?

A. Yes, sir.

Q. I take it one of you fixed the lunch?

A. Yes, there was a kitchen in the apartment.

Q. And you sometimes went there in the morning?

A. Yes, sir, sometimes.

Q. Now, Doctor, you had told Mrs. Hoover about your marital problems?

A. Yes, I had.

Q. And she told you about hers?

A. Undoubtedly.

Q. Did you tell her Barbara was frigid?

A. Yes, I suppose I did.

Q. Did Carole ever tell you her husband, Billy Hoover, was frigid?

A. I don't believe so, sir.

Q. Was there any discussion of her sexual problems with Billy Hoover?

A. I don't believe so, sir.

Q. Well, do you know if she was having sexual relations with Billy Hoover at this time?

A. She definitely was not.

Q. Did she tell you she was frigid?

A. No, sir.

Q. I take it you knew she wasn't.

A. Indeed, sir.

Q. Did she say why she was not having sexual relations with her husband?

A. I gathered she didn't feel that way about him.

Q. That was her choice?

A. Yes, sir.

Dr. Finch chose to regard the intimate questions with clinical detachment, sometimes even with an air of enjoyment. You couldn't say he was boasting, but you couldn't say he was bashful either. He was unfaithful to his wife with a Mrs. X, he said, and a Mrs. Y before he became enamored of Carole and began to concentrate on her. But for them it was the parked car in some lovers' lane, or Mrs. X followed him to San Francisco and made her charms available to him in his hotel on a strictly transient basis, or he took her to a motel, or he took Mrs. Y to a motel, or Mrs. Y welcomed his embraces in the apartment for which she was paying the tab.

Dr. Finch seemed almost astonished at Mr. Whichello's naïveté when the assistant district attorney asked him: "Did you tell these women you loved them?"

Sitting erect in the witness box, the defendant answered, "I think under the circumstances that would be routine."

"Did you and Carole have sexual relations before you rented the apartment?" asked Mr. Whichello.

"No, sir," the doctor said with emphasis, as if the very idea offended him.

"Did you at some time, though, discuss the apartment and having sexual relations there?"

"Yes, I must have."

"Did you propose it?"

"Undoubtedly I did," replied the doctor.

"Did you think it wise?" inquired the prosecutor.

"Undoubtedly I did."

"Did you think of your credit rating, Barbara's pride, feelings, and so forth?"

"Well, it was part of my agreement with Barbara that I

could do that any time I wanted and it would be all right."

"But it wouldn't be all right with the rest of the world, would it?" asked Mr. Whichello.

"I think it's fair to say I didn't expect the rest of the world to find out the way they're doing now," the doctor said.

When the questioning turned to Cody, Dr. Finch thought there was a "ten-percent chance" that the phony would be able to seduce Mrs. Finch.

"I knew Barbara had been frigid to me, but I didn't think that meant she would be frigid to every other man in the world," said the doctor.

"When you met Cody, did you get an impression of his cultural level?" Whichello asked.

"Yes, I did."

"You got an impression of his grammar and the level of his conversation?"

"Yes. At that time I had a higher opinion of him than I now have."

"I don't blame you," snapped the prosecutor. "Cody was a head shorter than she, wasn't he?"

"No, I don't think so. I would say he was five feet eight."

"Barbara was tall for a girl, wasn't she?" pursued Whichello.

The doctor pondered. "Well, I guess five feet eight is taller for a girl than it is for a boy," he answered.

Stepping closer to the witness box, Mr. Whichello asked, "Whatever you thought of Barbara, she was a lady, wasn't she?"

"Yes, she was."

"And did you really think this two-bit crook was going to be able to seduce her?"

"I told him exactly that, Mr. Whichello. I told Jack he was going to have one heck of a mess trying to pick up Barbara. I told him it wasn't going to be easy, but he said women were his business, women were his living, to just leave it to him."

Q. Now, you expected Cody to appear as a witness in some future divorce action, did you not, Doctor?

A. Yes.

Q. Did you feel he would make a qualified witness?

A. I was chiefly interested in the report he would make, in the evidence he would gather. I wanted to have the facts.

Later, the doctor told the court, "I don't mean this to be crude, but Barbara wasn't getting any sex at home and I thought that regardless of the fact that she was cold to me, she might not be cold to someone else."

He admitted he had nothing specific to go on, no idea of what male friend might be supplying Barbara with her "only human" quota of passion.

Dr. Finch remained courteous and unrattled through seven days of testimony. Most of the time he maintained an air of confident attentiveness. When the going was not too rough he leaned back, relaxed and smiled. Except for a few well-timed tears as he first described his wife's death, he maintained a facade of innocence.

He told a straightforward story under direct questioning, and when the cross-examination came he patiently went back over the ground, sometimes a trifle nettled, sometimes telling a little more than was asked. But in general he did not give much ground to the prosecution. He readily admitted the provable— his affair with Carole and other ladies in his life, his use of a false name in an ancient situation, his lies to his wife, his annoyance with his wife, his meetings with Jack Cody in Las Vegas, his presence at the scene of the slaying. But he produced his own version of the unprovable—what he wanted with Cody, how the gun went off, what his wife said in gentle forgiveness as she lay dying. In the emotional narrative of Mrs.

Finch's last words, the doctor undoubtedly achieved a first in murder trials: He had the victim apologizing for being shot.

Carole took the stand for an eight-question examination by her attorney and after denying any complicity to harm Mrs. Finch in any way, she faced the cross-examination of Assistant District Attorney Crail.

Scornfully, Mr. Crail asked Carole to go back over the scene in the Finch garage, when she and the doctor waited for Mrs. Finch to get out of her red Chrysler so they could ask her for more favorable divorce agreements.

"She said she didn't want to, or no, she wouldn't, or something like that—I don't recall her exact words."

"What is the next thing that happened?"

"The next thing that happened, she had a gun."

There was so much—too much—Carole could not remember. There were so many important points that she only explained as "not seeming important" to her at the time.

"I didn't notice" was a frequent alibi. " I don't recall, really."

Mr. Crail, the tough man of the state's team, treated her roughly.

And he scored.

He got Carole to admit the strange fact that although she was in a state of panic when Mrs. Finch pulled a gun on her and the doctor in the West Covina garage, she not only caught a bag of cartridges Dr. Finch tossed at her but she carefully stopped in her flight to put them in the leather case.

And Carole could not reconcile her early version of why she and the doctor had called on Mrs. Finch that night with her present explanation. In her original statement she said she and Bernie hoped to arrange a reconciliation with his wife, because he was not financially ready for the divorce. On the witness stand she said they wanted to persuade Barbara to go to Nevada for a quick divorce so they could marry without the yearlong wait required by California law.

Carole's greatest problem was Cody's testimony. She had had far more contact with him than Dr. Finch had; she hired him, she paid him. The burden of erasing the conspiracy charge fell on her shoulders. If she and Dr. Finch had hired Jack Cody merely to obtain divorce evidence, as they claimed, why did they pay him $1300 even though he did not produce a shred of evidence compromising Mrs. Finch? For what? Crail made her look bad, and she realized it every step of the way.

Carole Tregoff's few dark hours in the witness box changed the betting on the outcome of her trial. Many observers felt she had nudged her lover quite a bit closer to the gas chamber.

She proved one thing: If she did set out, as the state charged, to help the doctor kill Barbara Jean Finch, she overestimated her talent for homicide. She was a haunted, hunted, quavering witness—a tremulous contrast to Dr. Finch, who had coolly and calmly withstood his cross-examination.

Carole would take the big gamble—all or nothing at all—when her attorneys summed up. All three expensive lawyers would plead her innocent, and one of them would tell the jury, "If you find this girl guilty, send her to the gas chamber. If not, set her free. There is nothing in between."

Assistant District Attorney Crail rose to sum up the case for the State of California. He did it with the efficiency of an IBM computing machine and the cold passion of an avenging angel.

Addressing the jury in an ultimate effort to send the defendants to their death, he served up a harsh version of the killing and the roles played in the tragedy by the accused.

"Little Marie Anne goes into the house and calls the police. She said they arrived in six or seven minutes. She has Mrs. Finch to thank for being here to testify. If Mrs. Finch hadn't gotten out of the car and run in the direction of her father-in-law's house, what do you suppose would have happened to Marie Anne?" He looked at the jurors solemnly, then looked back briefly and scornfully at the surgeon, balancing in his brown leather swivel chair.

"It's a strange story," he told the jurors. "As many times as the defendant says Mrs. Finch had that gun in her hands, she never fired it. She pointed it many times, but she never fired it.

"We say to this—Mrs. Finch was afraid of a gun.

"We say to this—Mrs. Finch didn't have a gun."

He again affirmed the state's contention that the attaché case carried to the scene on the night of the tragedy was a "murder kit" brought up the hill to eliminate Mrs. Finch. "Take that kit into the jury room with you when deliberating," he said. "Examine it. Outside of the large syringe, is there anything in there that could be used in an emergency case? Go over the other items in the case and see if you can find any reason to believe that they were designed for any emergency surgery.

"Do any of you people believe that bag and its contents were ever meant to cure anybody?"

Mr. Crail paused significantly, and the jurors looked at him, spellbound.

He charged Carole and her lover with "a compelling motive" to kill Mrs. Finch—a motive powered as much by greed as by passion. He told the jury, quietly but mercilessly, that he believed they should die for it. "I say to you, ladies and gentlemen, by overwhelming evidence in this case, we have established beyond even a possible doubt the guilt of these defendants on both counts contained in the indictment.

"Murder is the unlawful killing of a human being with malice aforethought. If it is willed and planned as it was by these two, it is murder in the first degree. If they conspired together the murder of Barbara Jean Finch, they are guilty of murder in the first degree."

After brilliant closing arguments by both prosecuting and

defense attorneys, the jurors waited for final instructions from Judge Evans.

The courtroom doors were locked according to tradition, and the judge began, in his deep rumbling voice, to explain the rules under which their verdict must be returned.

Carole and Dr. Finch could receive identical or different verdicts. A door could open for one of them and close on the other. They were tried jointly, but the law did not link them inextricably.

Judge Evans permitted the jury to bring in any one—or two —of six possible verdicts:

GUILTY OF MURDER IN THE FIRST DEGREE.

GUILTY OF MURDER IN THE SECOND DEGREE.

GUILTY OF THE CONSPIRACY TO MURDER.

NOT GUILTY OF MURDER.

NOT GUILTY OF CONSPIRACY TO MURDER.

ACCIDENTAL HOMICIDE.

But the curtain was to drop abruptly on the sensational trial when after days of deliberation the jury announced that it was "hopelessly deadlocked." Ten wanted Dr. Finch convicted of murder; two insisted on an acquittal. Four voted guilty for Carole in both the murder and the conspiracy; eight voted not guilty. The same four believed Dr. Finch guilty of conspiracy to murder his wife; the same eight jurors found him not guilty of the conspiracy.

The jurors—even the bitter holdouts—agreed they would have found Dr. Finch guilty of manslaughter if that finding had been permissible. But at the urgent request of the prosecution, Judge Evans had not included the option of a manslaughter verdict in his charge to the jury.

A second trial began in November 1960, and again ended in a hung jury and a mistrial.

Why were these lovers still neither convicted nor acquitted?

Why had two juries failed to agree on their guilt or innocence?

The answers lay in the stormy, querulous deliberations of those juries—37½ hours of argument in the first trial; 71 hours of argument in the second.

The second trial had a most unusual judge. He told the jurors, after they had been deliberating for 63 hours, that in his opinion the evidence showed "a willful and deliberate taking of human life"—which is the key element in first-degree murder.

As the jurors filed back into the jury room to resume their wrangling, one of the jurors said, in a voice loud enough to be heard in the courtroom, "Did you hear what he said? He's got a lot of nerve!"

The third trial, which began on January 3, 1961, produced no headlines, no reporters, no pyrotechnics of any sort. Dr. Finch and Carole Tregoff were convicted on March 27 of murder in the second degree, and on April 5, 1961, they were sentenced to life imprisonment.

ABOUT THE EDITOR

Eric Corder was born in 1943, and has been writing professionally since his student days at New York University. The son of a Chicago crime reporter, murder and its permutations have been of enduring interest to him. He now lives in Woodstock, New York, with his wife (who is also a writer) and their two children. He spends his leisure time renovating a large old house and breeding and training German shepherds.